art maps

How to Paint Expressive Landscapes in Acrylic

by Jerry Smith

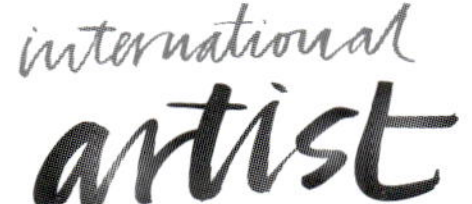

international **artist**

International Artist Publishing, Inc
2775 Old Highway 40
P.O. Box 1450
Verdi, Nevada 89439

Website:www.internationalartist.com

Edited by Paul Soderberg
Design by Vincent Miller
Typeset by Cara Herald

ISBN 1-929834-49-7

Printed in Hong Kong
First printed in hardcover 2004
08 07 06 05 04 6 5 4 3 2 1

Distributed to the trade and art markets in North America by:
North Light Books,
an imprint of F&W Publications, Inc.
4700 East Galbraith Road
Cincinnati, OH 45236
(800) 289-0963

Copyright warning!

Artist Jerry Smith has generously supplied some exceptional paintings for you to copy. He knows that it is only through practice that skill is built. However, when you make your own versions these paintings, please respect the artist's copyright. Other than for educational purposes, it is against the law to make copies of another artist's work and pass it off as your own. So, by all means show your finished versions to your family and friends, but please do not sign them as your own, exhibit them, or attempt to sell them as your own work.

Contents

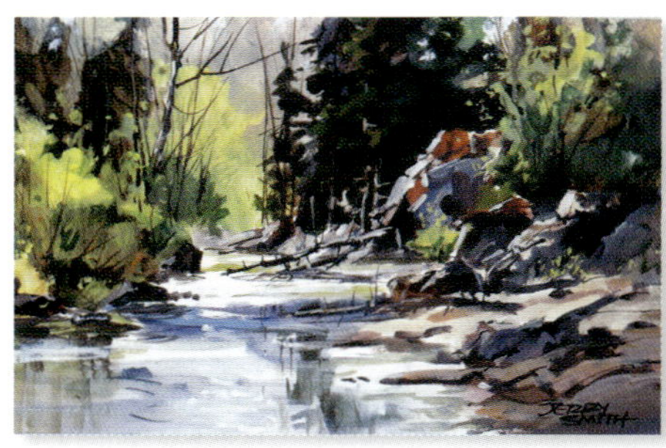

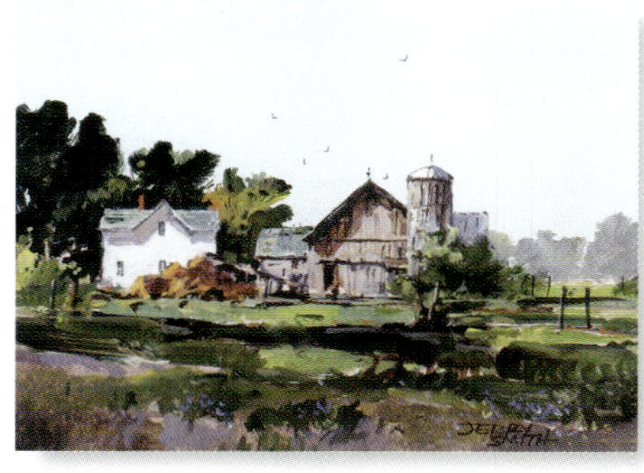

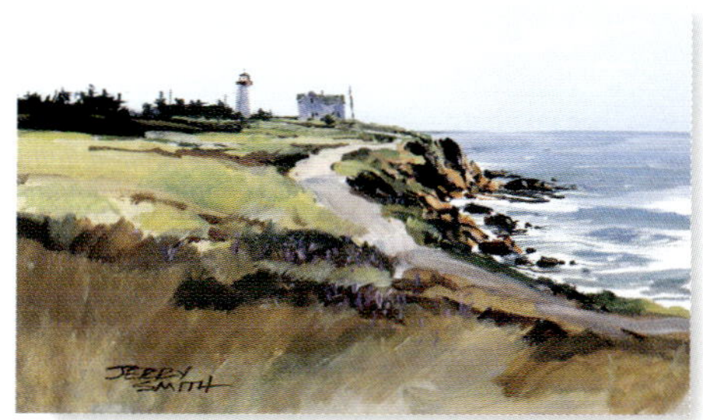

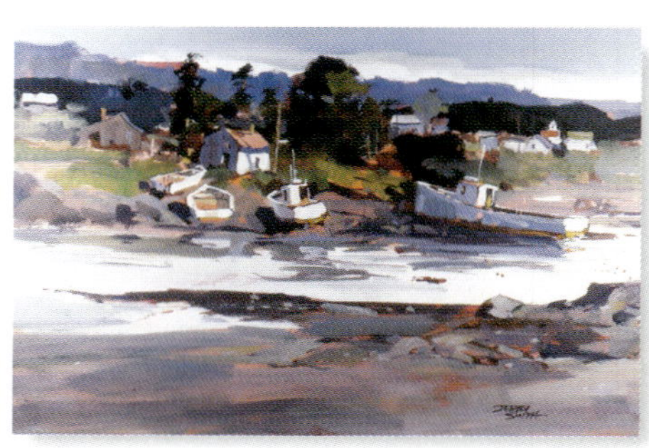

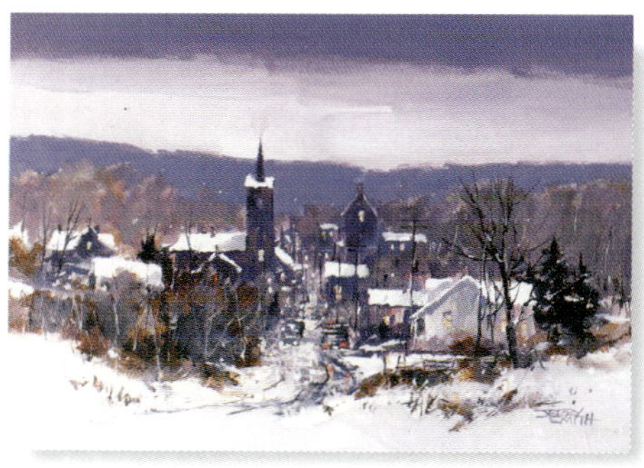

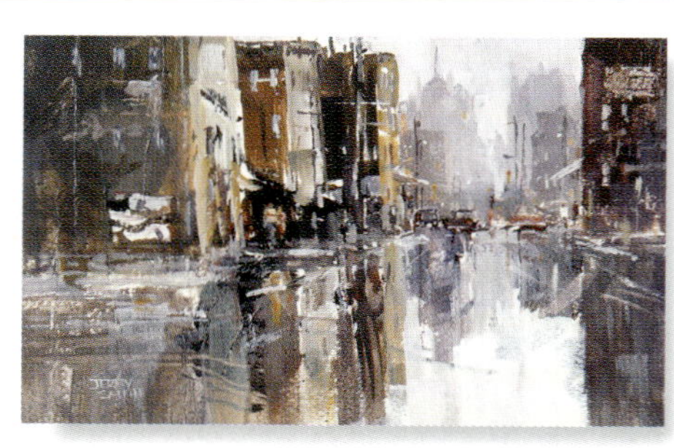

About the artist

When Jerry Smith was a small boy growing up in Indiana and anyone asked him what he wanted to be when he grew up, his response always was:"An artist." But in college he earned a degree in business administration, then went into the printing industry, and although he kept talking about being a painter, his career needed a boost. His wife gave it to him, he says:"One day she called my bluff by buying me a set of oil paints and some canvases. And I have now painted for more than 30 years."

Although he quickly found he preferred traditional transparent watercolor, he now divides his painting time between watercolor and acrylics.

Over these three decades of actually living his childhood dream, Smith has gone from very tight paintings to much looser ones."My current work with acrylics began with a foundation in abstraction. Over the years my work has been primarily representational, but I've always set aside periods for experimentation and exploration, especially during the slower winter months. I try to put the business and production of art aside so as to experiment with new materials and to just see where my imagination might take me.

"During one such period, I noticed that my abstract efforts with acrylics and collage were pointing back toward representation. Many of them had begun to look like cityscapes, street scenes, and other recognizable subjects. This was very liberating for me, the realist-at-heart, to find myself able to start a painting with a bold, abstract approach, and then let the subject matter evolve."

Smith is a Cardinal Fellow of the Watercolor Society of Indiana, and a member of the Indiana Artists Club, the Hoosier Salon, the Indiana Heritage, the Indiana Plein Air Painters, and the Brown County Art Guild. He is a former instructor with the Indianapolis Art Center and currently teaches regional watercolor workshops. He has recently restored a century-old storefront building in Crawfordsville, Indiana, where he maintains his studio and gallery.

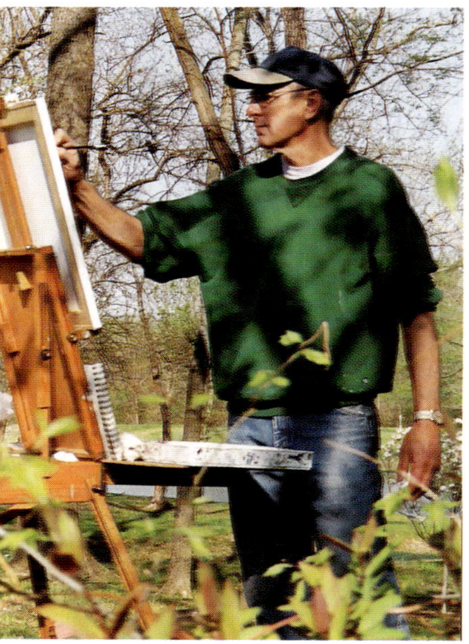

DEDICATION

This book is dedicated to my wife, Cindy, who gave me a push to pursue a career in painting, who has spent countless hours sitting on rocks reading while I sketched and painted, and who for more than 30 years has accompanied me down every byway and dead-end road I could find.

Introduction

If you have chosen painting as your means of expression, you are a member of the unique fellowship of artists that dates back to the cave renderings of prehistoric times. If you've just joined this fellowship, however, you might be finding it difficult to get started on a painting, with a blank white paper or canvas staring back at you. The painting projects in this book will help you get yourself into the painter mode by showing you how to analyze any painting's basic design. By completing each project, you will strengthen your painting skills and enhance your own creative expression.

These painting projects call for acrylic paint, and you could view this book as an introduction to the uniqueness, versatility, and expressive possibilities of this recent art medium: acrylics.

A child of the plastics industry, acrylic paint has quickly proved itself to be a superlative medium for everything from abstracts to photorealist paintings.

Acrylic paints have seven properties that set them apart from other mediums. **1. rapid drying**, which makes them great for painting in layers, and which also makes completed paintings **easy to transport**, since they're already dry. **2. bold, intense color**, which is easily toned down or modified. **3.** they are **very correctable** all the way through to the final stages of painting. **4.** they are **easily combinable** with other water mediums and even with collage material (as you'll see in Projects 11, 12, and 13). **5.** acrylics may be **used on all kinds of surfaces**, including watercolor paper, illustration board, Masonite, and canvas. **6.** being water-soluble, they allow **very easy clean up**. **7.** Perhaps most exciting property of acrylic paints is their **versatility**. They can be used either transparently or opaquely, they can be applied dark over light or light over dark, and they may be used either thick over thin, or with thin glazes over thicker paint.

While this book focuses on painting landscapes, the system it presents can be applied to any other subject. Each of the 15 projects presents a different acrylic painting. Each then focuses on the most significant aspects of that painting's design, and shows you the techniques that will enable you to paint that painting. The first objective of each project is to break the painting into its component parts and identify the various painting elements and principles. Next, a simple and logical method of mapping out a design is shown. Then, you'll learn how to transfer the design to your paper or canvas.

The paintings of most beginners look weak when they are finished. This is because they were started with a lack of confidence or uncertainty about what was to be achieved and how to develop an idea. These projects will give you a solid goal in mind and get you off to a good start, at which point you'll be free to use your paint in a more bold and expressive manner. When that happens, the end result will be paintings with stronger statements.

I believe that the best paintings are those that come from the heart. My experience is that when you're looking for something to paint, the best subjects will find you. The best ones are subjects that seem to be crying out to be painted. When you and such a subject find each other, all that remains is for you to paint it. Will you be ready? Yes, because of what you will learn through this book's 15 painting projects.

The most important thing to remember at the outset, though, is that belonging to the ancient and unique fellowship of artists means that you, like me and every artist, will constantly be analyzing your own paintings to find ways to make the next one better. That is the joy of being a painter: it's a journey that never ends.

So, welcome to the wonderful world of painting expressive landscapes in acrylics. Now let's get started!

Materials you will need to paint every project in this book

Paint

Here are the acrylic colors I use fairly consistently. The palette consists of at least one warm and one cool of each of the primary colors, along with some secondary colors and earth tones. Earth tones are generally graying agents, and while they are useful in mixing subdued colors they should be avoided when intense color is desired.

While it's true that all colors can be derived from the primary colors, there are some subtle variations made possible through the use of secondary colors.

Painting Surface

The beauty of acrylics is that you can work on a variety of painting surfaces, from watercolor paper that has been coated with gesso; gesso primed canvas; unprimed illustration board (acid-free drawing paper mounted on heavy cardboard); primed museum board, or even old discarded watercolor paintings. There are a couple of projects where I recommend watercolor paper or canvas, but mostly I used boards. Experiment with these surfaces to experience the different feels and results each will give.

Other materials

2B pencil

ruler

palette

spray bottle to keep your palette moist

acrylic spray fixative

acrylic gloss medium

satin polymer varnish

white tissue paper (the thinner the better)

Brushes

1/4", 1/2" and 1" flats

nos. 4, 6 and 12 rounds

small rigger 1 or 2

Acrylic paint

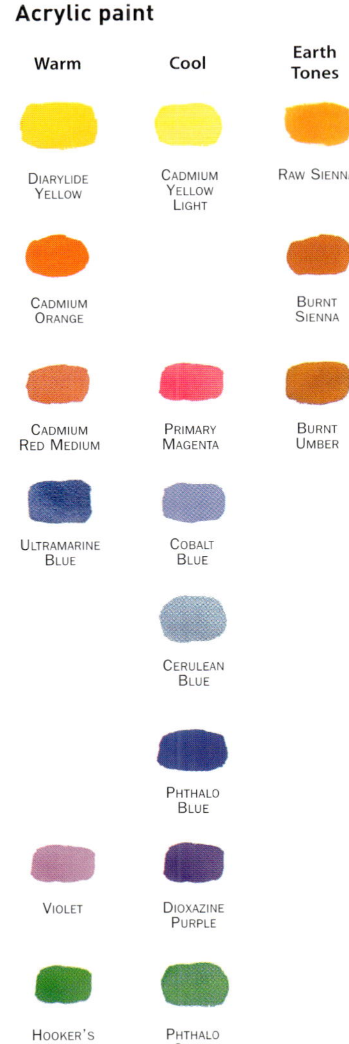

art map 1

Painting with contrasting colors

Before you begin, read the entire project through so you know what's going to happen next.

The goal in this first project is to paint this stream in Oak Creek Canyon, Arizona, in which the lights and darks harmonize to convey the tranquillity and mystery of untouched nature. This project also teaches you the forgiving nature of acrylics, and how the layering process allows you to take a loose approach to create expressive landscapes.

How art maps work
Working with an art map will help you get the design and the balance of the painting right in the first place. It is frustrating to get most of the way through a painting, only to realize that the entire scene doesn't fit on the paper, or that the main object is in the wrong place and the design no longer works. Using the art map approach, you avoid that frustration and end up with a satisfying painting.

If you become used to drawing up an art map first, you will be able to immediately and accurately place the major shapes to best advantage, and you'll get their proportions right.

Think about it: what does any road map do? It shows you the way to go from where you are to your destination, which in this case is a beautiful painting.

1. The image to be transferred using the art map.

Read the instructions to see how to map this image across to your working surface.

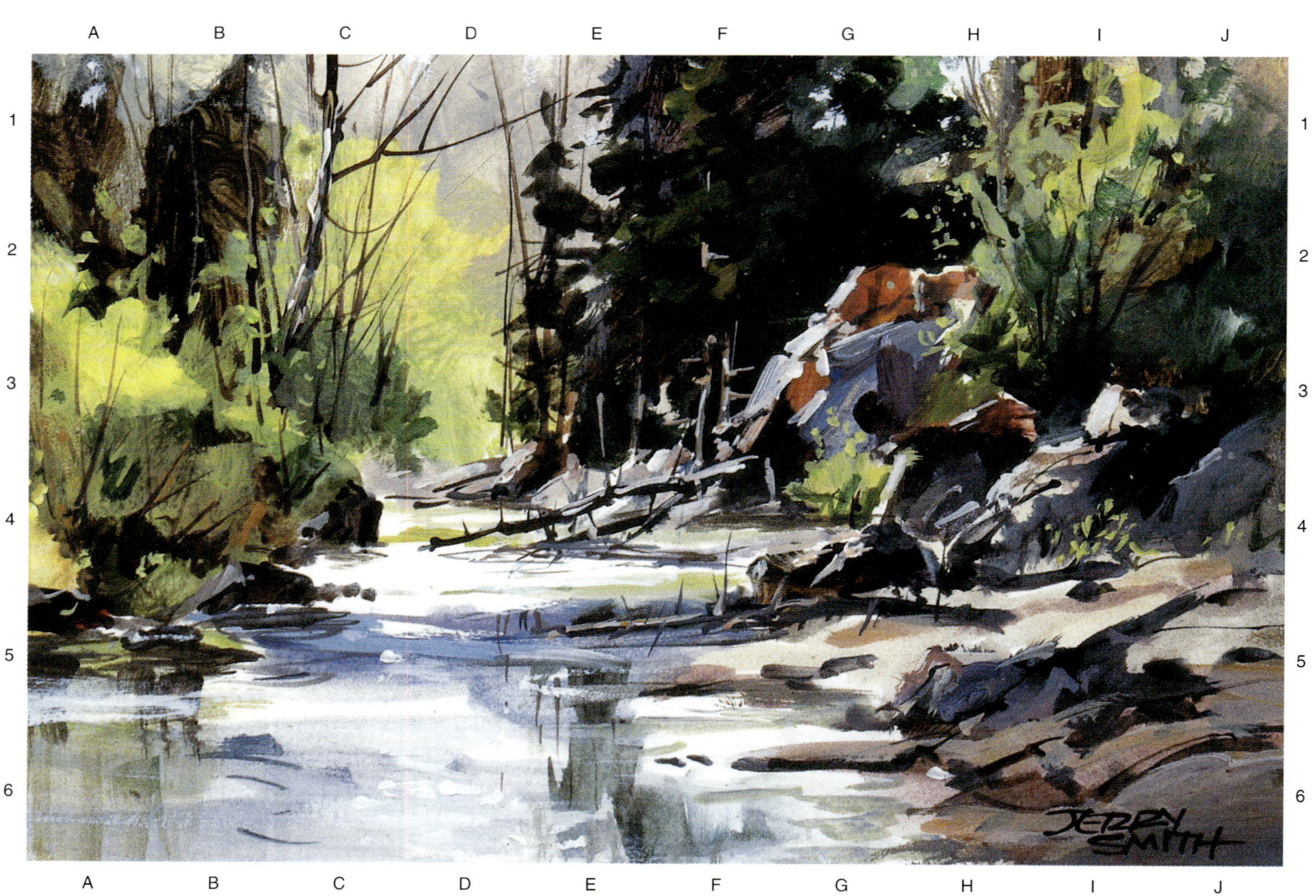

2. Map the image

The first step is to decide how big you want your painting to be. My original is 6 x 9" (15 x 23cm), but the grid allows you to make yours proportionately larger or smaller. The important thing is that your grid must have the same number of squares as mine: 60 (six down, ten across). To draw the grid, use a 2B pencil and a ruler. You can draw it LIGHTLY directly onto your painting surface. Once you've drawn your grid, put in the numbers and letters along the edges to make the next step easier.

3. Use the art map to transfer the image

Now, still drawing very LIGHTLY with your pencil, copy the main contour lines of the object as shown in each square onto your working surface. It's not necessary to get every detail—just a simple line drawing will do. I recommend LIGHTLY and gently erasing the grid lines in the open, lighter areas before continuing.

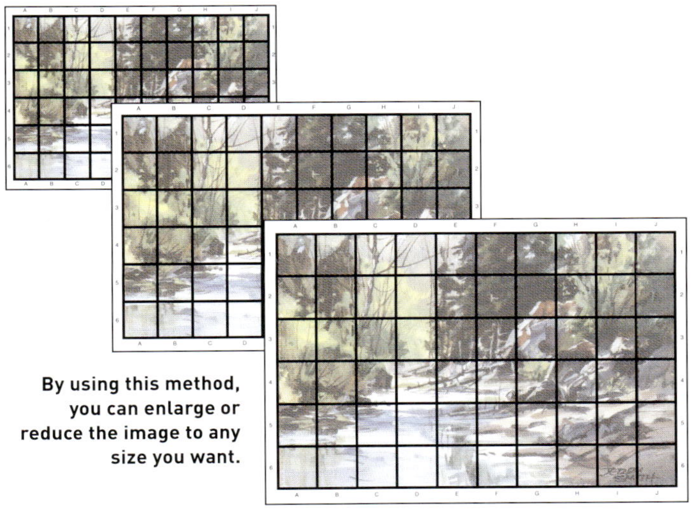

By using this method, you can enlarge or reduce the image to any size you want.

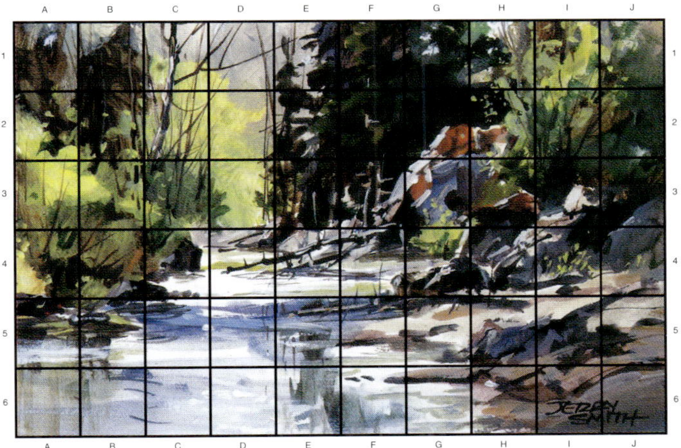

This is how your art map should look.

Here I've done the drawing in dark ink so you can see the idea, but you will do this lightly in pencil on your working surface.

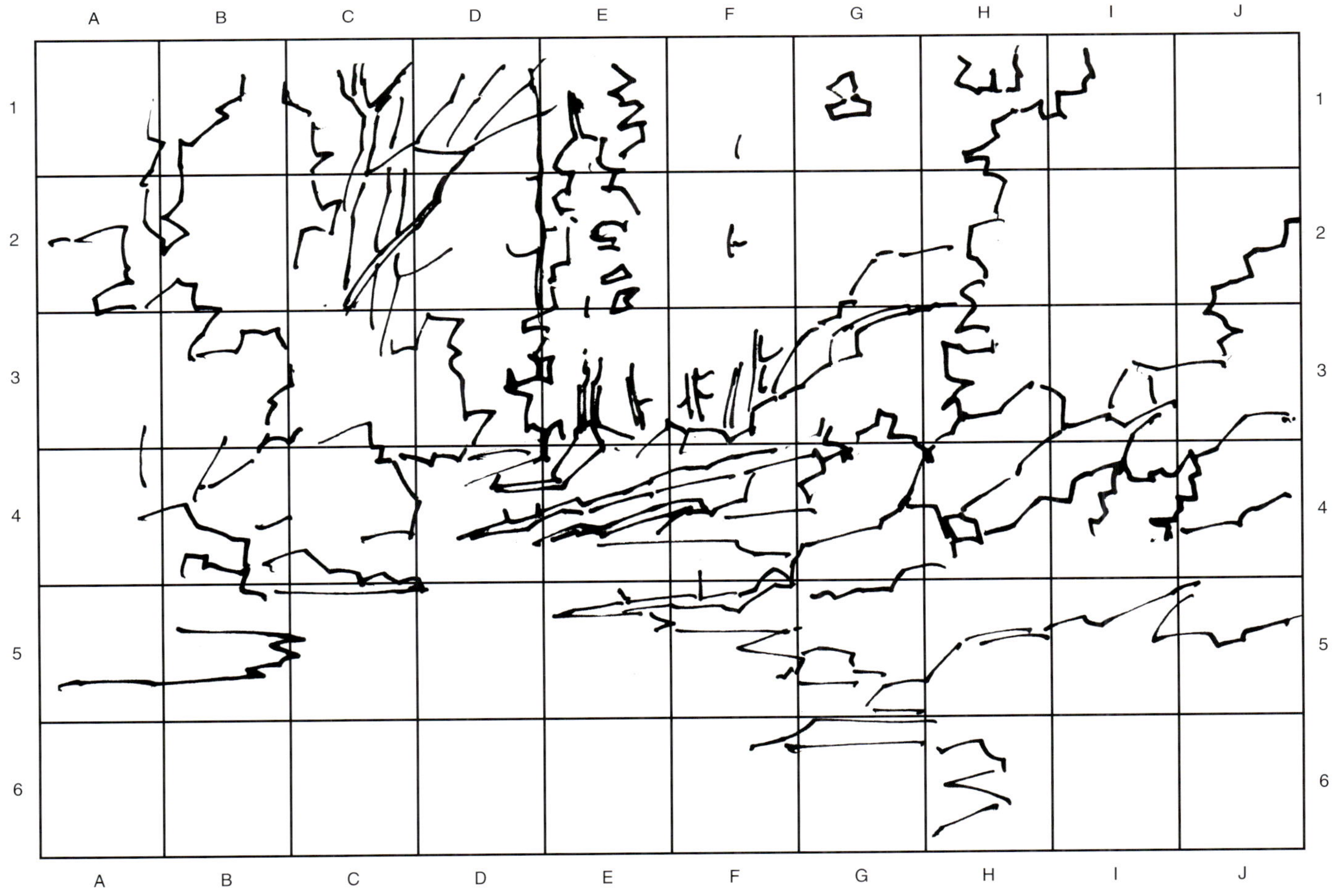

Study these pages before you start painting

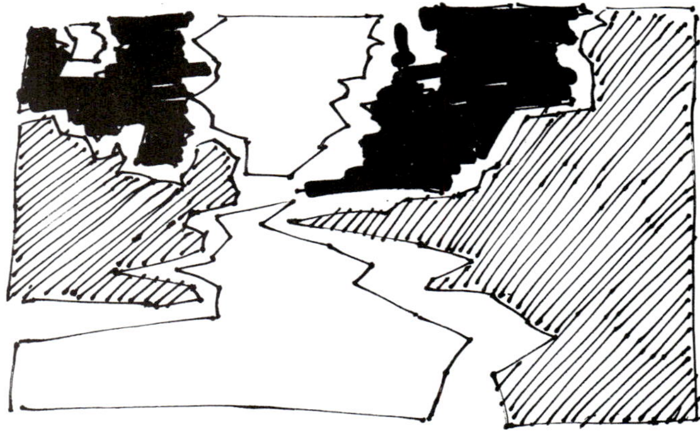

Shape map
Note how the larger, dominant shapes on the right are balanced by the more intricate shapes on the left. Also note how this composition plays horizontal lines against vertical lines and angular shapes. The predominantly horizontal lines of the stream and stream bed, as well as the horizontal format of the overall painting, create a feeling of tranquillity. The trees and shadows break the flow of the horizontals and create a sense of mystery.

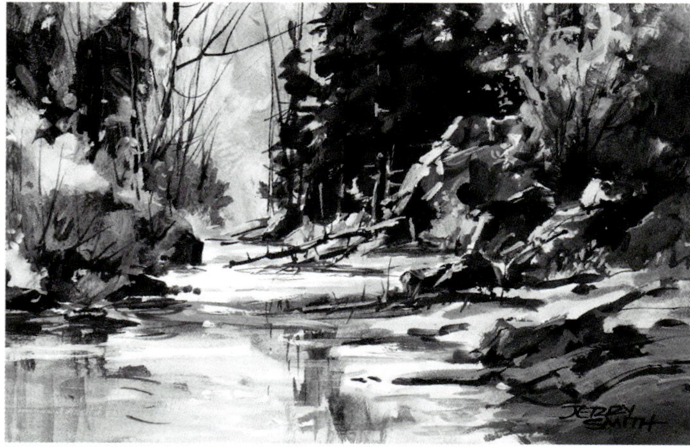

Tonal value map
Learning to see the tonal values—the lightness and darkness of the colors—is essential. In this black and white version of the painting, you can see how I arranged the values with a purpose. I put the lighter values toward the center to keep the eye moving within the painting, and used darker values toward the edges to prevent the eye from leaving the canvas.

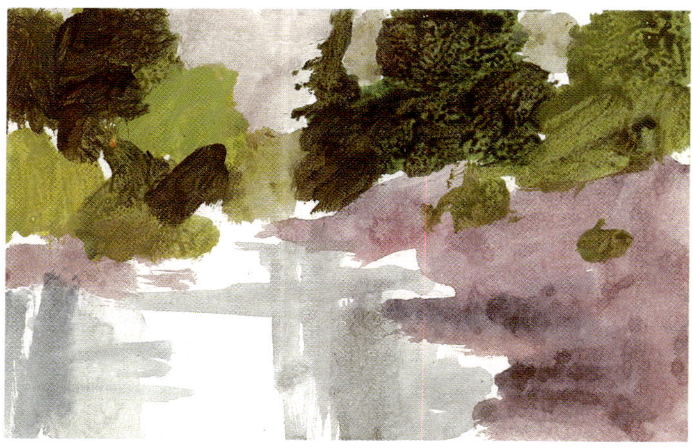

Movement map
Notice how the foreground stream leads your eye to the center of interest, while jagged edges on the banks and reflections keep your eye from moving too rapidly into the picture. Linear shapes like the bare tree branches stand out and contribute interest at the focal point. The corners of the painting are fuzzier with less detail than in the center, again drawing the eye into the picture. See how the composition and the selection of shapes and colors leads your eye from point to point in a clockwise oval, always drawing your attention to where the stream disappears into the trees. This is the goal of any artist—to keep the viewer's eye moving around within the painting.

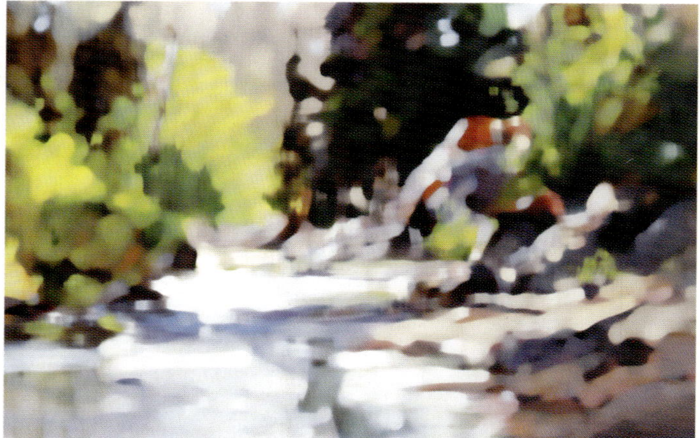

Color map
This computer generated image suggests what you see when you squint. You can see that the foreground water and background trees are virtually the same value, although different colors. This adds to the tranquil, mysterious mood, and also makes the darker-valued colors stand out.

materials you'll need

painting surface
canvas, or illustration board or museum board with one coat of gesso

brushes
¼", ½" and 1" flats

nos. 4, 6 and 12 rounds

small rigger 1 or 2

other tools
2B pencil

ruler

palette

spray bottle to keep your palette moist

your acrylic palette for this painting

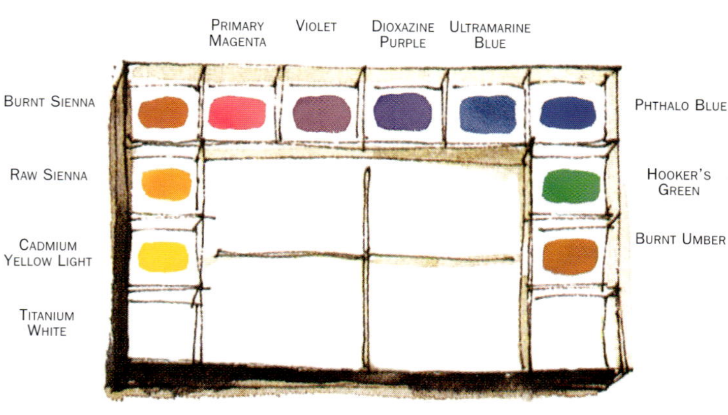

Consider the following elements

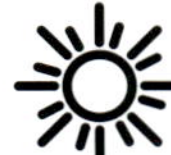

Light source

Note the direction of light. It's most evident on the rocks and banks where there are flat planes. Darks and lights are juxtaposed at the focal point or center of interest. Dark areas are tied together. It's not necessary to paint each tree individually.

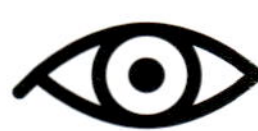

Viewpoint

Showing the stream disappearing into the forest creates a feeling of mystery, which is just right for the mood and feeling I was trying to convey.

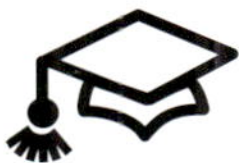

Bright idea

You can leave brushstrokes in the gesso underpainting to enhance the finished texture of the painting.

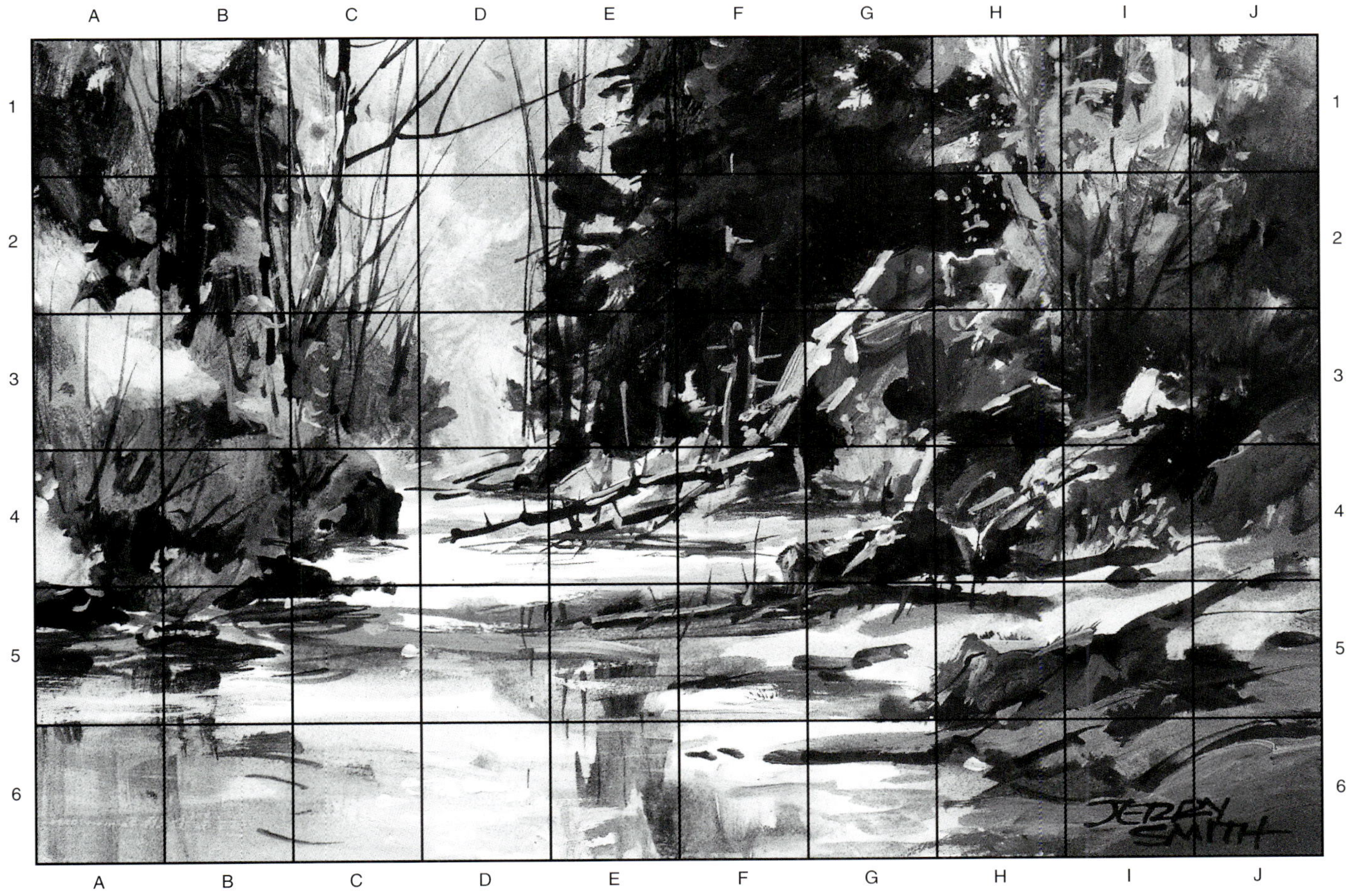

Read me!

Brushes: Acrylic paints are rather hard on brushes. Old watercolor brushes that have lost their point or edge can still be serviceable acrylic brushes, especially for initial washes and underpaintings.

Palette: Because acrylics will build up on a wooden palette, I use a plastic palette designed for acrylic paints. This has a resealable lid to keep paint moist while painting and between painting sessions.

Mixing area: Although a limited amount of mixing can be done directly on the palette, it's best to have a separate mixing surface, such as a piece of Masonite or Plexiglas, or a disposable palette.

Put it all together

4. Block in the painting

To start your painting, paint in the lights and midtones.

5. Paint in layers

Layer dark shapes and accents over the top of the initial block-in.

6. Texture

A painting's various textures should reflect the subject, ranging from subtle ones for water to thicker ones for rocks. Your options for achieving these textures range from leaving the unpainted gesso surface or applying a thin wash of color (as in parts of the foreground stream) to applying thicker, opaque paint on top of the initial washes (as in the rocks and tree trunks).

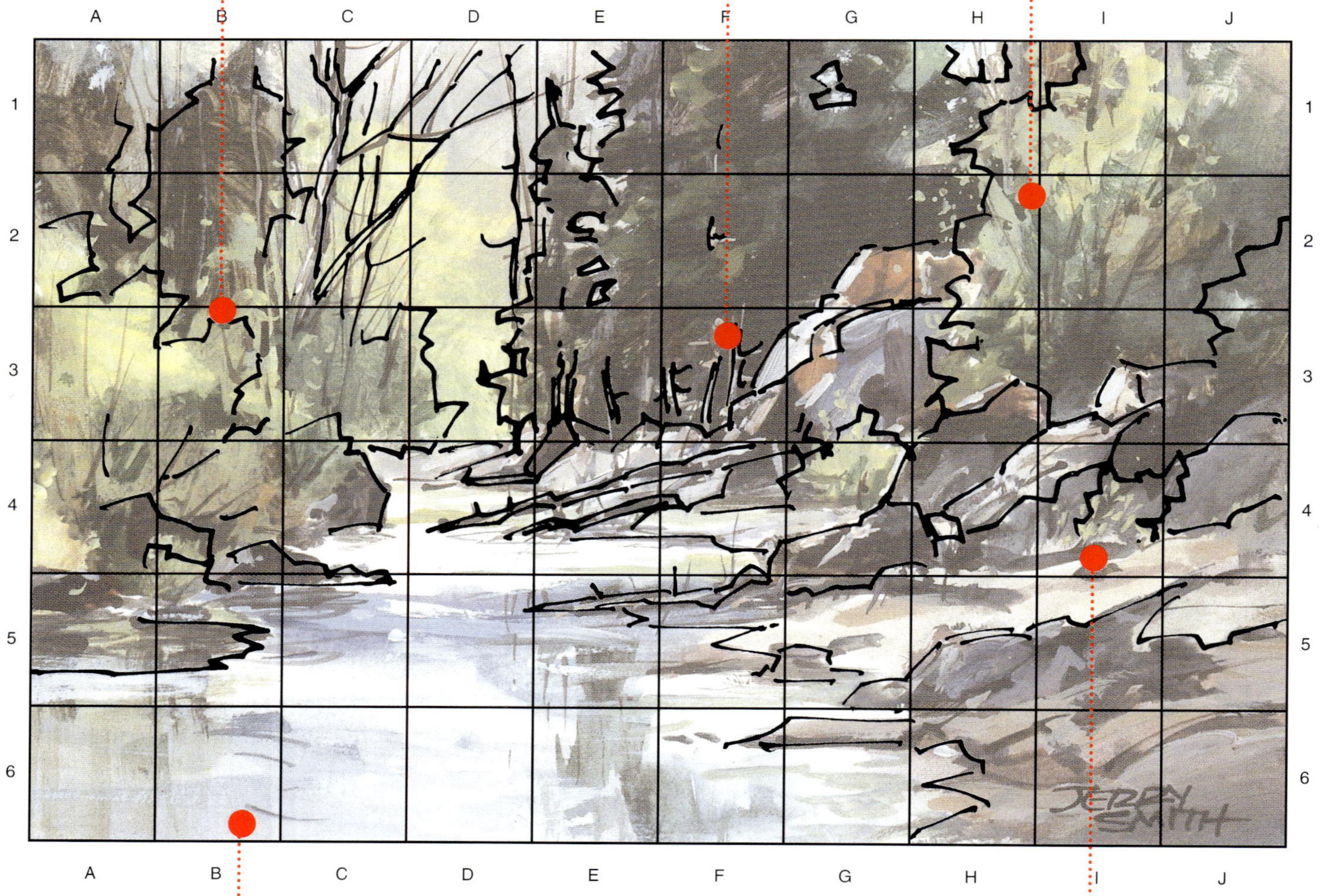

A B C D E F G H I J

1 2 3 4 5 6

A B C D E F G H I J

7. Add highlights

Additional highlights can be applied with thicker mixtures of paint.

8. Paint the details

In the final stages use your rigger brush to touch in the details.

Learning points

- Light and dark colors, such as the deep blues and bright yellows in the water, give a painting a lot of impact. They're guaranteed to attract a viewer's eye.
- Another point to learn from this painting is the importance of a good value plan.
- This first painting project should also have taught you the forgiving nature of acrylics, and how the layering process allows you to take a loose approach in order to create expressive landscapes.

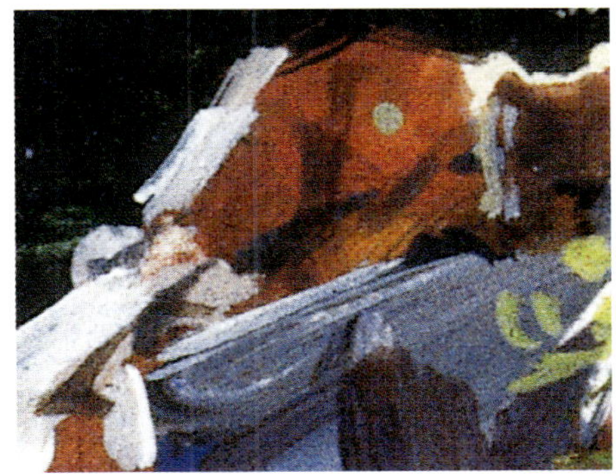

Detail

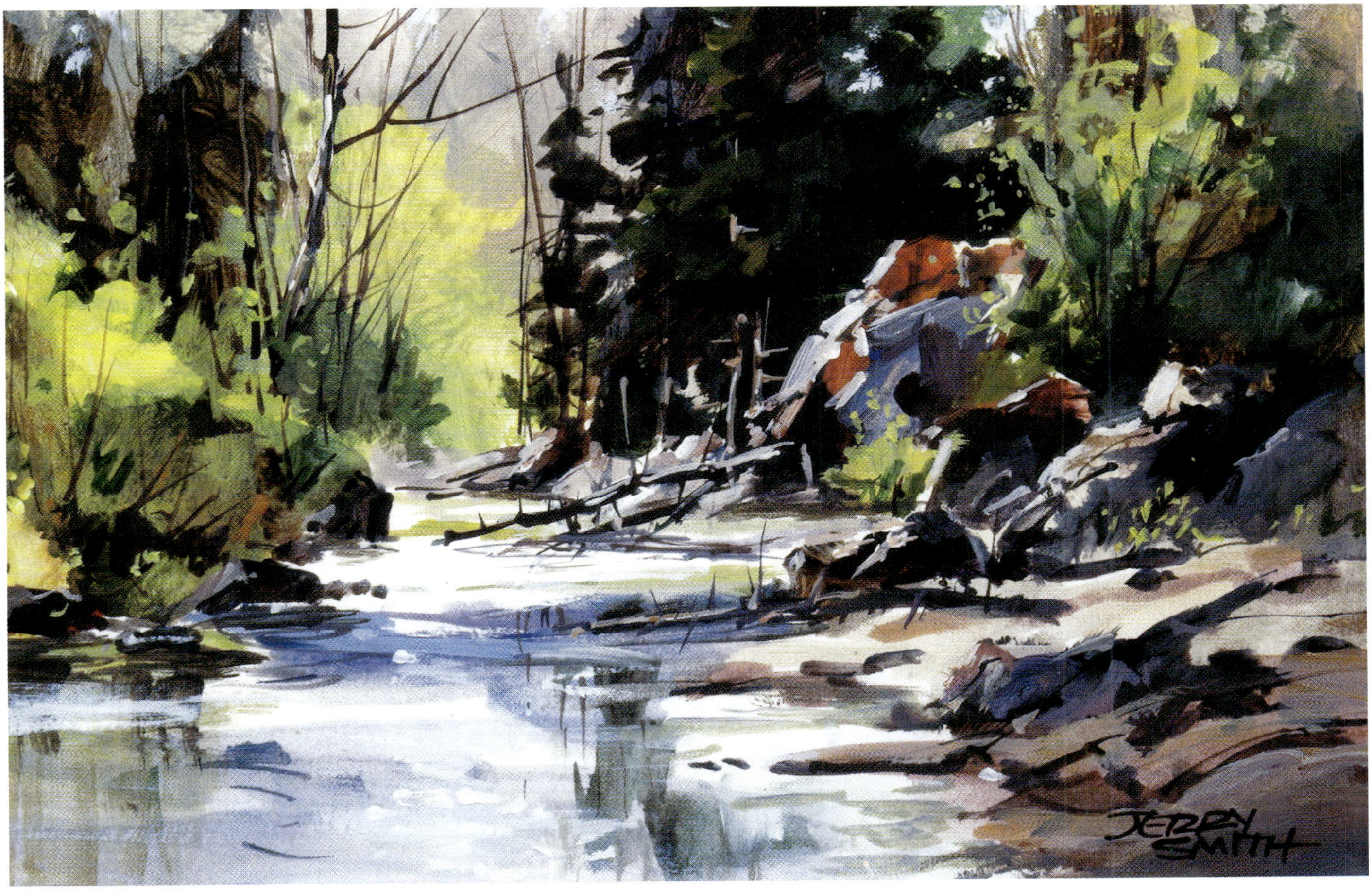

***Oak Creek Canyon*, acrylic, 6 x 9" (15 x 23cm), by Jerry Smith ©**

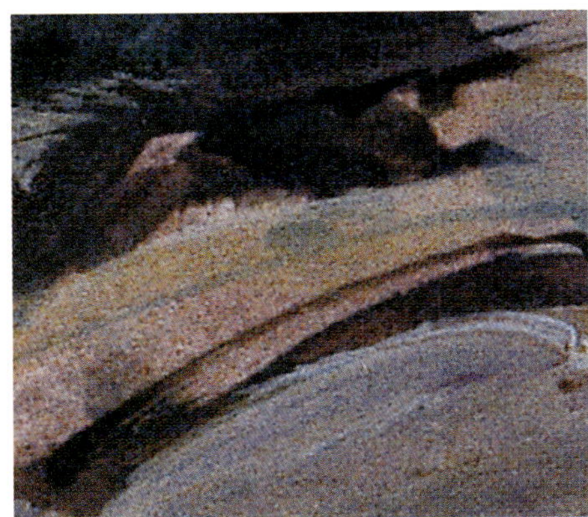

Detail

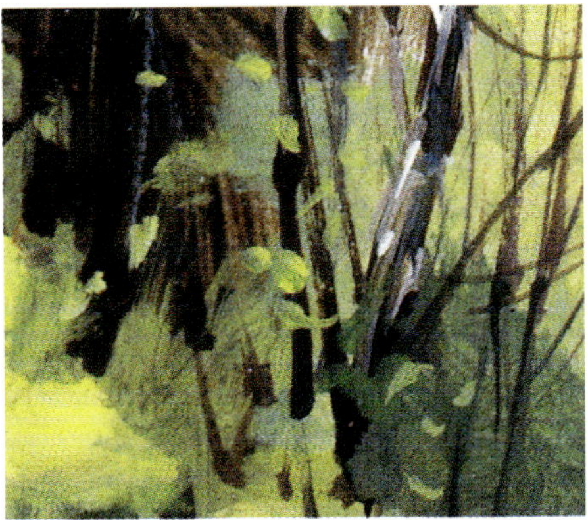

Detail

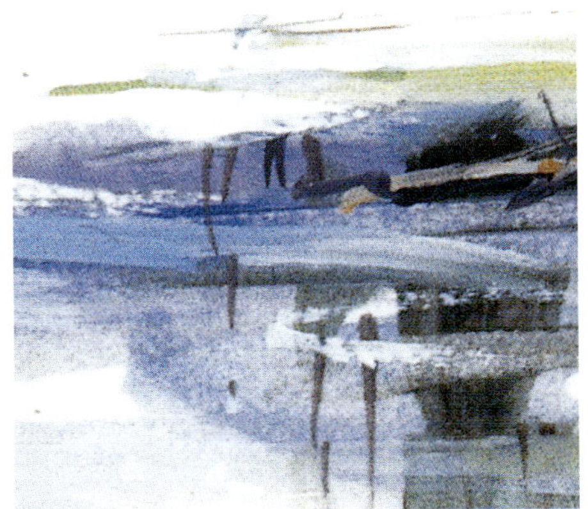

Detail

art map 2

Creating depth

Before you begin, read the entire project through so you know what's going to happen next.

A very important aspect to landscape painting is achieving the illusion of distance and three-dimensional space on a two-dimensional surface. This is accomplished by first thoughtfully planning your colors and values.

While the processes and materials for this project are very similar to those of the first project, the focus of this project is creating spatial depth in a painting with color and values, and by thinking of your subject in terms of receding planes.

1. The image to be transferred using the art map.

Read the instructions to see how to map this image across to your working surface.

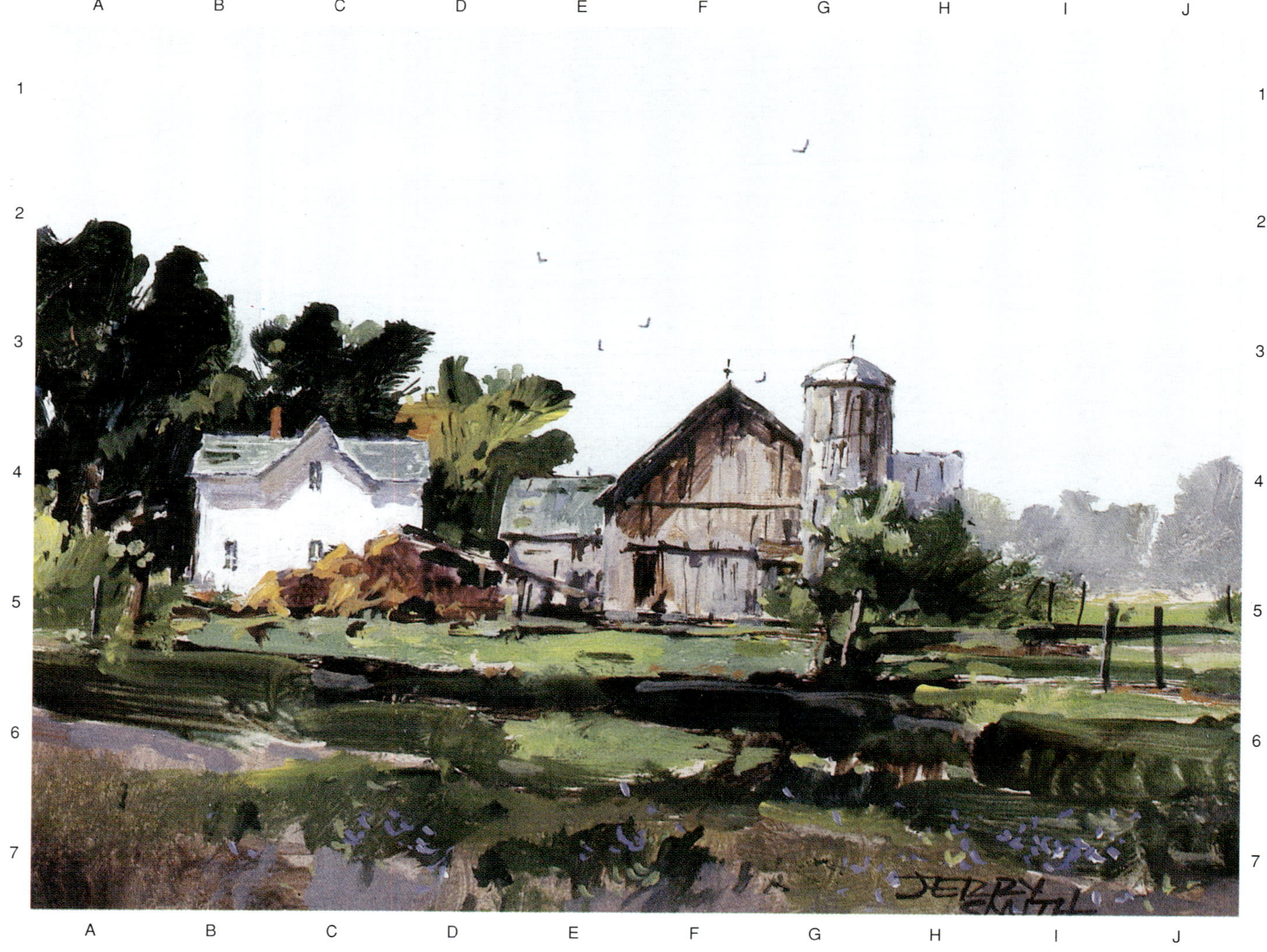

2. Map the image

With a 2B pencil, begin by LIGHTLY drawing a grid on your working surface that has the exact same number of squares as my grid. Your support can be the size of my original, or you can choose something proportionally larger or smaller. Your art map will be 7 squares down and 10 squares across. Put in the letters and numbers along the edges tc make the next step easier.

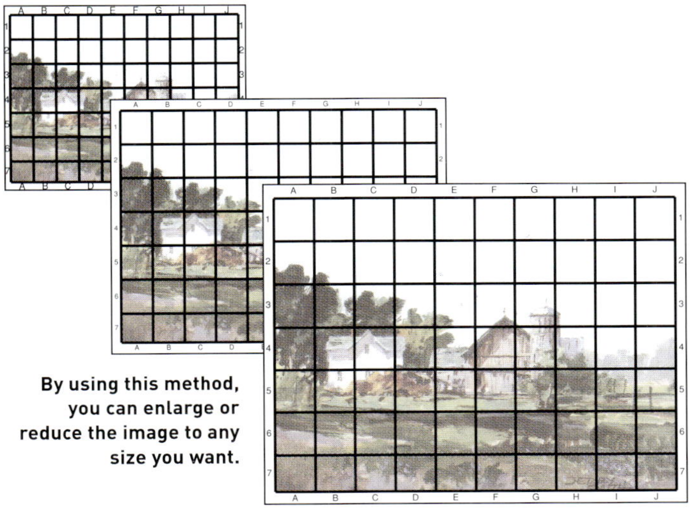

By using this method, you can enlarge or reduce the image to any size you want.

3. Use the art map to transfer the image

Now, still drawing very LIGHTLY with your pencil, copy the main contour lines of the object as shown in each square onto your working surface. It's not necessary to get every detail—just a simple line drawing will do. I recommend LIGHTLY and gently erasing the grid lines in the open, lighter areas before continuing.

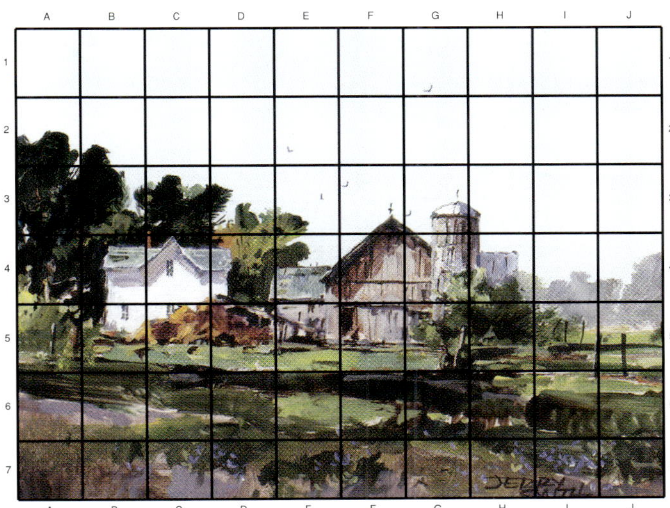

This is how your art map should look.

Here I've done the drawing in dark ink so you can see the idea, but you will do this lightly in pencil.

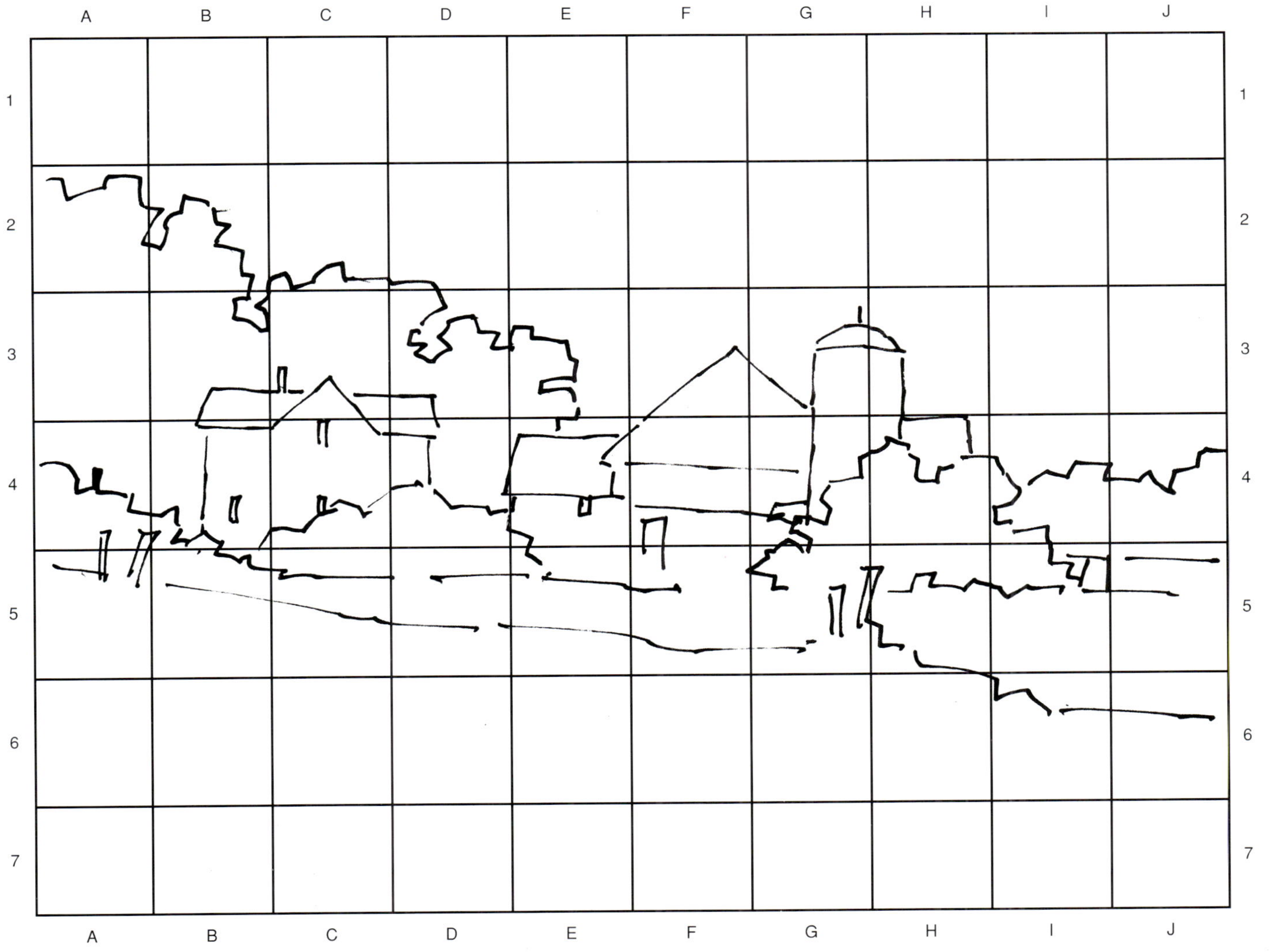

Study these pages before you start painting

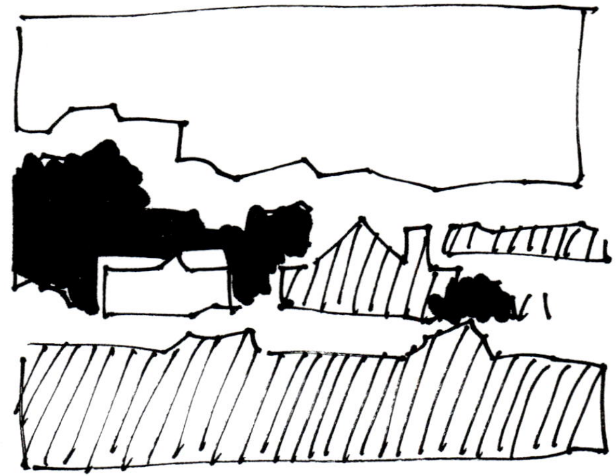

Shape map
Loose, horizontal shapes in the foreground keep this rather large area from becoming too static.

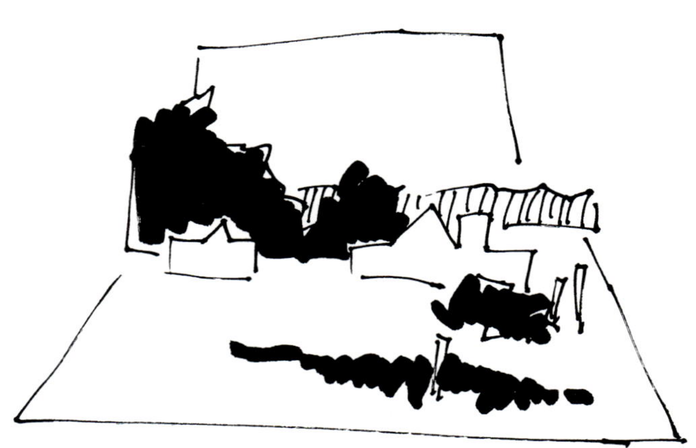

Planes
Receding planes are the key to creating depth on a two-dimensional surface.

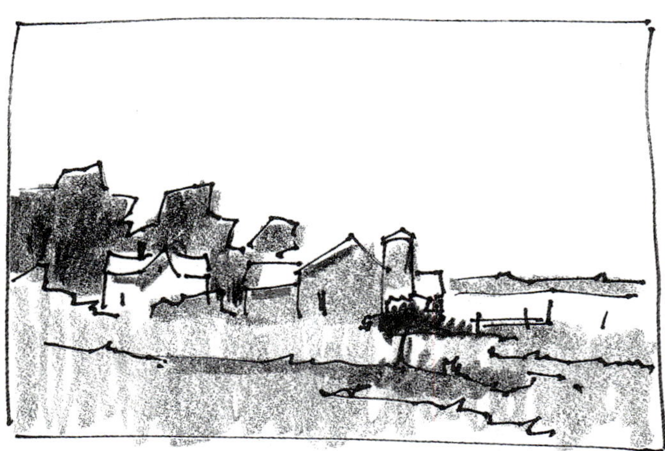

Preliminary sketch
Note the sharp value contrast created by the dark trees surrounding the white house. Thumbnail sketches are useful tools for getting your design plan organized before you paint. The horizon line divides sky from land approximately one-third from the bottom. Placing the horizon line exactly in the middle of the canvas should be avoided because a symmetrical composition destroys the illusion of depth. The greatest value contrast (white house against dark trees) is placed off-center. Note how the posts and dark foreground shapes help lead the eye through the painting.

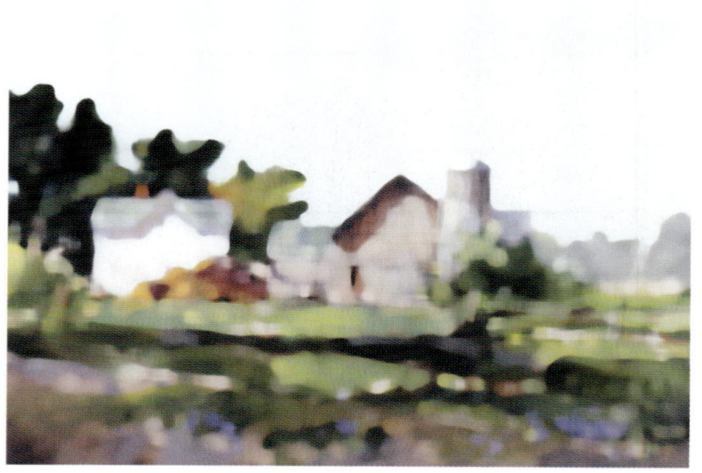

Color map (how you would see the colors if you were to squint)
This painting has a red/green color plan with the greens dominating. Note the variety of greens used. Nothing kills a summer painting quicker than using one constant green throughout the painting.

materials you'll need

painting surface
Canvas or board

brushes
¼", ½" and 1" flats
nos. 4, 6 and 12 rounds
small rigger

other tools
transfer paper or graphite paper
tracing paper
2B pencil
ruler
palette
spray bottle to keep your palette moist

your acrylic palette for this painting

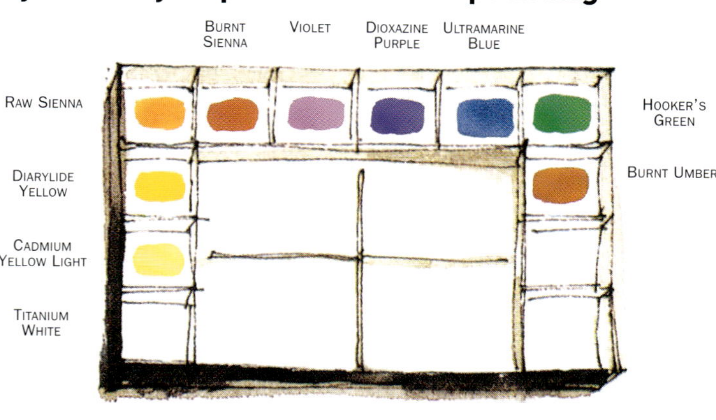

Consider the following elements

Light source

Shadows under roof overhang indicate the sun is overhead and slightly to the left. Some liberties may be taken with shadows, but they must be consistent throughout the painting to be believable.

Bright idea

Avoid tangent lines—two or more lines, such as the trunk of a tree and the edge of a building, placed so close to each other that they confuse the viewer. Note the absence of tangent lines in the painting, where background tree shapes interlock with the buildings, and no single group of lines confuses the viewer.

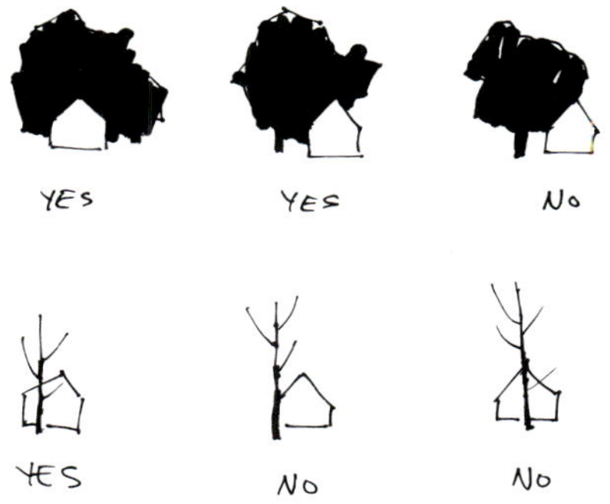

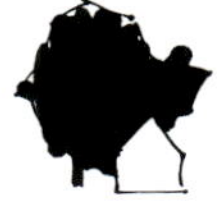

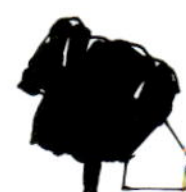

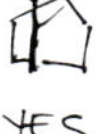

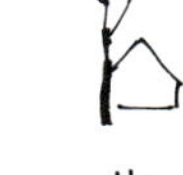

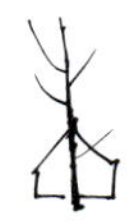

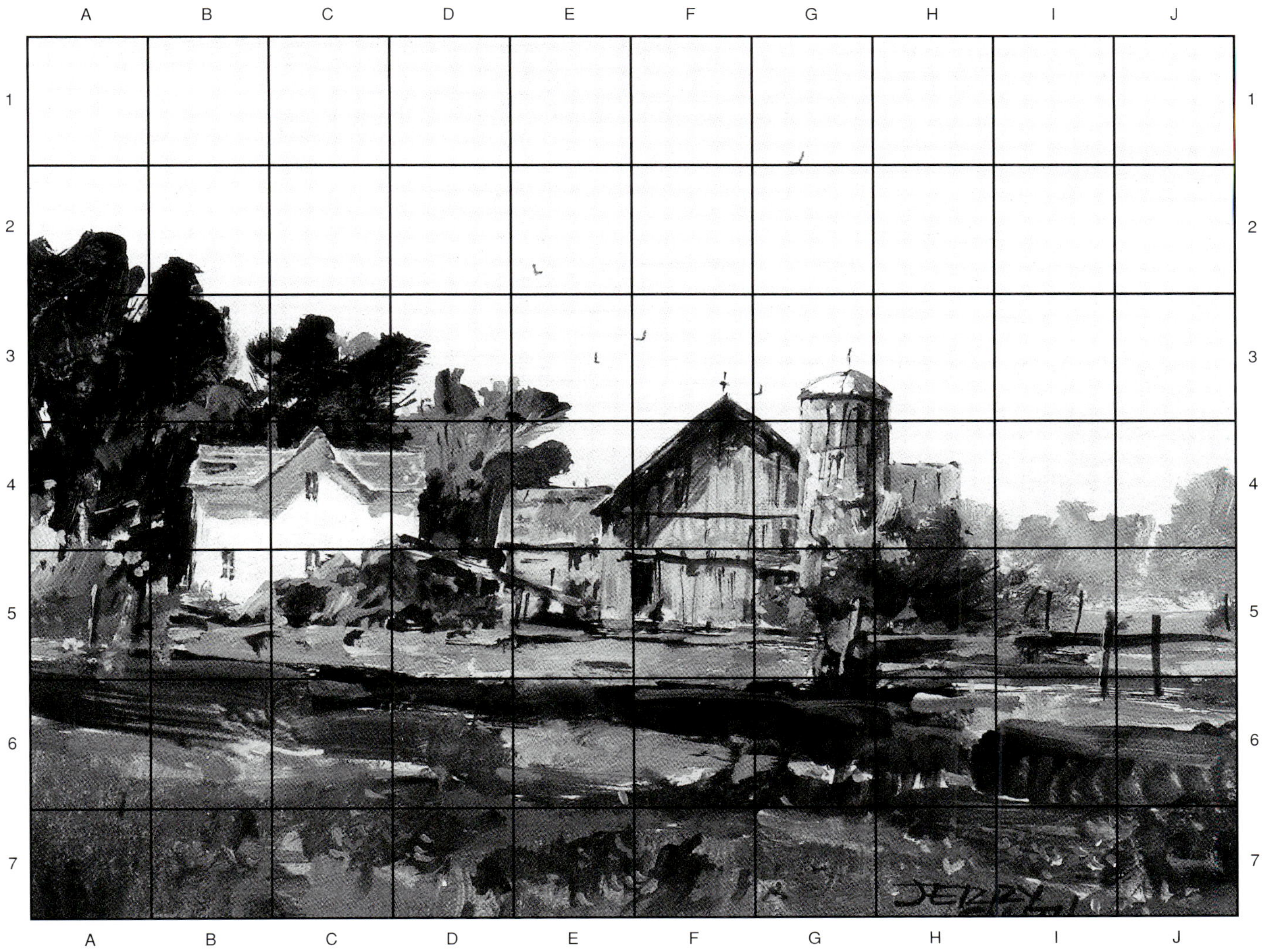

Use tone for impact

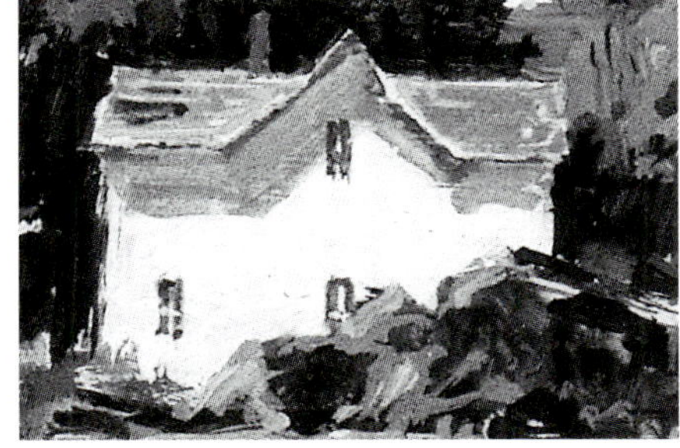

Put it all together

4. Paint the sky—twice

For the sky color, thoroughly mix a large enough quantity for two coats. Paint the first coat down to the horizon, allow it to dry thoroughly, and then paint the second coat. The second coat provides full coverage and eliminates brushstrokes.

5. Paint in the trees

Working from back to front, paint the distant trees in flat, cool color to push them into the distance. You don't want texture and bright color here!

6. Add color accents

Small spots of color can add variety and a spark of life to a large, dark foreground. "Checkmark" birds also add life and provide a transition from sky to landscape.

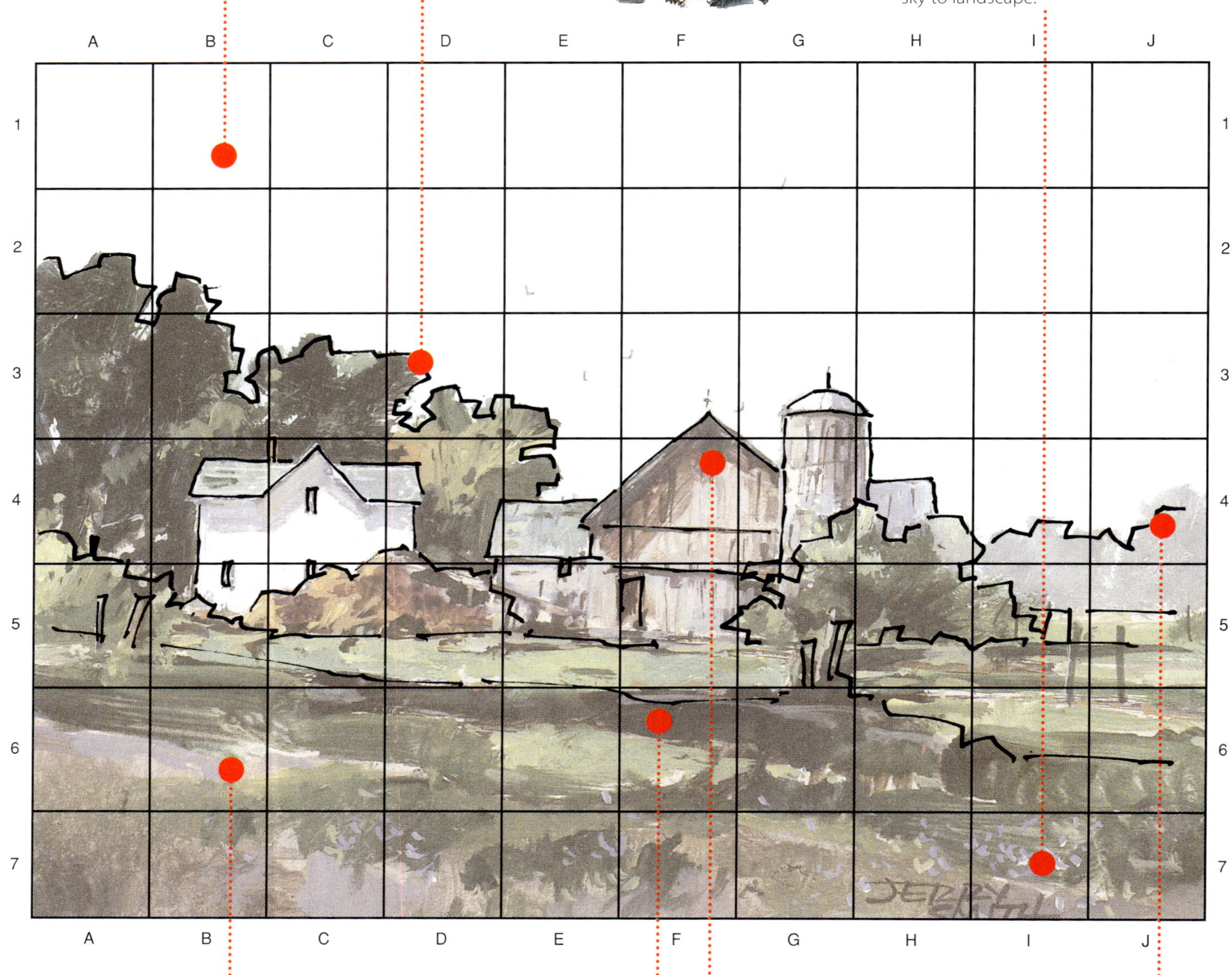

7. Paint the foreground

Create the foreground texture by starting with warm, earthy washes, then dry-brushing shadows and grass texture over them. The brushy gesso primer coat also contributes to the effect.

8. Beware of shadows

Be careful not to get shadows so dark that they appear opaque rather than transparent.

9. Unify the painting

For the balance of the painting, work back and forth from the middle distance to the foreground, which serves to unify your painting as it progresses.

10. Leave the roofs till last

Save the rooftops to paint in the final stages. Since they can be basically any color, you can use them to either repeat colors or create color contrast.

Learning points

- Color and value can be used to create depth and lead the viewer's eye through your painting.
- Texture and detail can be implied with bold brushwork.
- Nothing kills a summer painting more than the use of one green throughout.

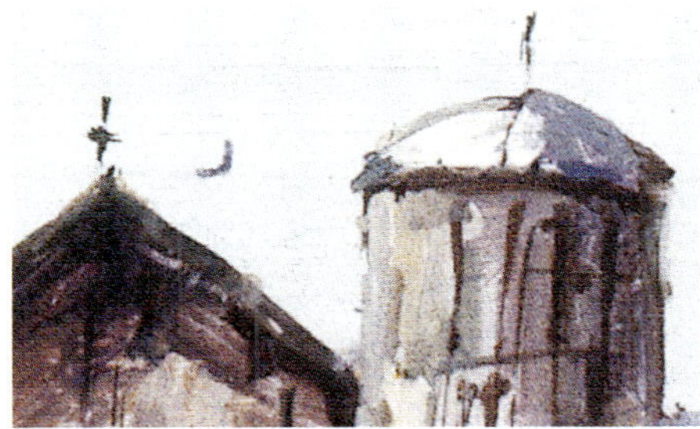

Detail

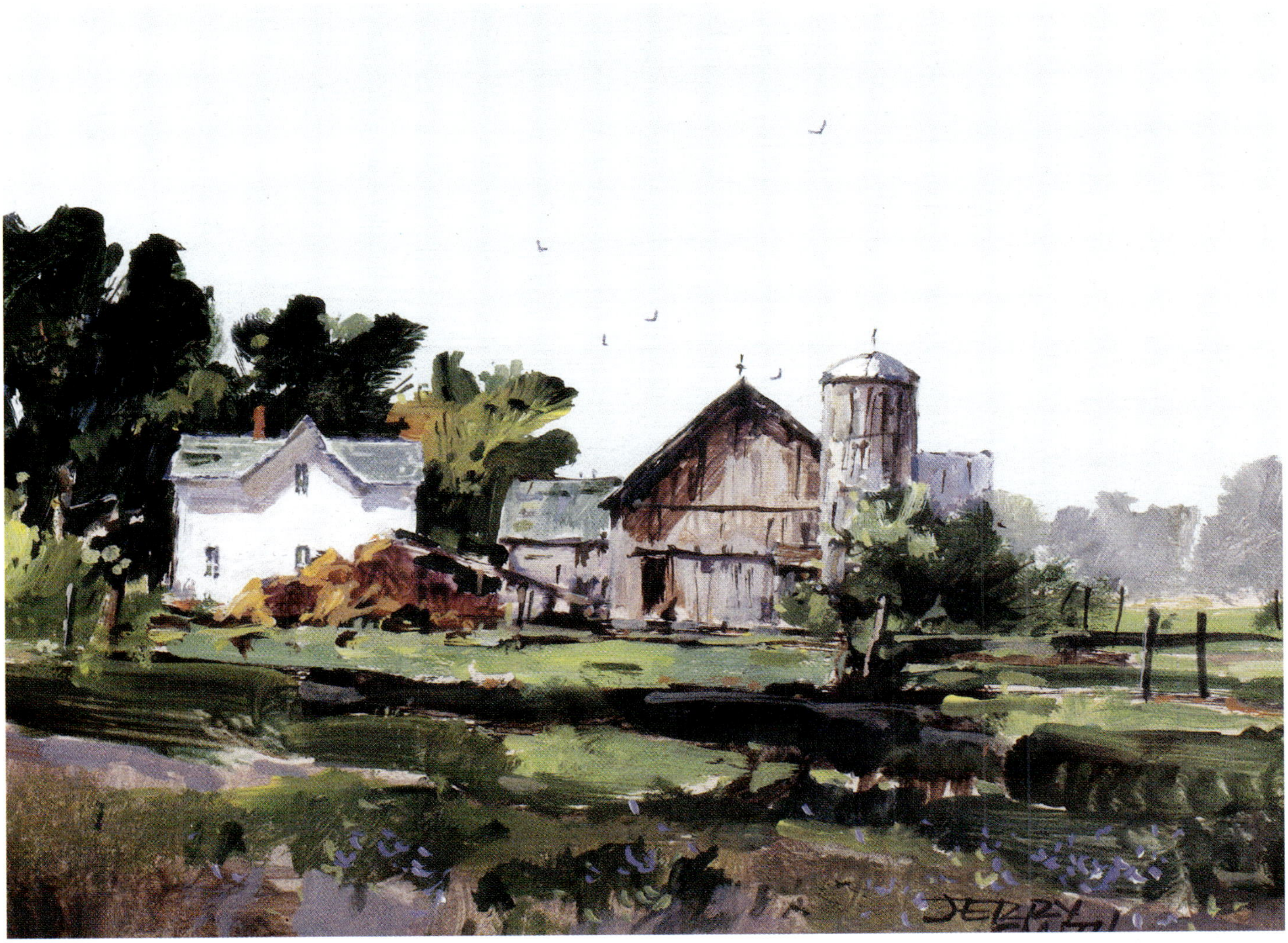

***Summer Green*, acrylic, 6 x 9" (15 x 23cm) by Jerry Smith ©**

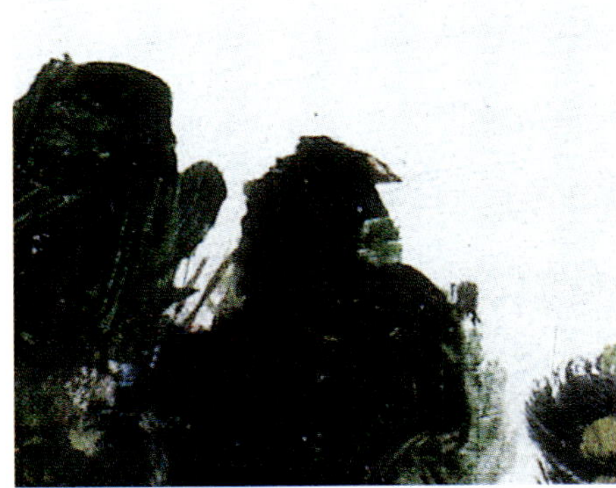

Detail

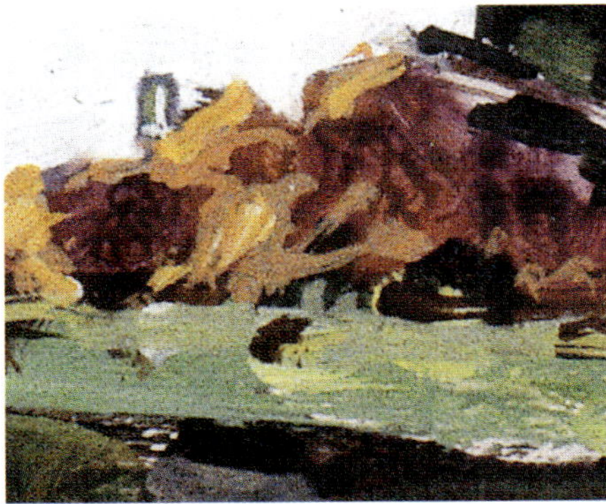

Detail

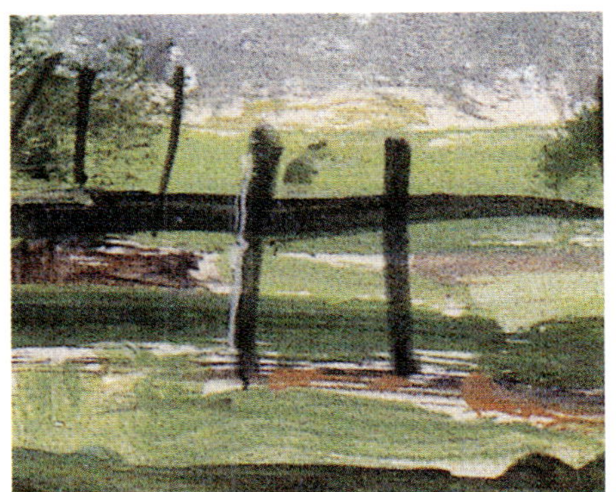

Detail

art map 3

Harnessing the power of light

Before you begin, read the entire project through so you know what's going to happen next.

Landscape painters are always inspired by the rich light and deep shadows that occur during the late evening. The light changes very rapidly during this period, but for a short period of time the effects are powerful.

This painting features the village of Stonington, Maine, in strong evening light.

1. The image to be transferred using the art map.

Read the instructions to see how to map this image across to your working surface.

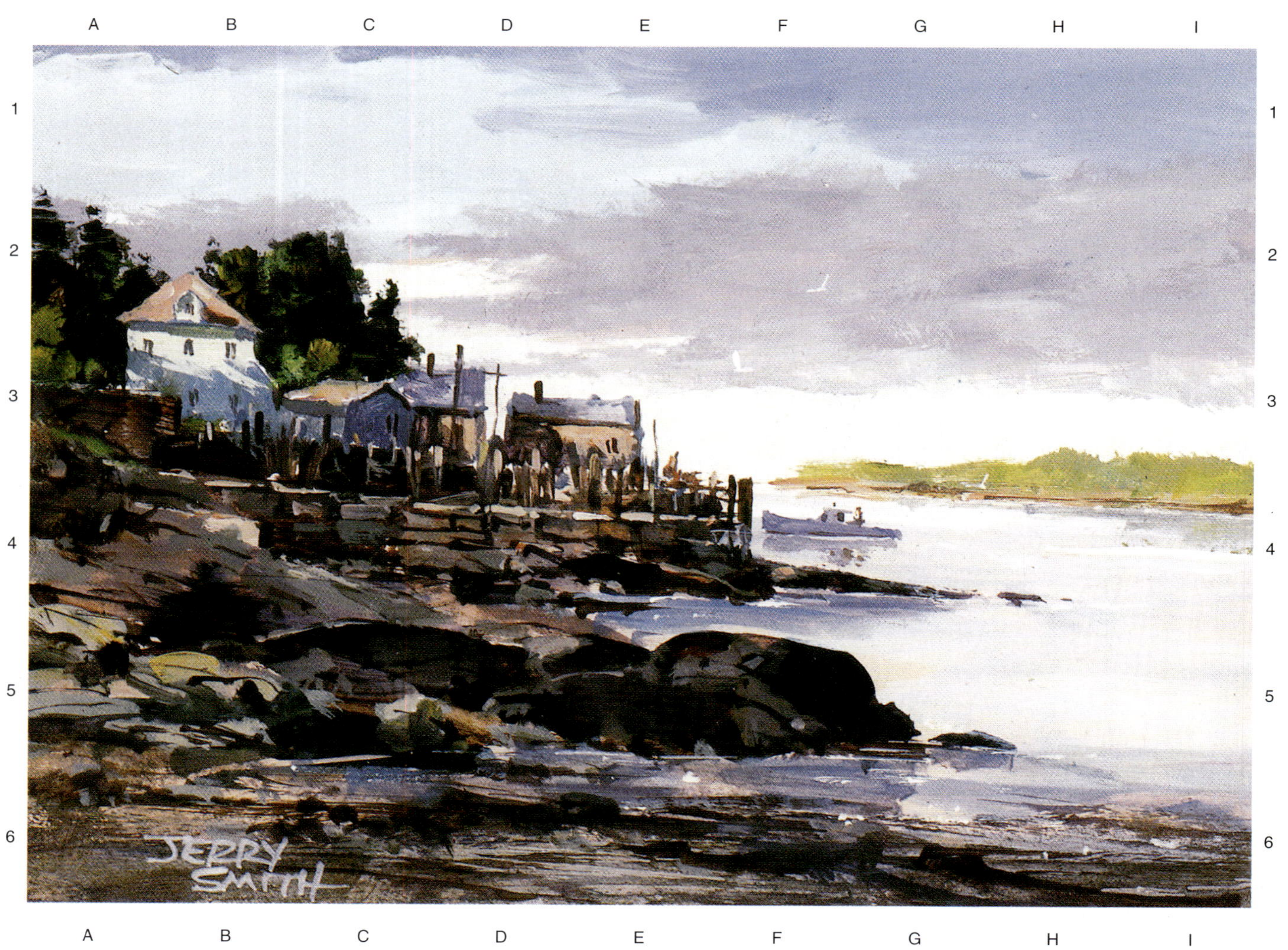

2. Map the image

With a 2B pencil, begin by LIGHTLY drawing a grid on your working surface that has the exact same number of squares as my grid. Your support can be the size of my original, or you can choose something proportionally larger or smaller. Your art map will be 6 squares down and 9 squares across. Put in the letters and numbers along the edges to make the next step easier.

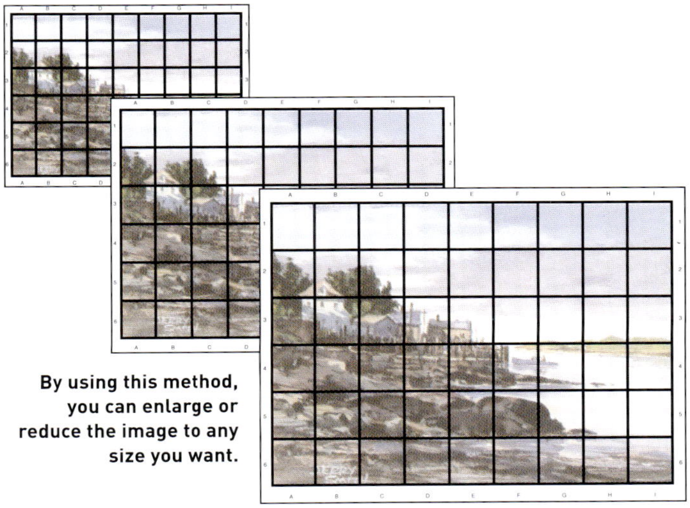

By using this method, you can enlarge or reduce the image to any size you want.

3. Use the art map to transfer the image

Now, still drawing very LIGHTLY with your pencil, copy the main contour lines of the object as shown in each square onto your working surface. It's not necessary to get every detail—just a simple line drawing will do. I recommend LIGHTLY and gently erasing the grid lines in the open, lighter areas before continuing.

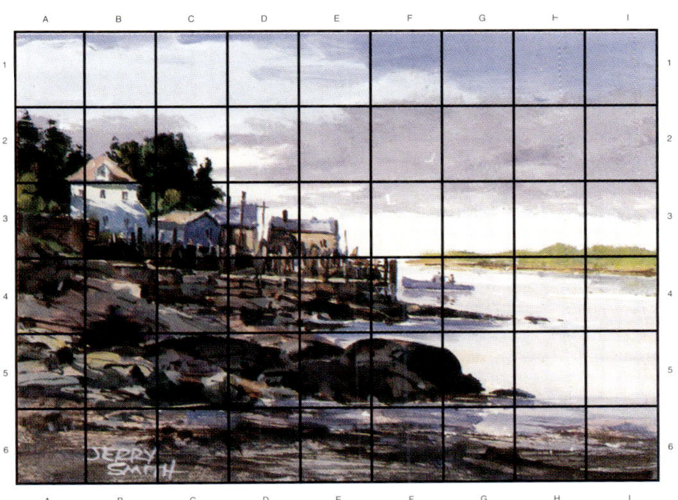

This is how your art map should look.

Here I've done the drawing in dark ink so you can see the idea, but you will do this lightly in pencil.

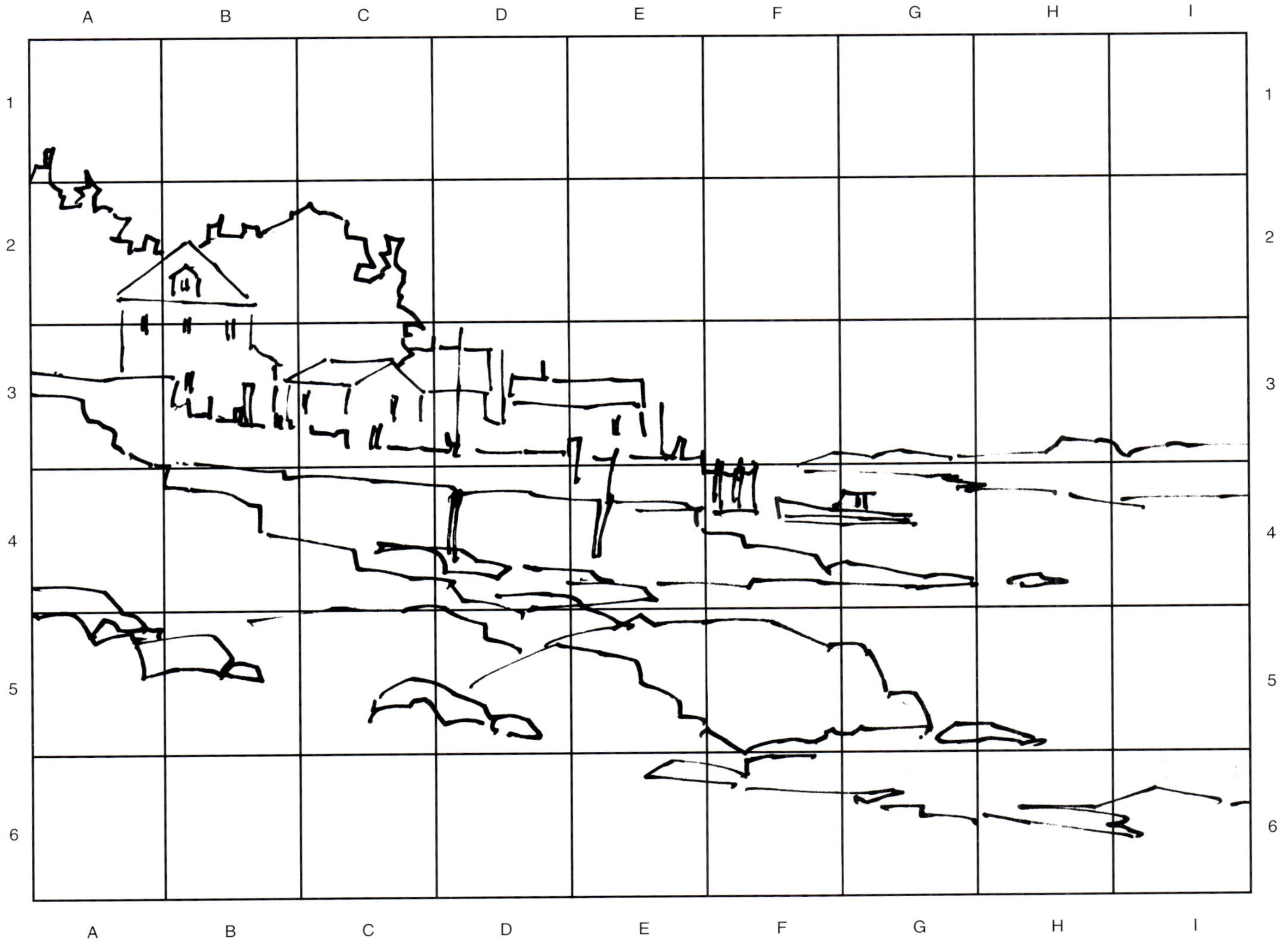

Study these pages before you start painting

Shape map
The large dominant shape on the left is balanced by two smaller shapes on the right that point to the focal area. Clouds can sometimes be a significant element in your composition. Loose rock shapes also walk the viewer into the painting.

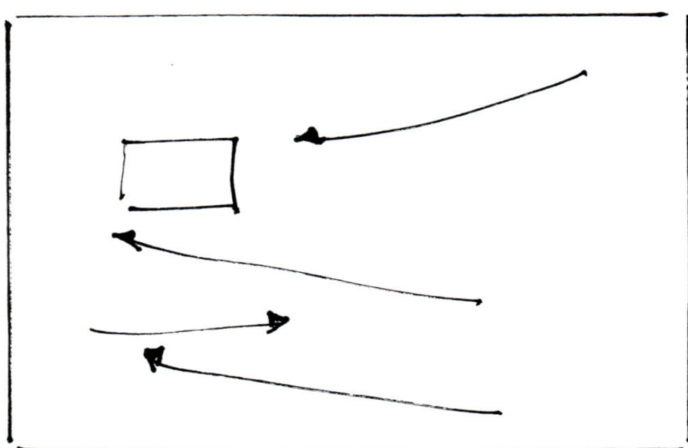

Design map
Zigzag design walks the viewer through the painting toward the center of interest.

Cloud shapes interlock with each other and direct the eye toward the focal point. Lost and found edges keep the foreground from becoming too busy. A variety of sizes, shapes and colors of rocks also enhances the foreground. Foreground colors carried into buildings help unify the painting.

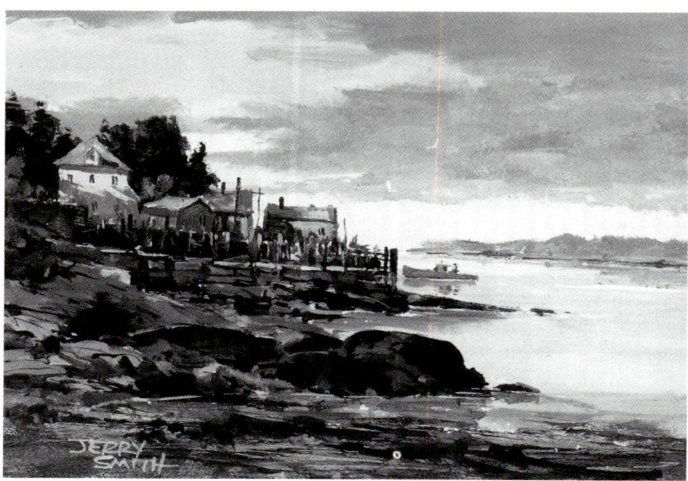

Tonal value map
Look at how the painting's lights and darks work to engage the viewer. The darks are tied together. It's not necessary to separate every tree and every rock. A large stand of trees or group of rocks can be massed together. The value contrast pulls the eye toward buildings, the dock and the boat.

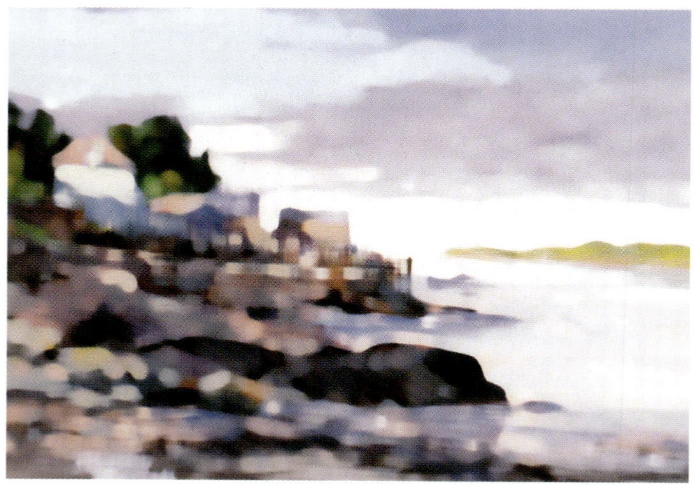

Color map (what you would see if you were to squint)
This painting has a red/green color plan with the greens dominating. Remember to vary your greens.

materials you'll need

painting surface
canvas or board

brushes
¼", ½" and 1" flats
nos. 4, 6 and 12 rounds
small rigger

other tools
2B pencil
ruler
palette
spray bottle to keep your palette moist

your acrylic palette for this painting

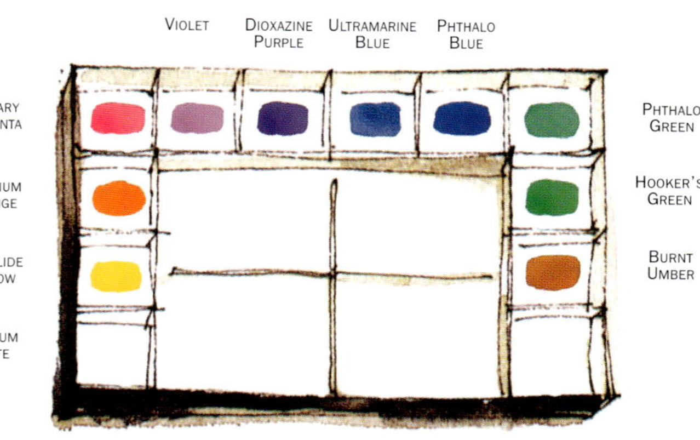

Consider the following elements

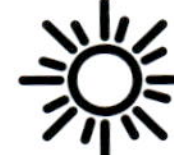

Light source

The light source is low in the sky and from the left side, casting shadows to the right.

Bright idea

Long shadows describe the mood and time of day. The entire foreground was taken down in value to place it in shadow. The warm light on the buildings and distant island makes the shapes "pop."

Planes

There is a definitive illusion of recession achieved by making a definite foreground, middleground and background.

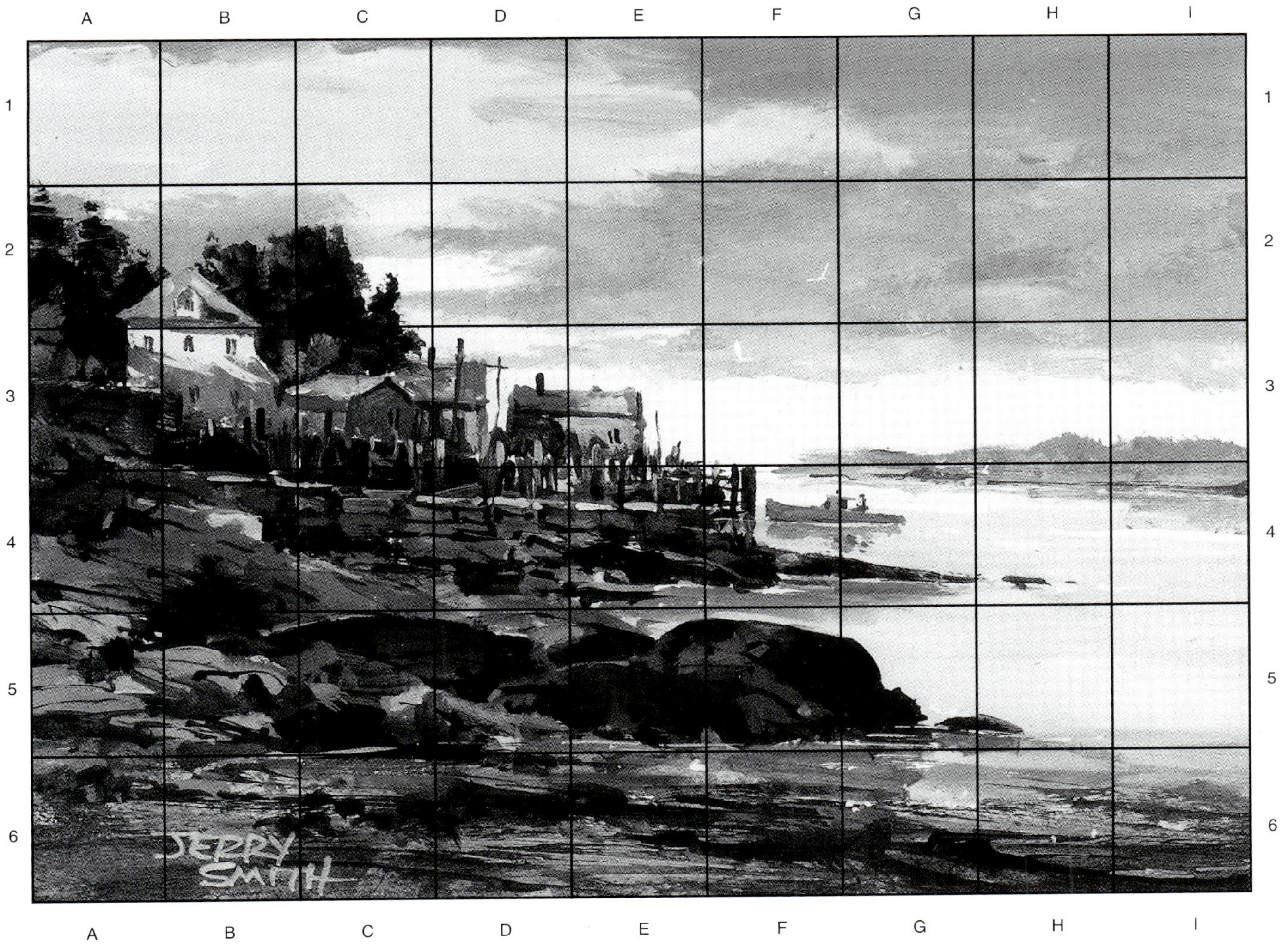

Put it all together

4. Start with the sky

Block in the sky and then refine it in three or four layers before moving on to the rest of the painting. Note that the sky is much lighter at the horizon, providing a nice contrast for the trees and buildings.

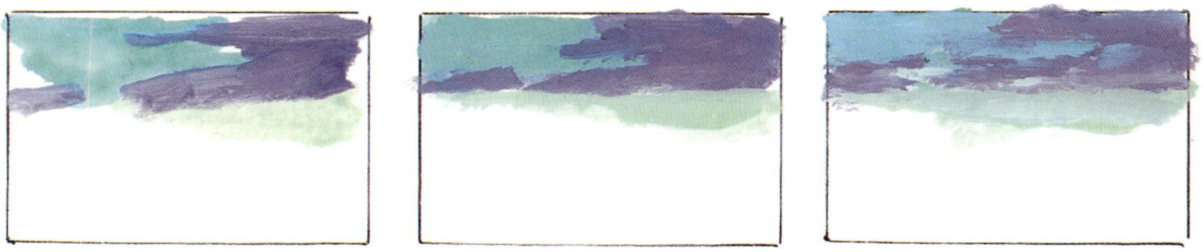

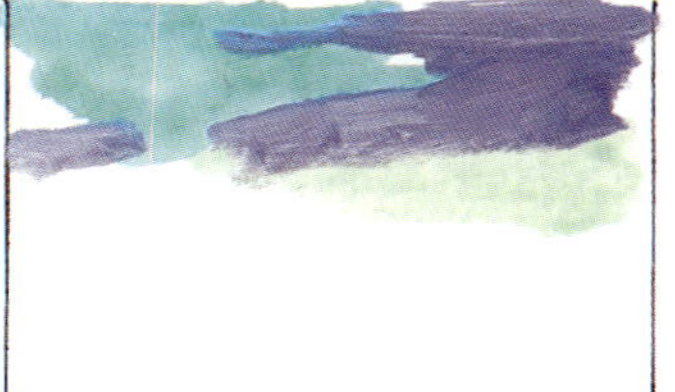

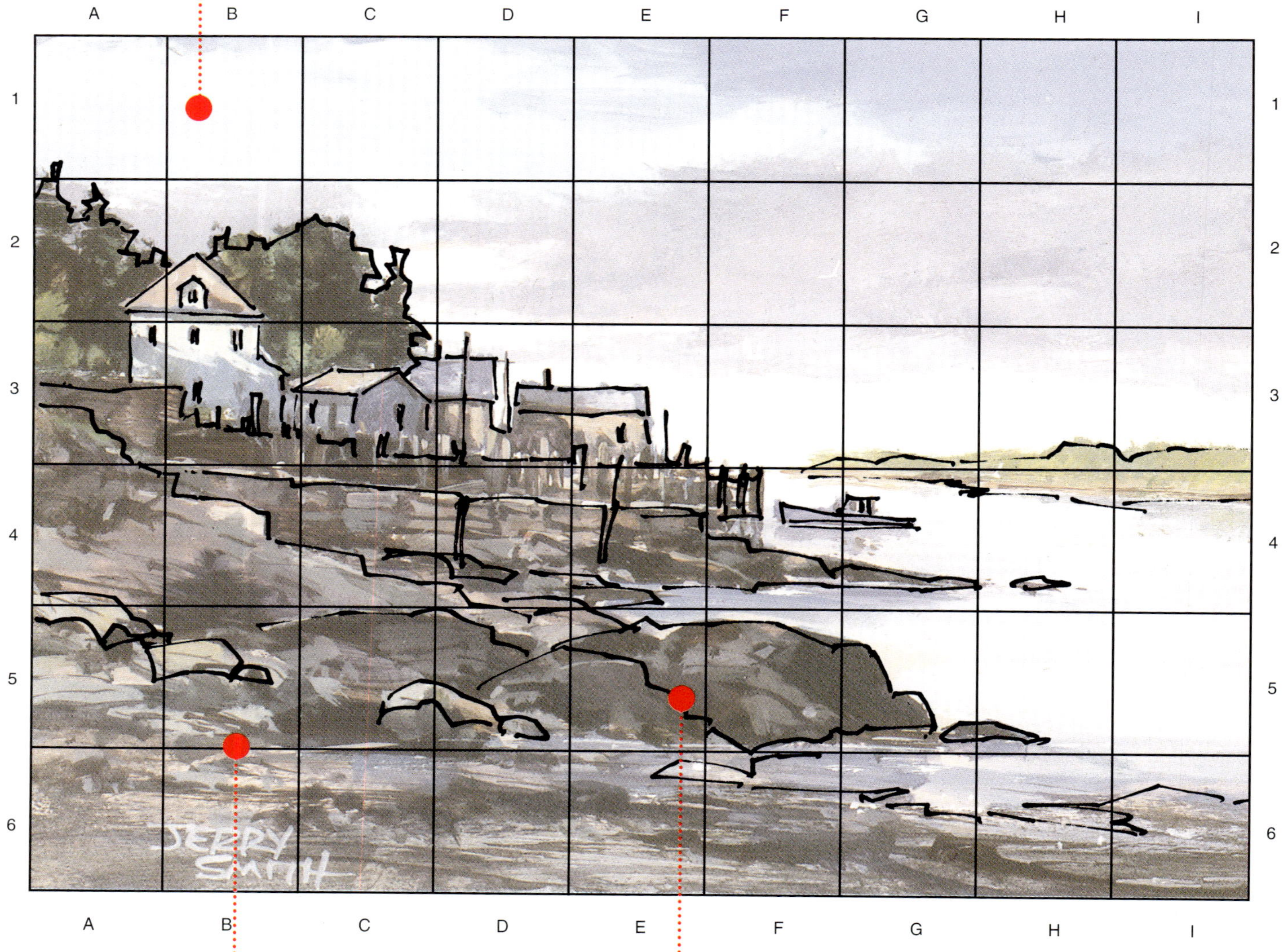

5. Block in the foreground

Using a violet-gray midtone, block in the entire foreground. Much of this underpainting will show through in the completed painting.

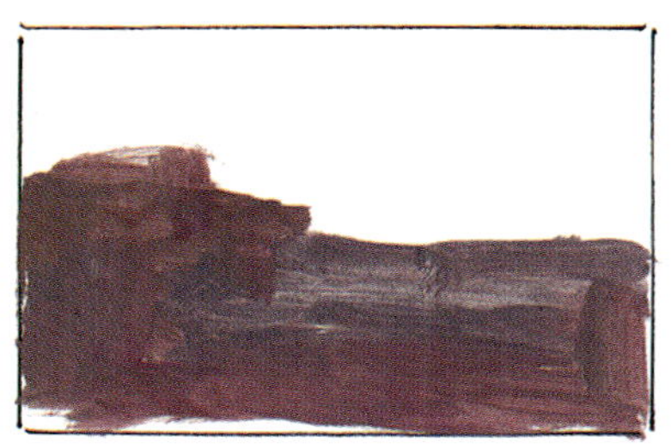

6. Modify sunlight and shadows

For sunlight or shadows, modify the base color by adding warm or cool colors.

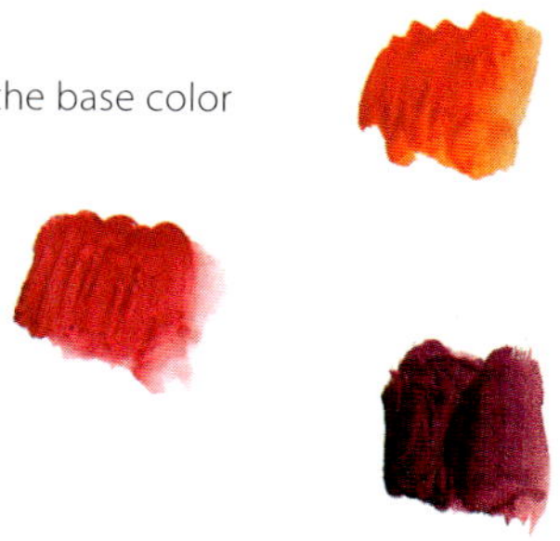

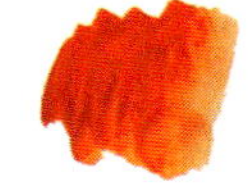

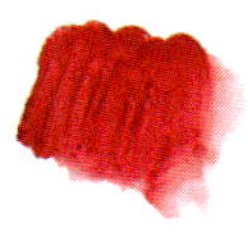

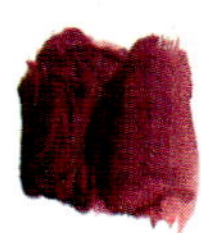

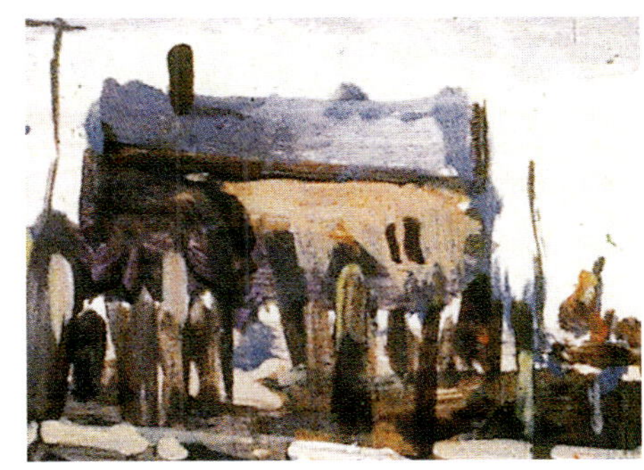

Detail

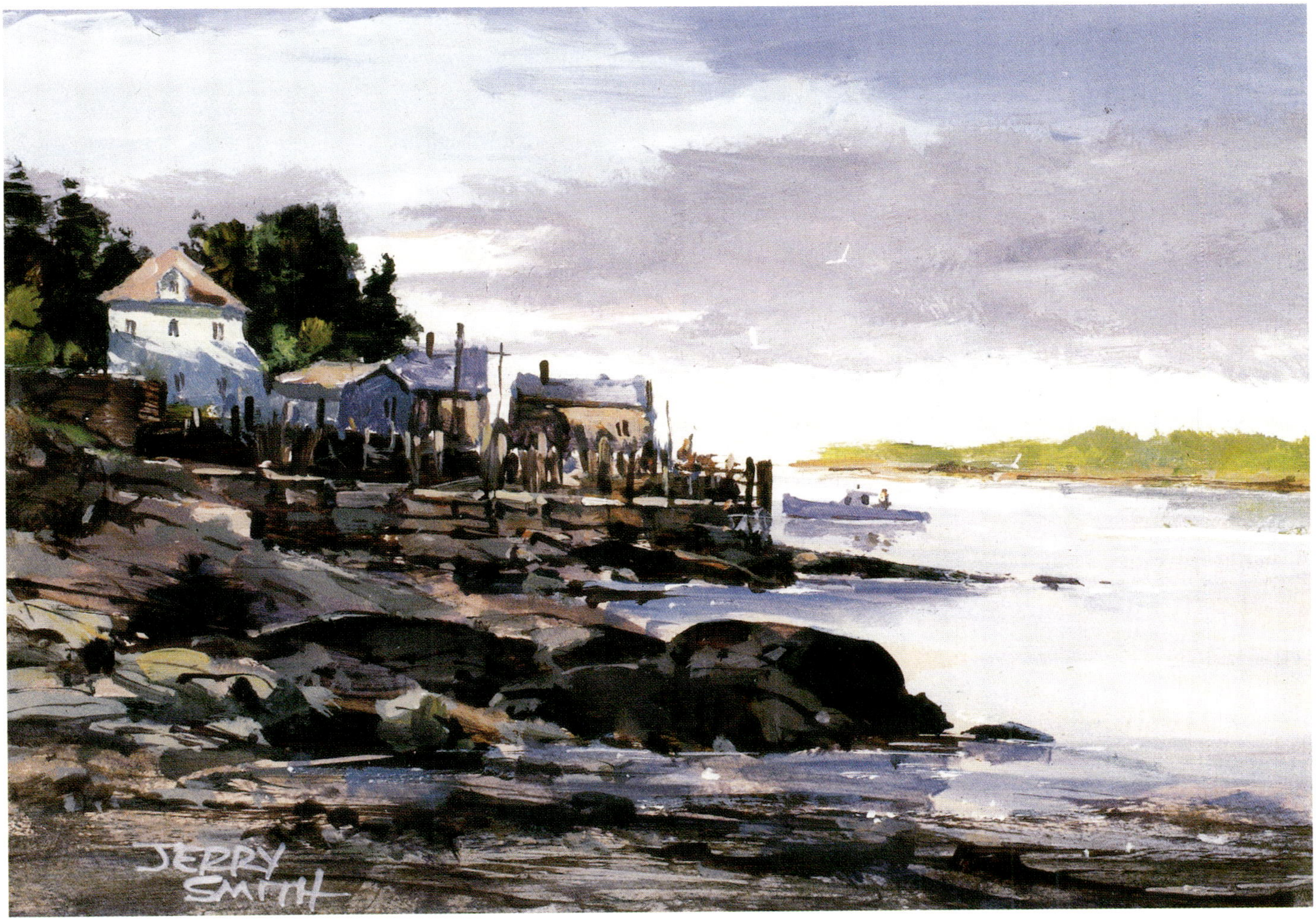

Stonington Evening, acrylic, 6 x 9" (15 x 23cm) by Jerry Smith ©

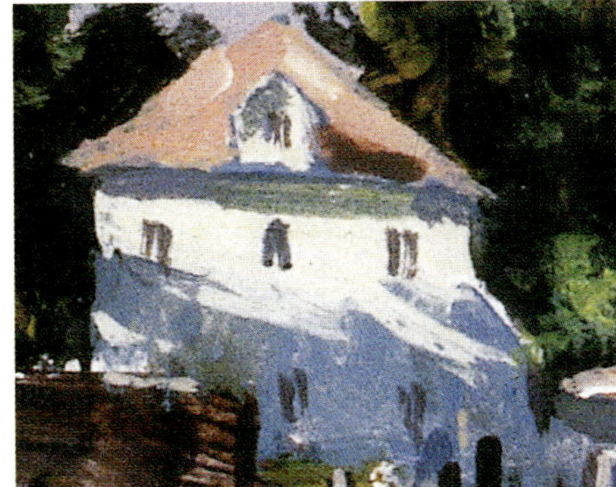

Detail

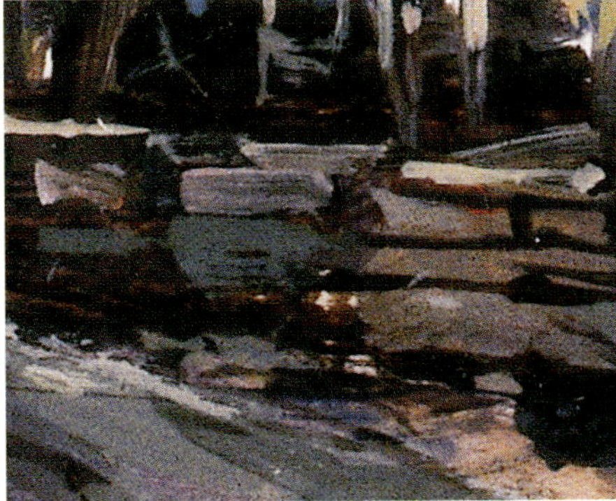

Detail

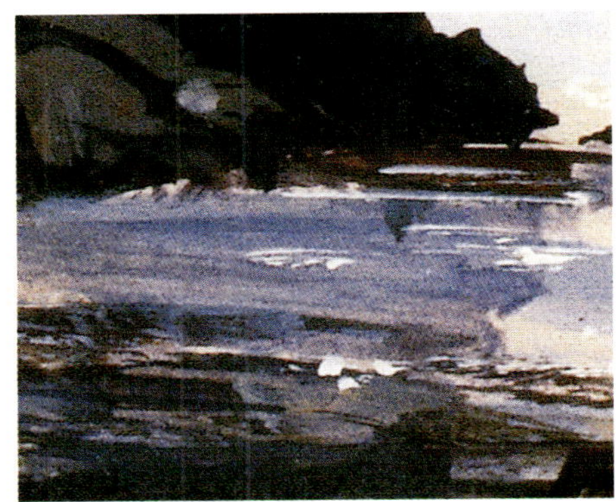

Detail

Before you begin, read the entire project through so you know what's going to happen next.

art map 4

Juxtaposing shapes and color

Another important aspect of painting is unity. All of the various elements of your painting must work together. One of the ways to achieve unity is to pull your painting together with shape and color. The painting in this exercise features relatively soft light and a complementary yellow/violet color plan.

The painting approach and techniques will be essentially the same as in the previous projects. You could try painting this one on unprimed watercolor paper, giving the completed painting more of a watercolor look.

Try drawing only a few significant shapes and doing the rest with paint. Don't forget acrylics are very forgiving if you make mistakes.

1. The image to be transferred using the art map.

Read the instructions to see how to map this image across to your working surface

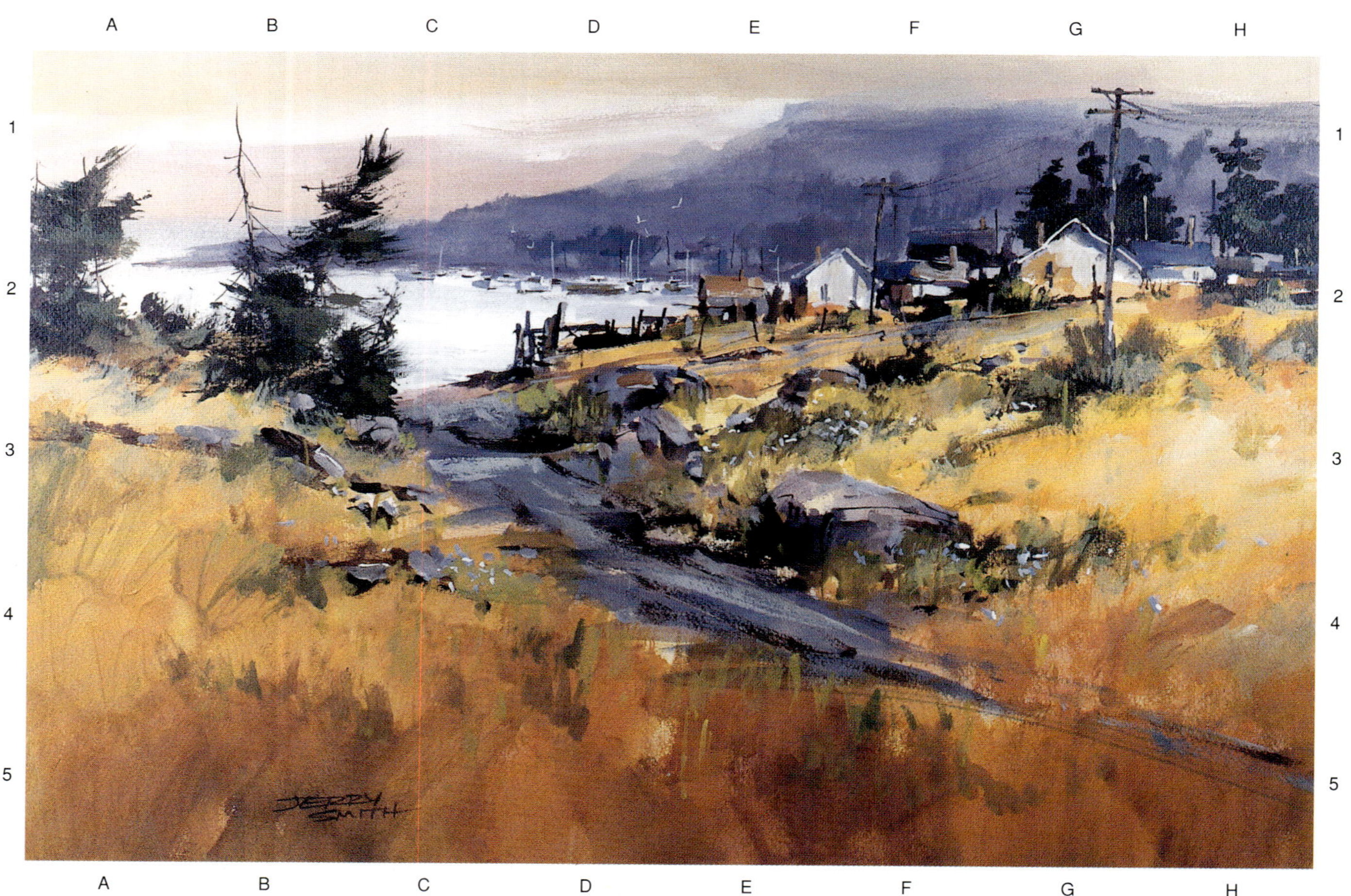

2. Map the image

With a 2B pencil, begin by LIGHTLY drawing a grid on your working surface that has the exact same number of squares as my grid. Your support can be the size of my original, or you can choose something proportionally larger or smaller. Your art map will be 5 squares down and 8 squares across. Put in the letters and numbers along the edges to make the next step easier.

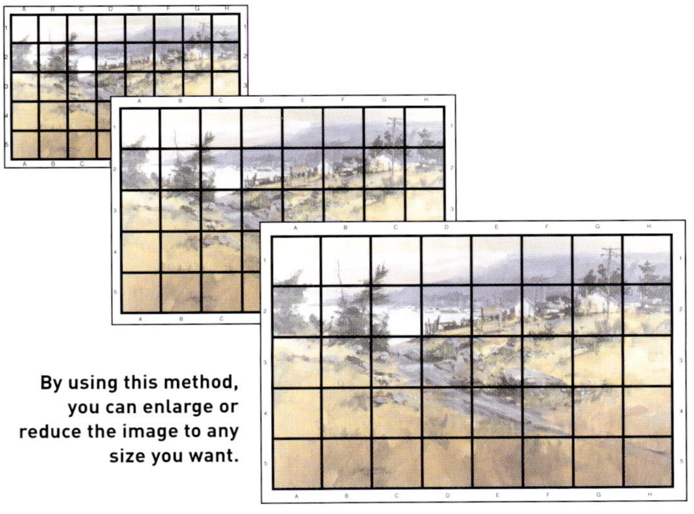

By using this method, you can enlarge or reduce the image to any size you want.

3. Use the art map to transfer the image

Now, still drawing very LIGHTLY with your pencil, copy the main contour lines of the object as shown in each square onto your working surface. It's not necessary to get every detail—just a simple line drawing will do. I recommend LIGHTLY and gently erasing the grid lines in the open, lighter areas before continuing.

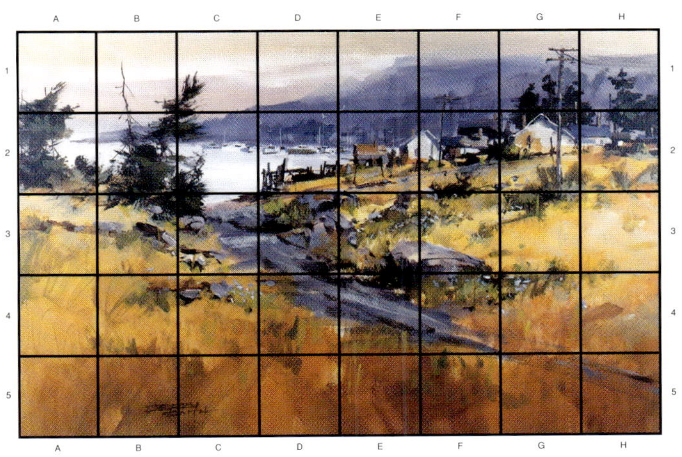

This is how your art map should look.

Here I've done the drawing in dark ink so you can see the idea, but you will do this lightly in pencil.

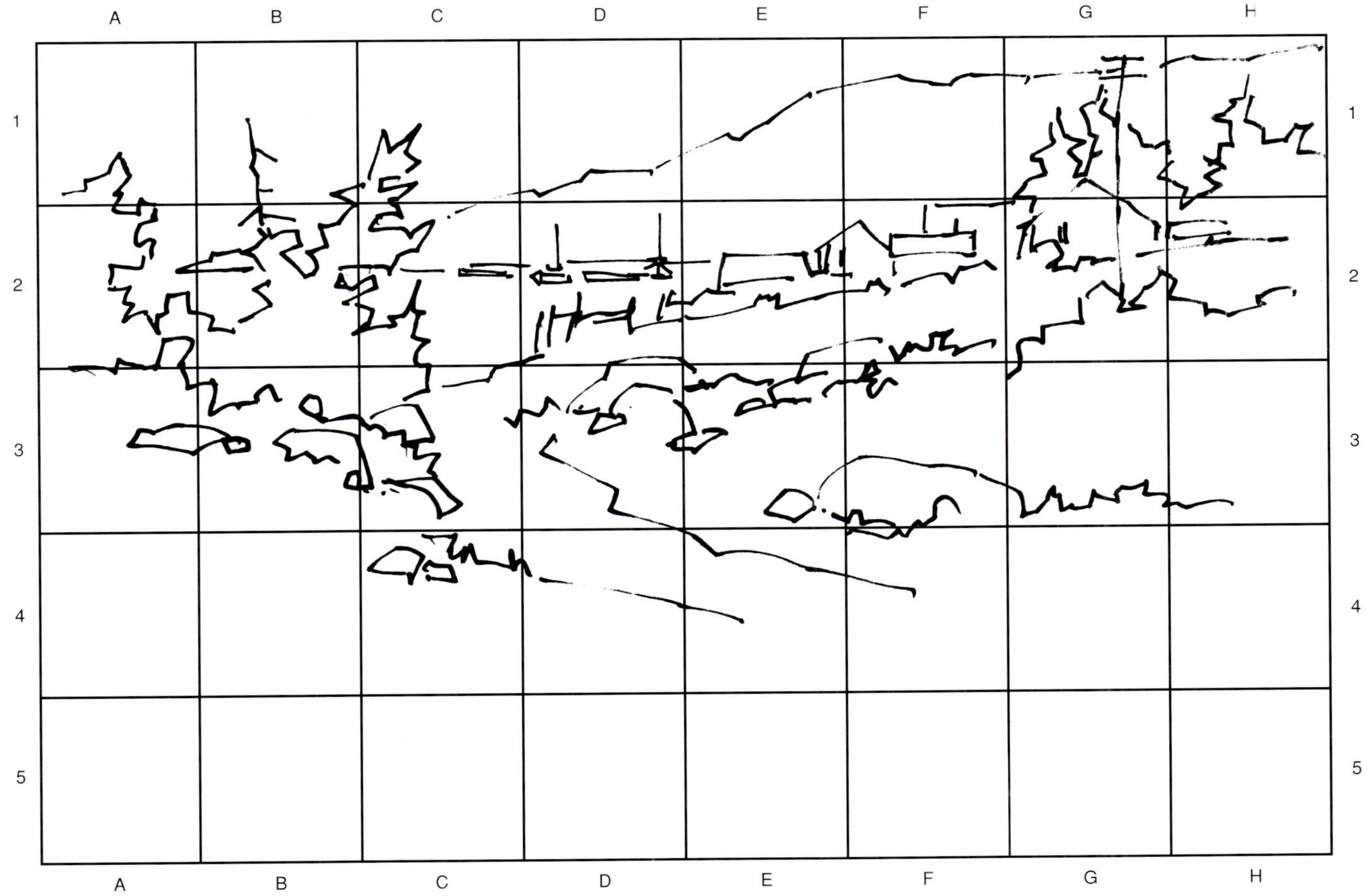

Study these pages before you start painting

Note the interlocking shapes throughout the painting. Loose strokes representing grass interlock with rocks and road to pull the foreground together. The vertical trees, posts, and chimneys pull the foreground, middle distance, and background together. Building shapes interlock, making them work together as one unit. As the viewer's eye works through the painting, the distant boats interlock with the background hills. Even the sky and background hills have some "lost and found" edges that pull them together. Finally, a few background colors carried into the foreground and vice versa also help pull the painting together.

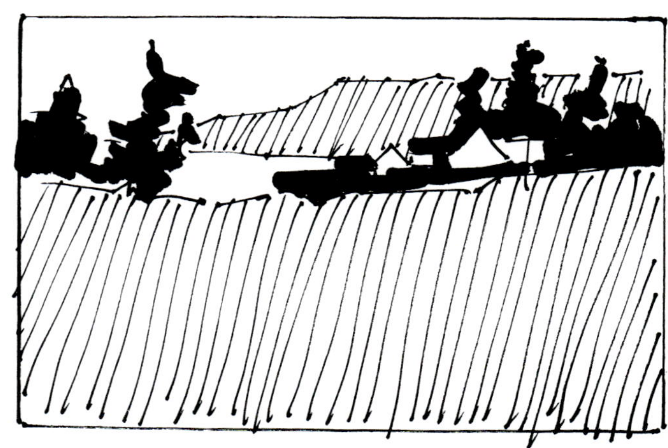

Shape map
Note the broken, uneven edges at the base of buildings and trees. This allows these shapes to gracefully merge with the land.

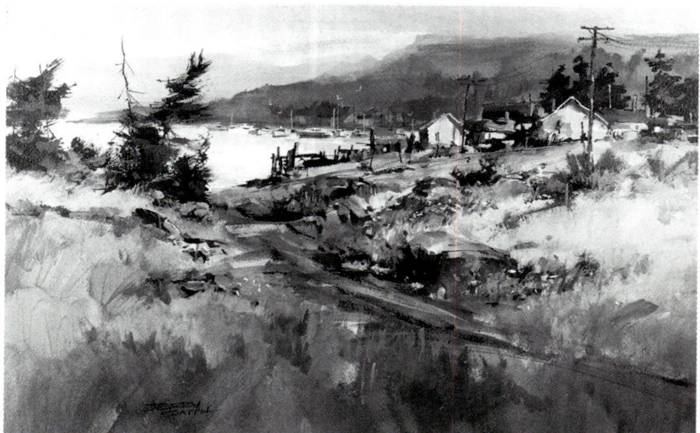

Tonal value map

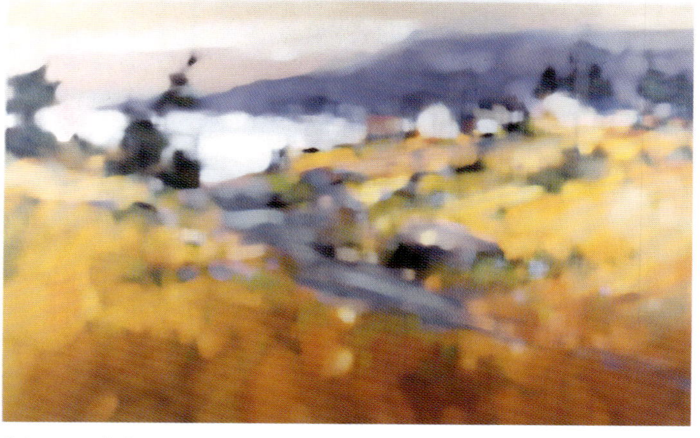

Color map (what you would see if you were to squint)
The painting has a yellow/violet color plan with the yellows dominating. A variety of greens are used throughout as accent colors.

materials you'll need

painting surface
This painting was done on a half sheet (15 x 22"/38 x 56cm) piece of stretched 140lb (300 gsm) watercolor paper. Stretching the paper ensures having a flat surface to work on, especially when applying initial washes of paint. If your paper is 300lb (638 gsm), stretching is not necessary.

brushes
1/4", 1/2" and 1" flats
nos. 4, 6 and 12 rounds
small rigger

other tools
2B pencil
ruler
palette
spray bottle to keep your palette moist

your acrylic palette for this painting

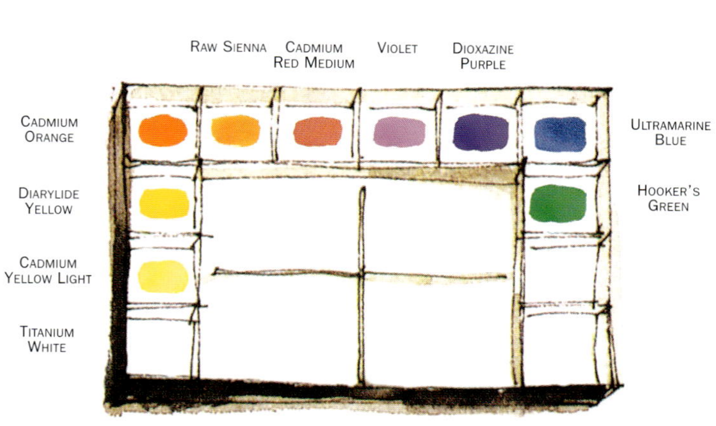

Consider the following elements

How to prepare watercolor paper

If your paper is less than 300lb you will need to stretch it. Soak your paper in water or with a large, natural sponge. Mount it as shown in the diagram, let it dry overnight, and you'll have a great surface to work on the next day.

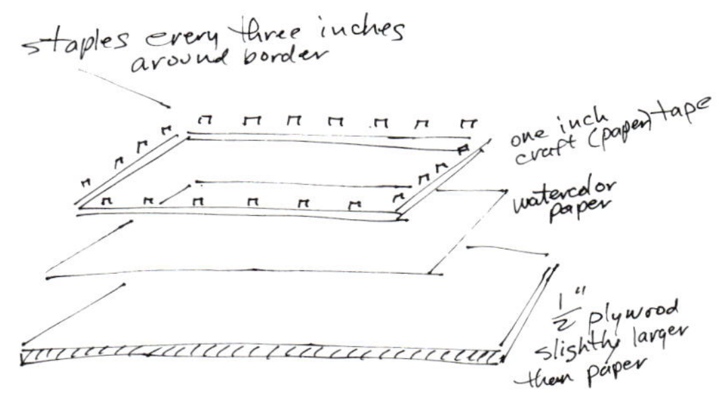

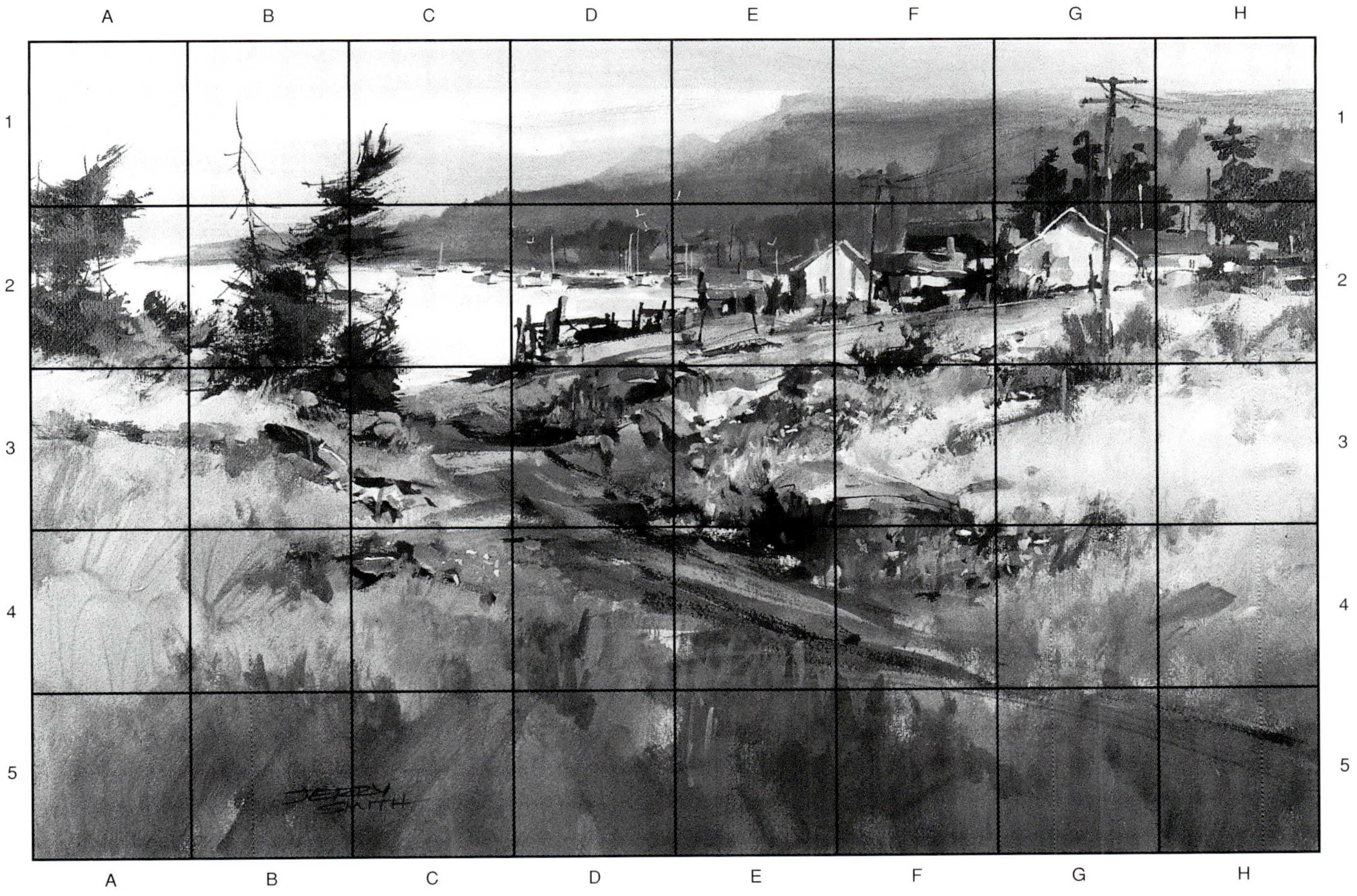

A B C D E F G H

1 2 3 4 5

Put it all together

4. Block-in

This painting begins with big washes of paint similar to watercolor washes. The advantage of acrylics is that you will later be going over these washes, so you don't have the worry about making mistakes at this stage.

5. Apply the initial washes

The initial washes are applied very loosely allowing them to blend in some places. Be on the alert for those "happy accidents" that occur when flowing colors come together.

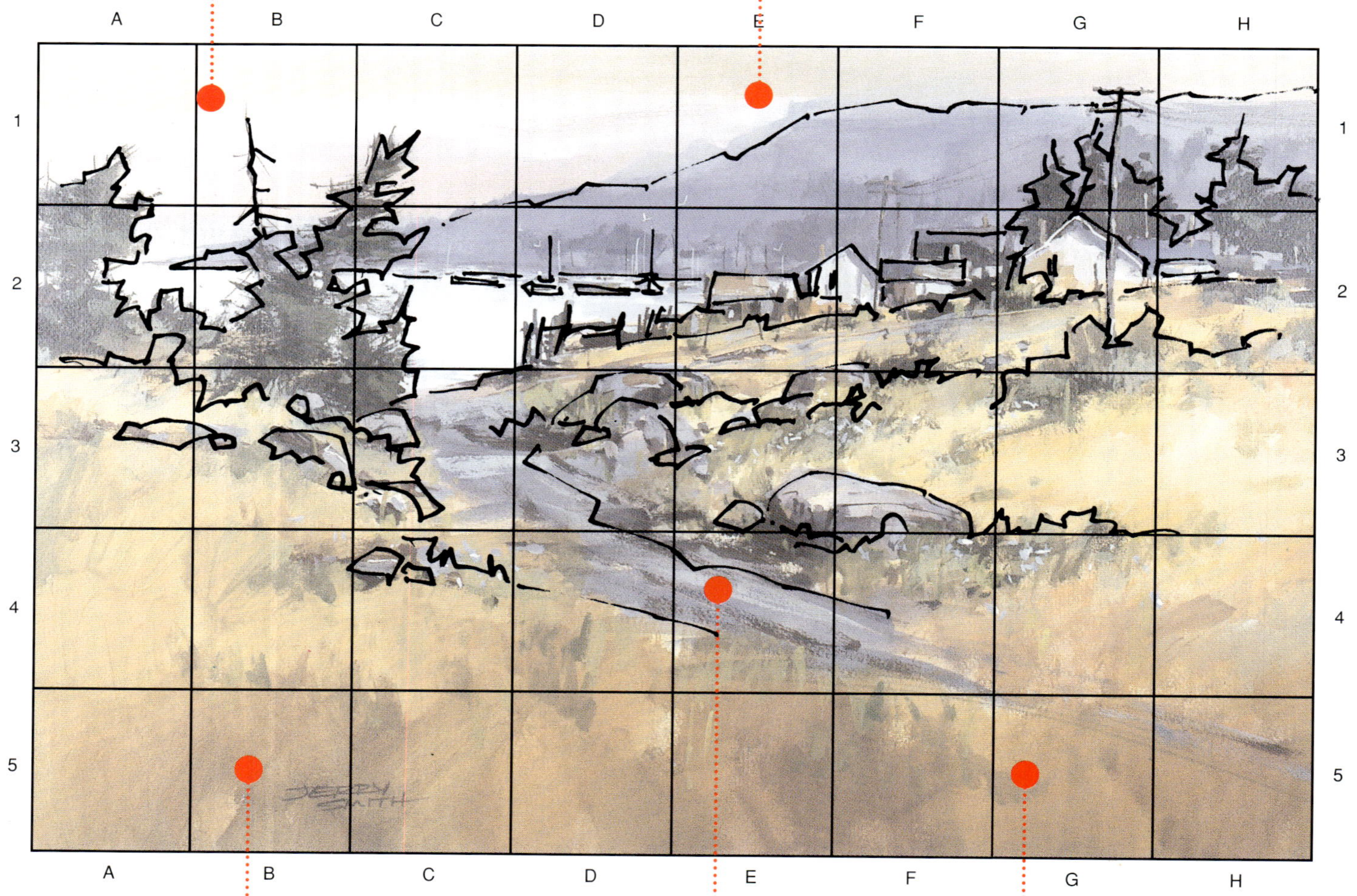

6. Overpaint to add detail

Overpaint with darks and lights to refine the painting and add detail. Note the various grays and neutral colors that can be obtained by mixing complementary yellows and violets.

7. Overlap to lock shapes

Colors overlapping from one shape to another lock shapes together. Dark shapes such as trees and rocks are given dimension by overlapping them with strokes of a lighter value.

8. Imply the grass

Much of the foreground texture is represented by the loose brushwork in the underpainting, but now a few bold, expressive strokes will the impression of a large grassy foreground.

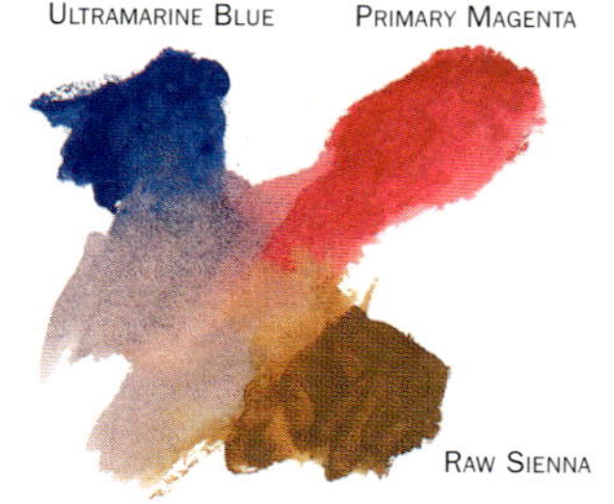

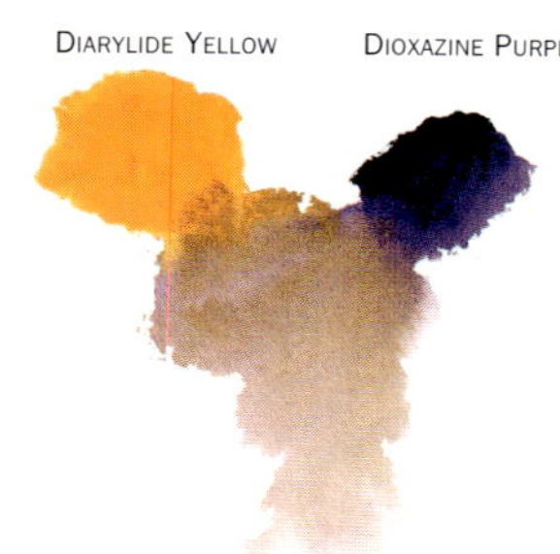

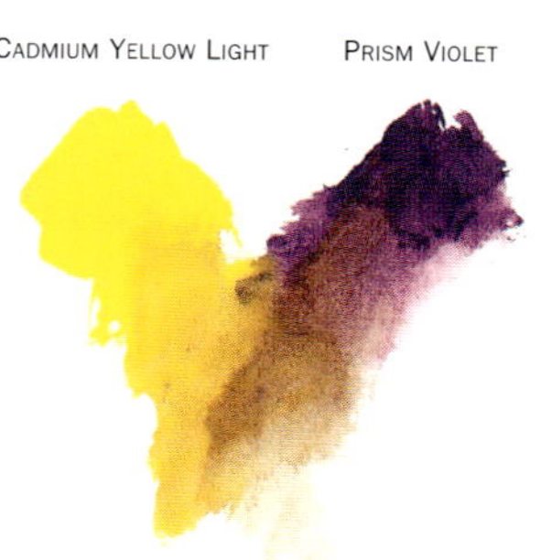

Learning points

- Be ready to capitalize on "happy accidents."
- For unity, tie shapes and colors together.

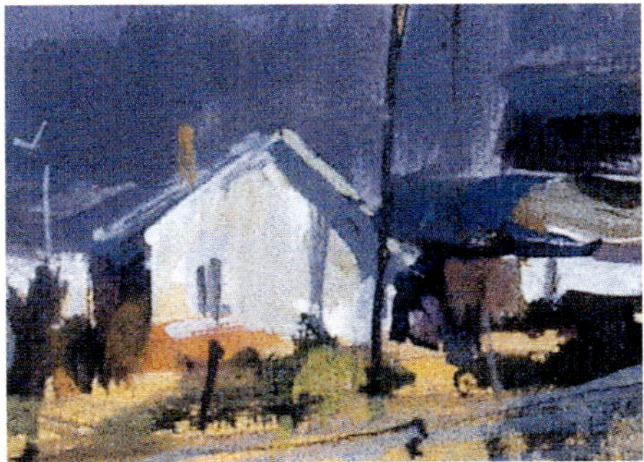

Detail

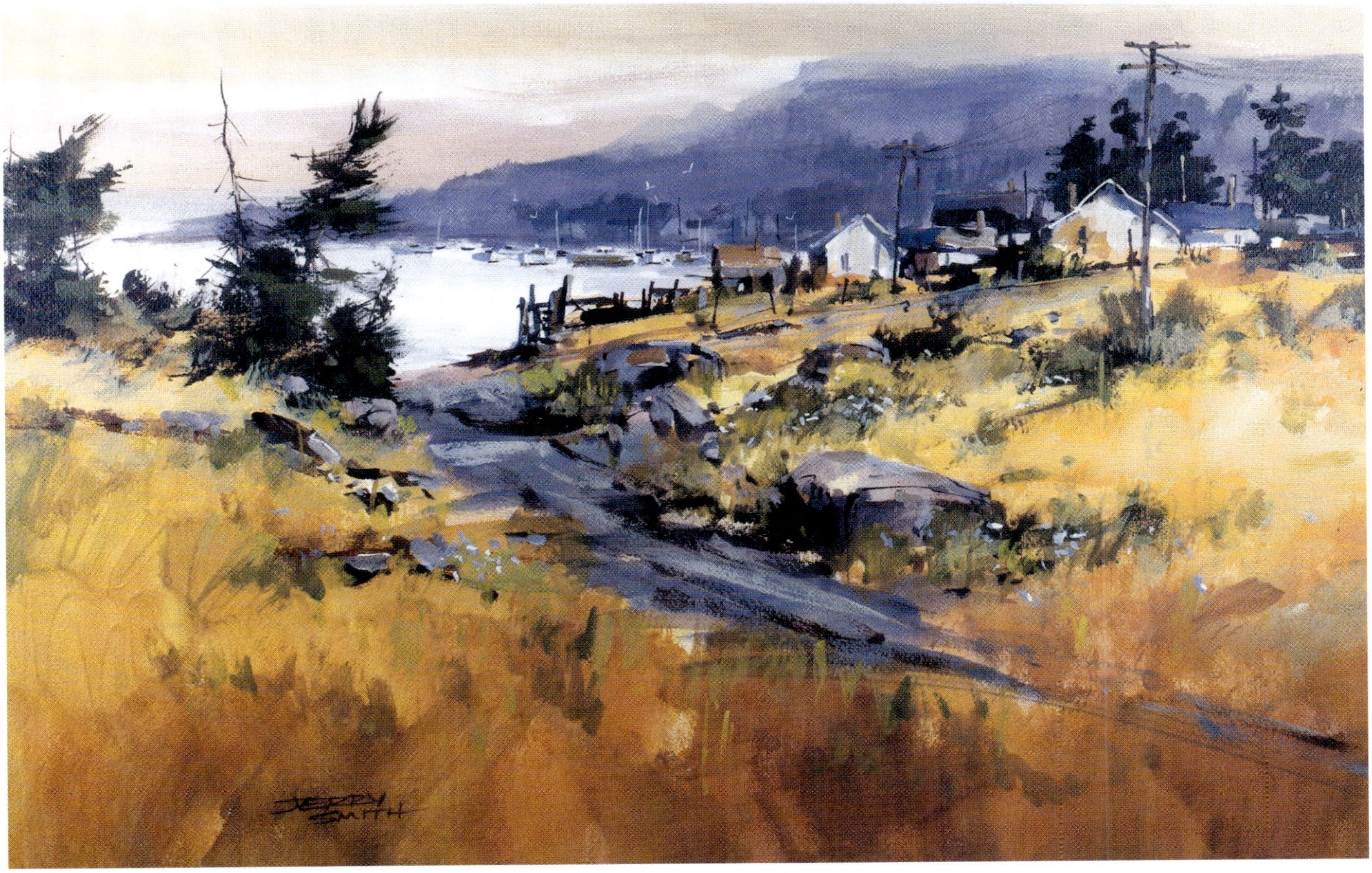

***Harbor Gold*, acrylic, 15 x 21" (38 x 53cm) by Jerry Smith ©**

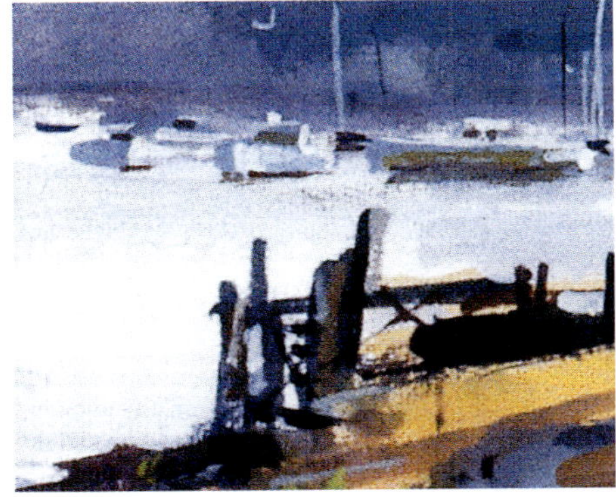

Detail

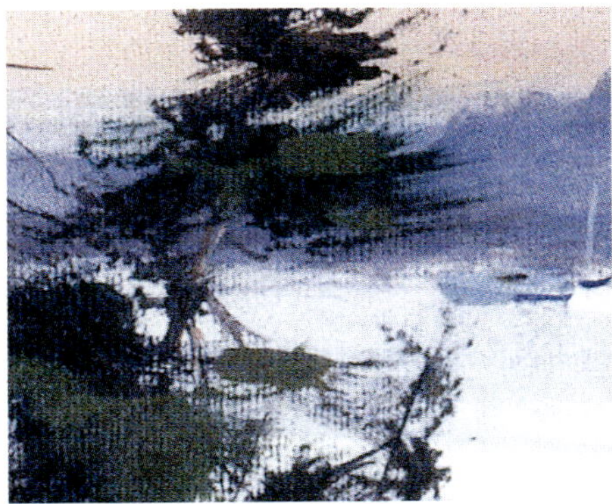

Detail

Detail

art map 5

Using grays and earth tones

Before you begin, read the entire project through so you know what's going to happen next.

A painting dominated by grays and earth tone colors doesn't have to be dull and lifeless. Subtle colors can focus concentration on other aspects of the painting such as value and texture. Snow scenes in particular offer a great opportunity for dramatic contrasts in values, shapes and textures.

The setting for this painting is a creek that runs through my home county. Sugar Creek has provided limitless painting material for me in all seasons. At almost any point on the creek you can spot white sycamore trees standing out dramatically against the background. In this painting the sycamores provide a way to repeat and carry through the bright whites displayed by the snow banks. This exercise also offers the opportunity to paint simplified, yet believable, water reflections.

1. The image to be transferred using the art map.

Read the instructions to see how to map this image across to your working surface.

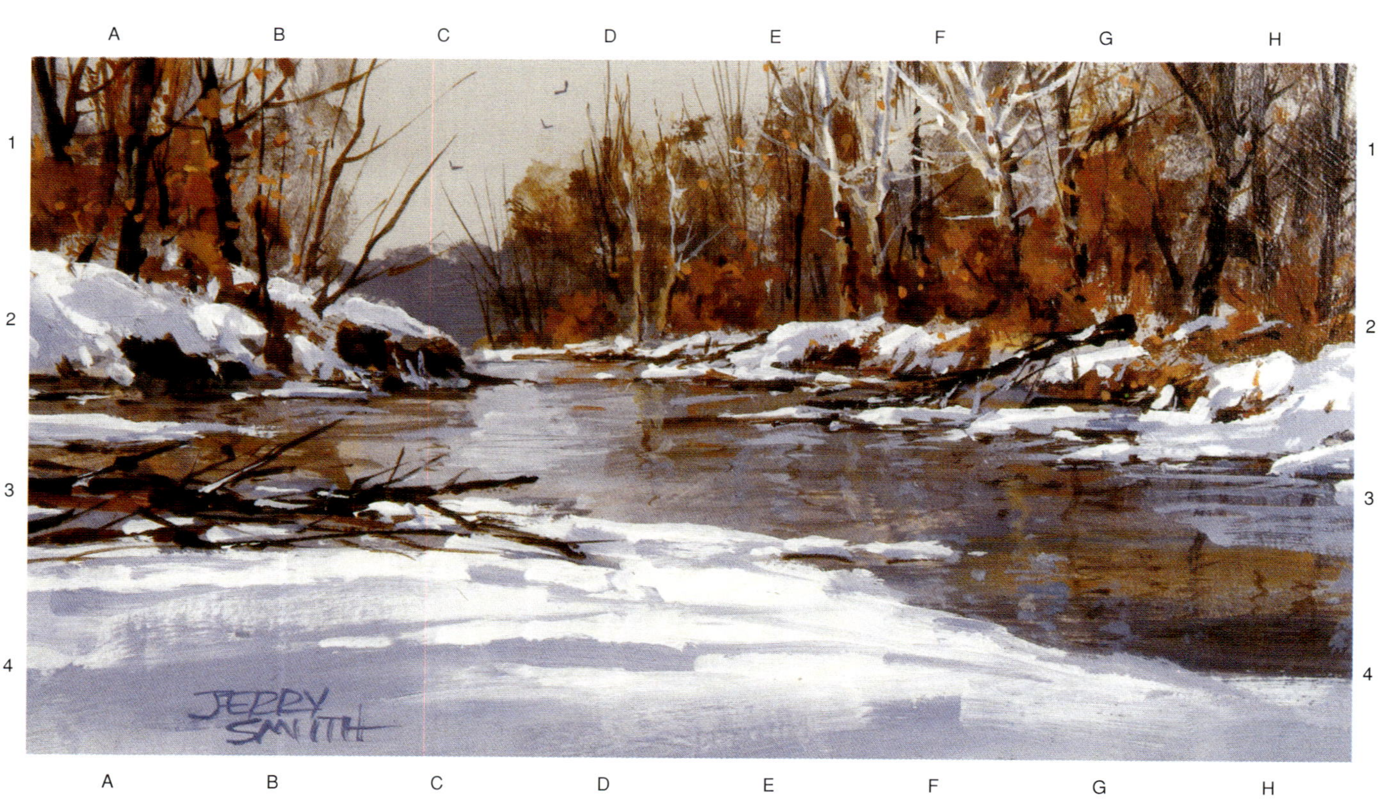

2. Map the image

With a 2B pencil, begin by LIGHTLY drawing a grid on your working surface that has the exact same number of squares as my grid. Your support can be the size of my original, or you can choose something proportionally larger or smaller. Your art map will be 6 squares down and 9 squares across. Put in the letters and numbers along the edges to make the next step easier.

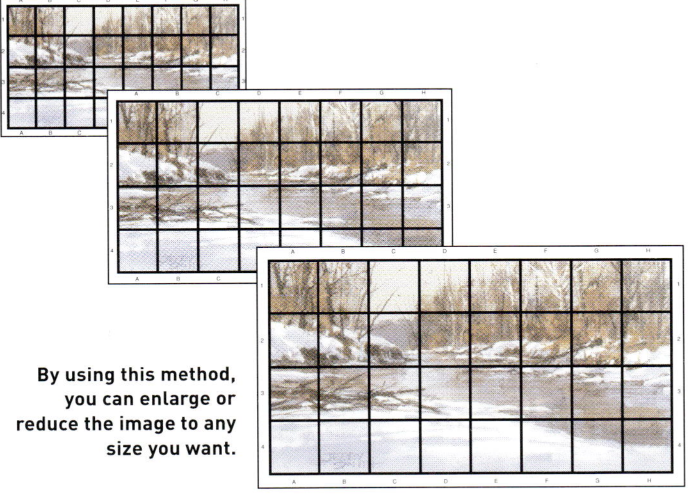

By using this method, you can enlarge or reduce the image to any size you want.

3. Use the art map to transfer the image

Now, still drawing very LIGHTLY with your pencil, copy the main contour lines of the object as shown in each square onto your working surface. It's not necessary to get every detail—just a simple line drawing will do. I recommend LIGHTLY and gently erasing the grid lines in the open, lighter areas before continuing.

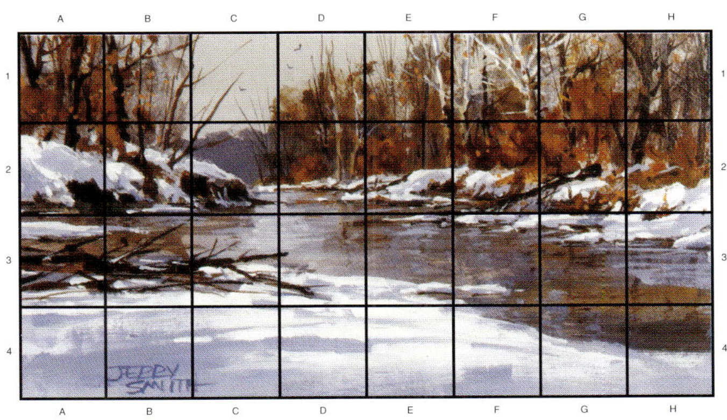

This is how your art map should look.

Here I've done the drawing in dark ink so you can see the idea, but you will do this lightly in pencil.

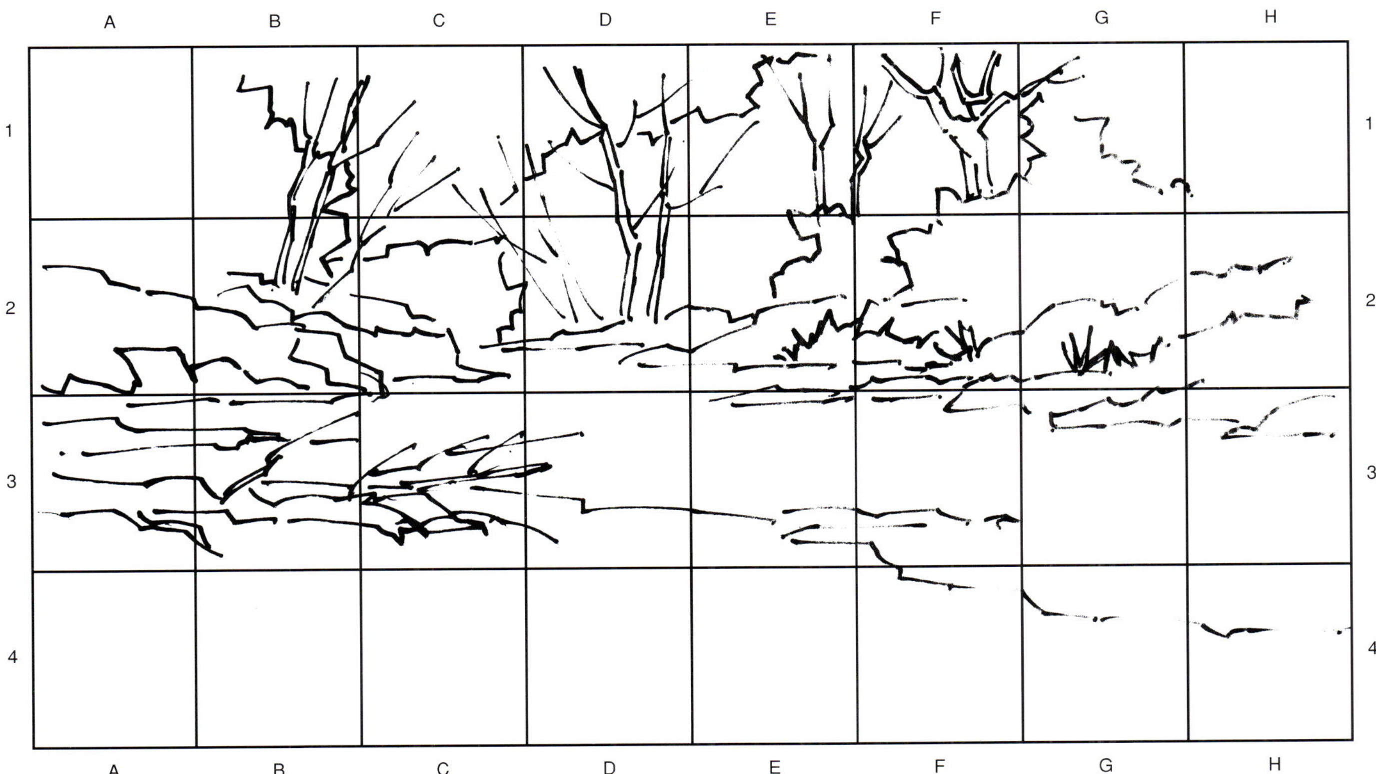

Study these pages before you start painting

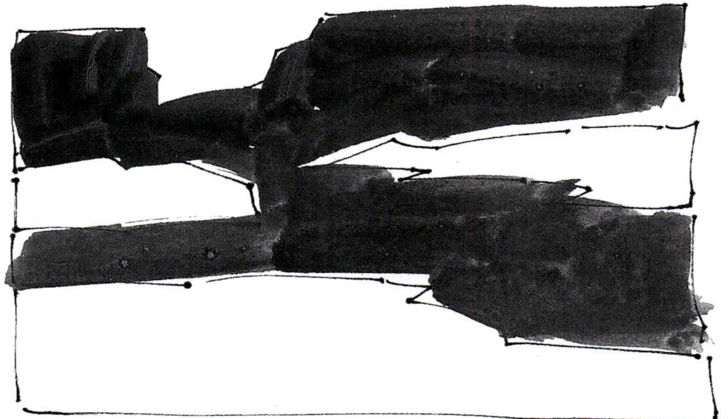

Shape map
Large shape in lower left is balanced by long dark shape at upper right. Note the simplification of wooded areas. Large sections are painted as one big shape. Then just a few individual trees are painted to give the impression of a deep wood.

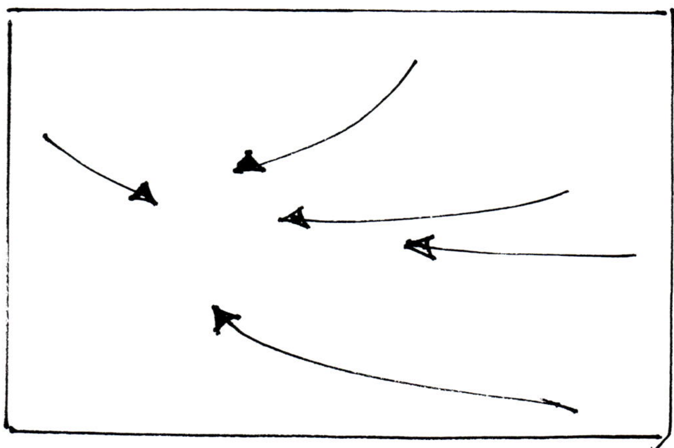

Design map
This painting is designed to lead eye gradually downstream and into the painting.

The horizon split is off-center with the larger section on the bottom. Branches and fallen trees serve as directional vehicles to move eye through the painting. Foreground shadows frame in the bottom to hold the viewer's eye in the painting.

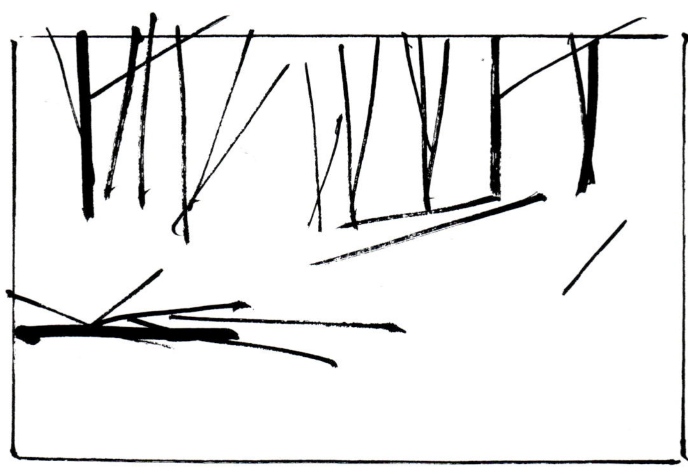

Line map
Line and calligraphy play a significant role in this painting.

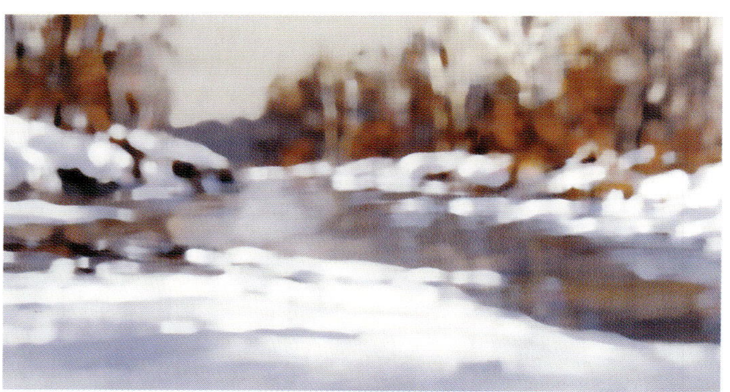

Color map (what you would see if you were to squint)

materials you'll need

painting surface
canvas, board or paper

brushes
$^1/_4$", $^1/_2$" and 1" flats
nos. 4, 6 and 12 rounds
small rigger

other tools
2B pencil
ruler
palette
spray bottle to keep your palette moist

your acrylic palette for this painting

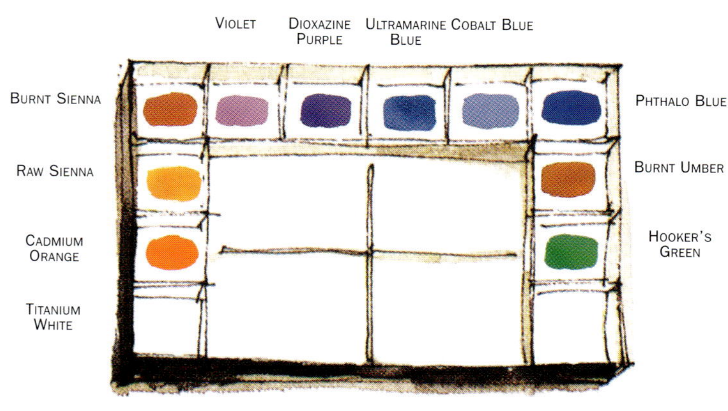

Consider the following elements

Bright idea

Drybrush with a lot of paint and just enough water to make it flow for the desired effect. The best effects are achieved by holding the brush almost horizontal to the support while scrubbing paint onto the surface.

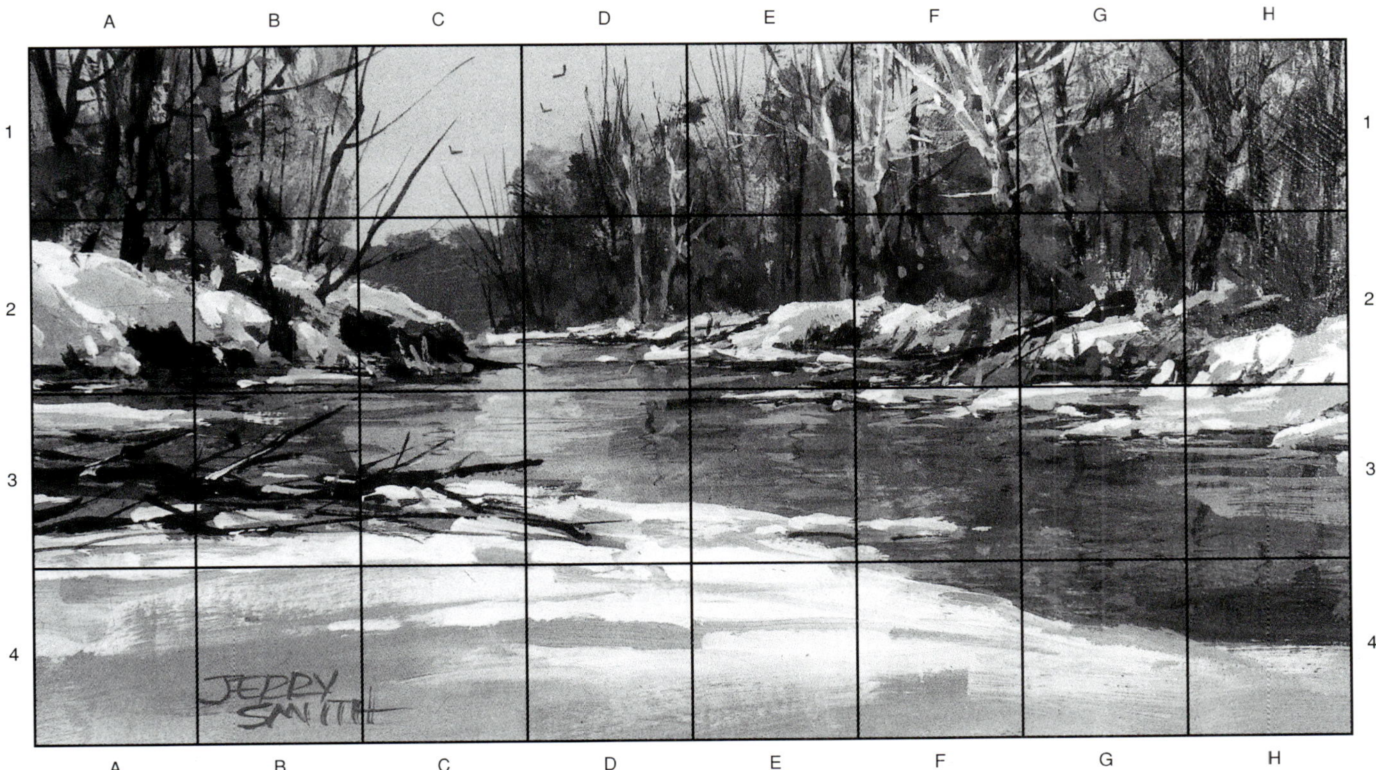

Read me!

Water tends to neutralize both color and value. Dark color reflects lighter and light color reflects darker. Reflections in moving water are broken, rather than a perfect mirror image.

Planes

Always consider developing a design that has a definite foreground, middleground and background.

Put it all together

4. Start with the sky

Paint the flat sky with two coats, allowing drying time after each coat. The value of the sky is relatively light, but dark enough to make the white snow and trees sparkle.

5. Add the trees

Next, working from back to front, paint in the most distant trees with cool, flat color. This is needed as a stopper to hold the viewer's eye in the painting. To achieve the impression of a deep wood, use dry brush texture to paint the background trees in large masses. Then add just a few individual trees using #4 round and rigger brushes.

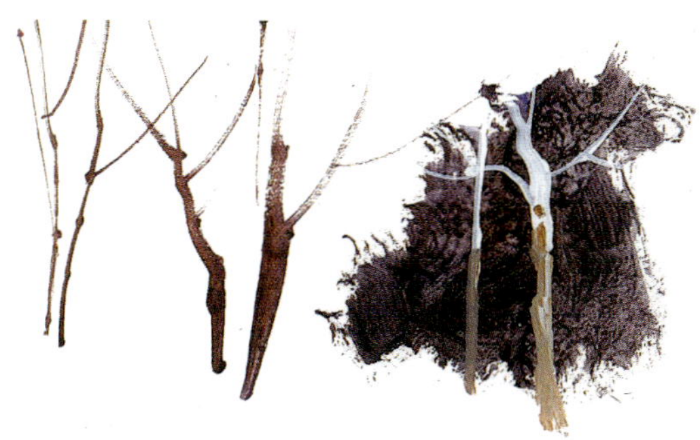

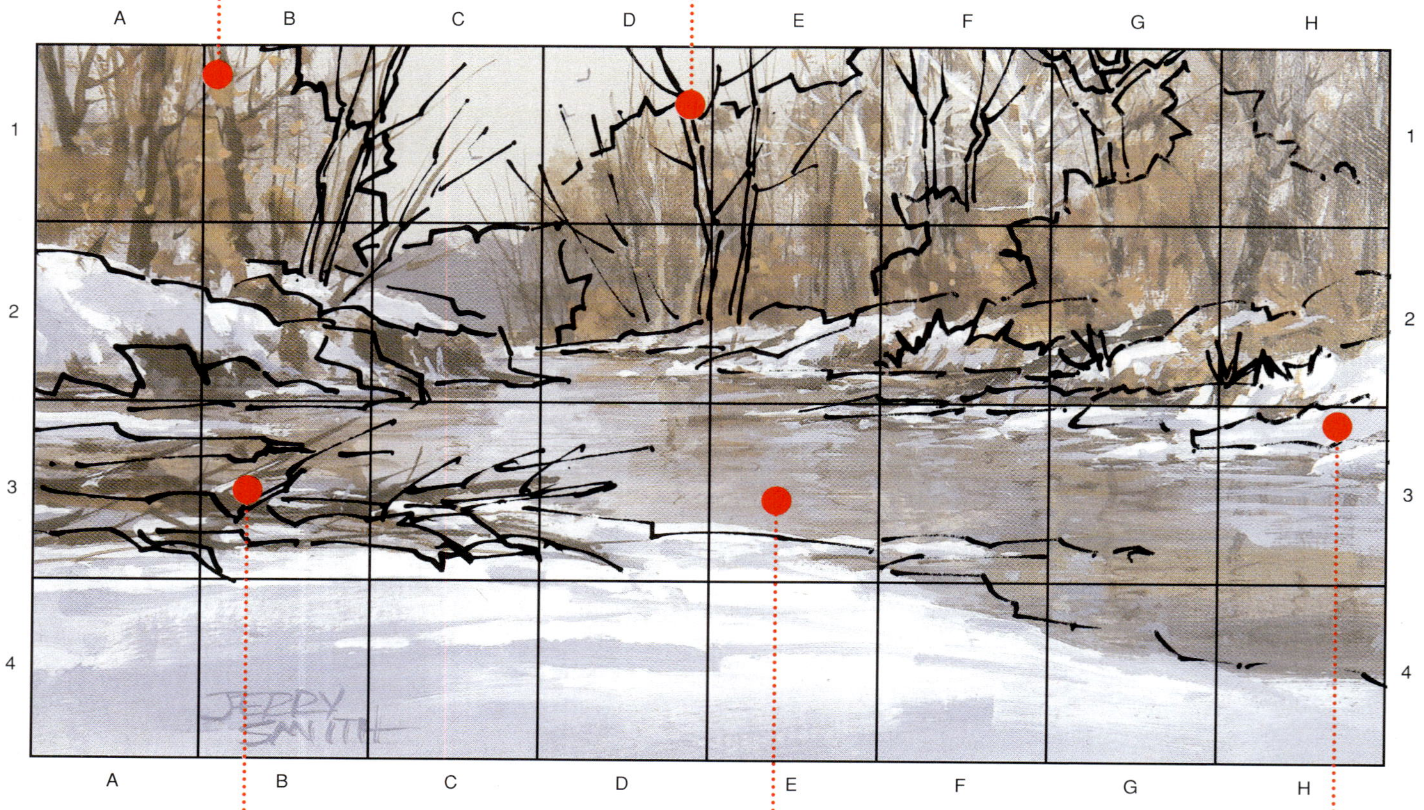

6. Use care with the shadows

Paint the shadows on the snow consistent with the light source. You can leave areas of the gessoed surface as a white to contribute to the effect.

7. Block in the stream

The entire stream is blocked in with color similar to the sky in a slightly darker value.

8. Paint the brights and the highlights

For the bright whites on the banks, use pure Titanium White mixed with a touch of warm yellow. Brighten the water where sky reflection is prominent.

Learning points

- Discover the beauty in browns and grays.
- Suggest a lot of detail with minimum efforts.
- Paint believable reflections without overworking.

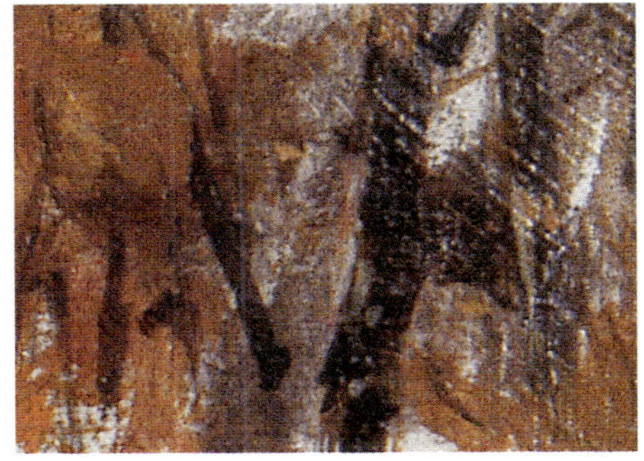

Detail

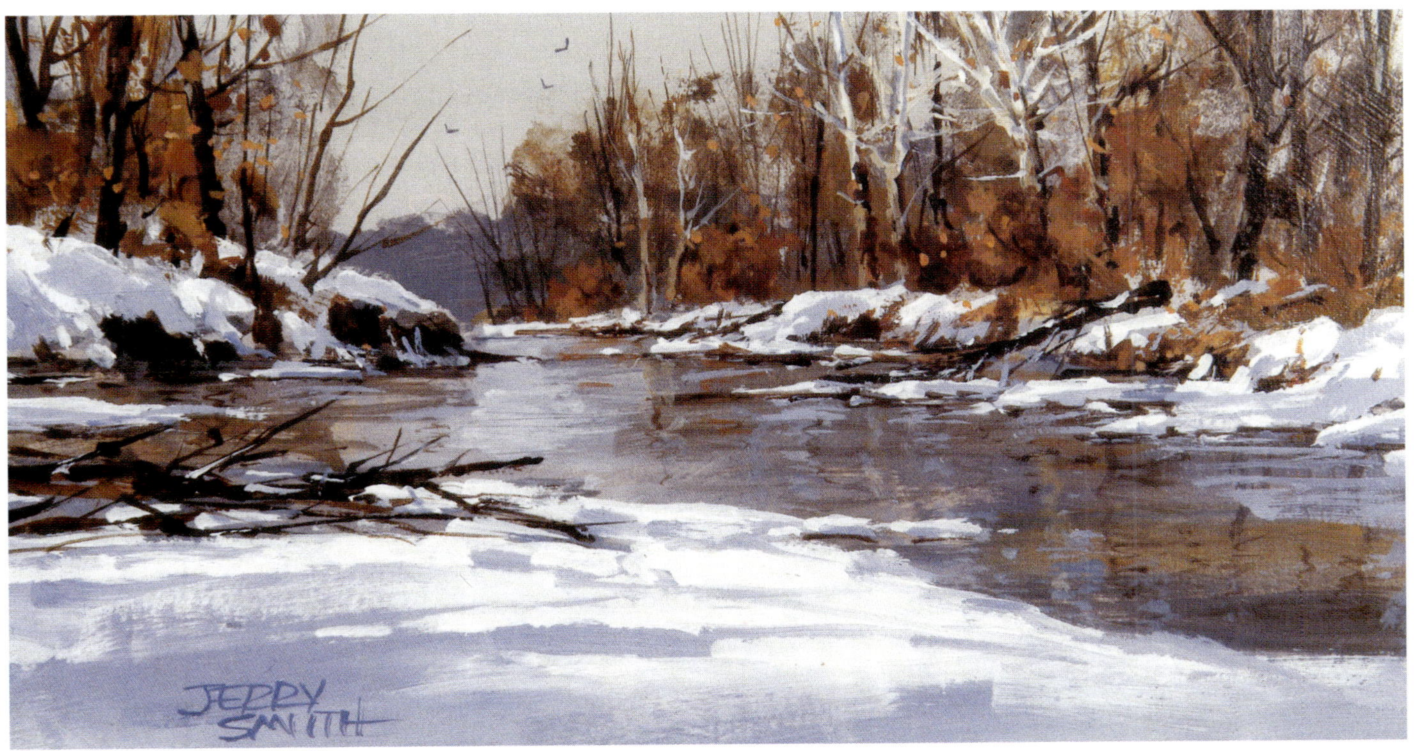

Sugar Creek Winter, acrylic, 7 x 11" (18 x 28cm) by Jerry Smith ©

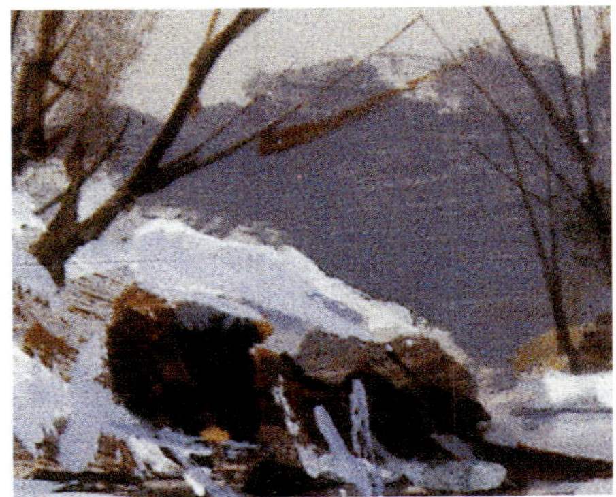

Detail

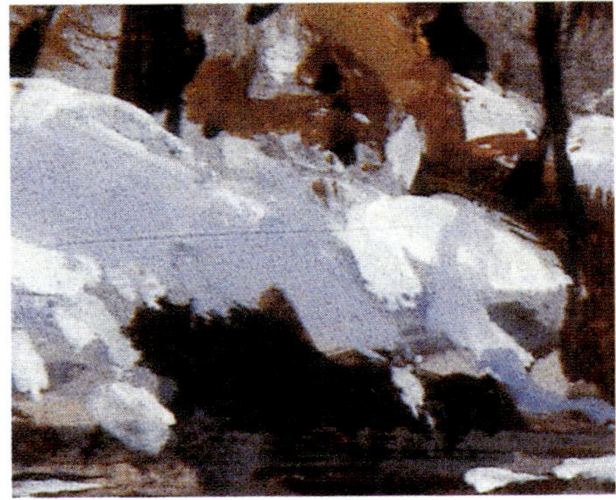

Detail

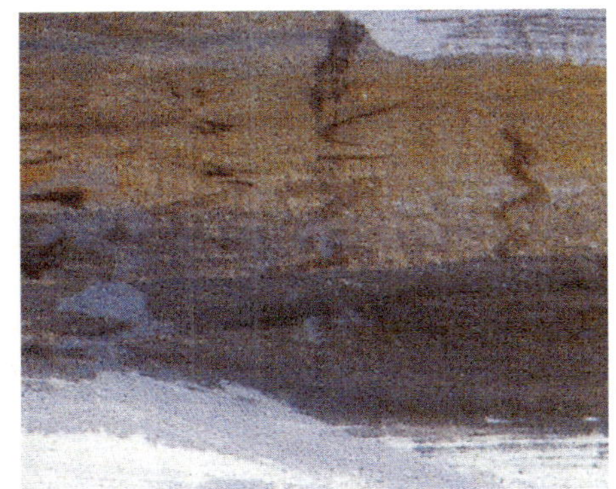

Detail

Before you begin, read the entire project through so you know what's going to happen next.

art map 6

Conveying tranquillity through horizontals

A dominance of horizontal lines and shapes in a painting creates a sense of calm. This was the mood when I did a watercolor sketch on location in Nova Scotia. I wanted to carry this feeling into the painting. The sky is relatively flat, but even the small horizontal clouds help convey the mood while directing the eye toward the lighthouse.

1. The image to be transferred using the art map.

Read the instructions to see how to map this image across to your working surface.

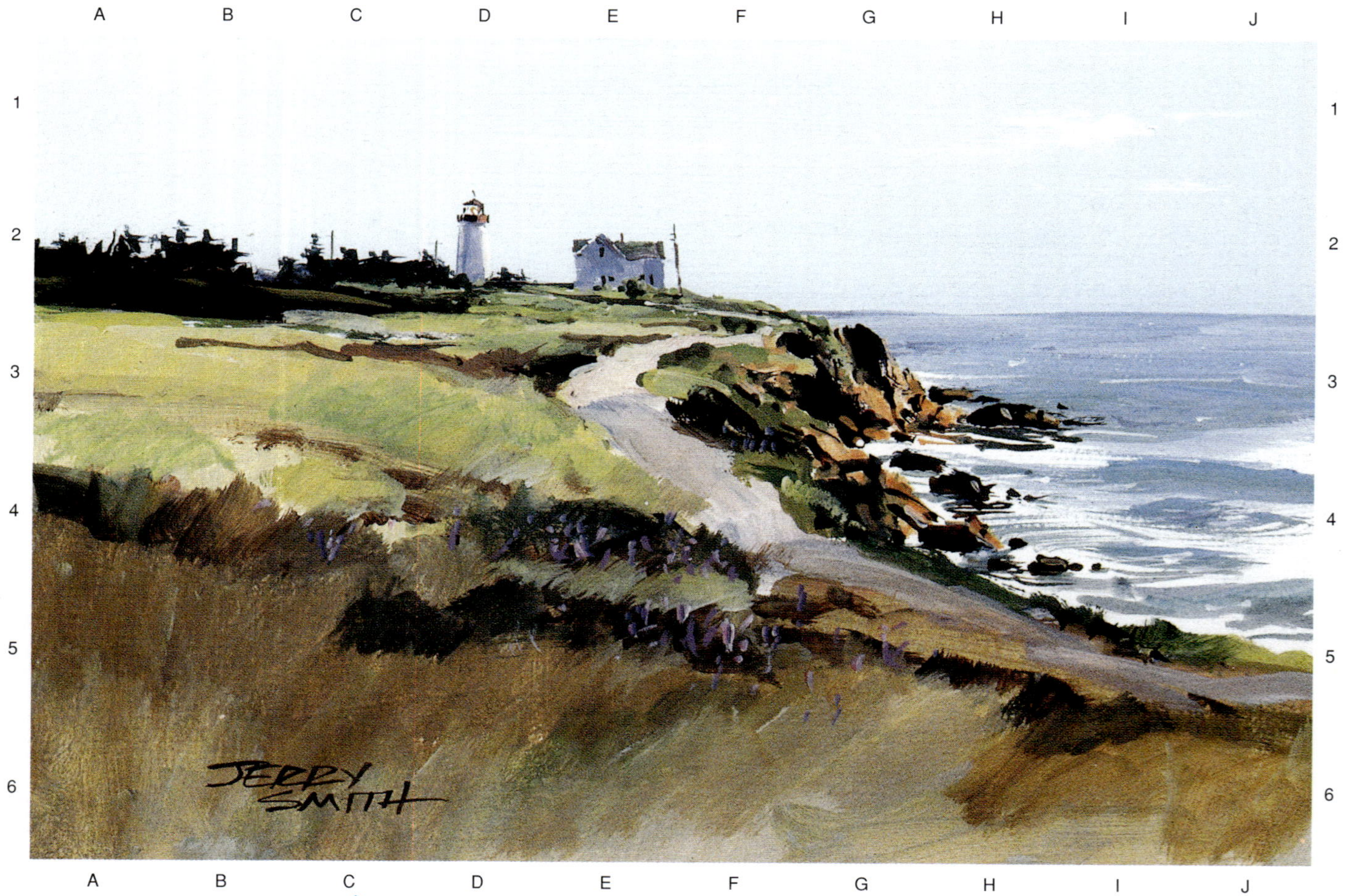

2. Map the image

With a 2B pencil, begin by LIGHTLY drawing a grid on your working surface that has the exact same number of squares as my grid. Your support can be the size of my original, or you can choose something proportionally larger or smaller. Your art map will be 6 squares down and 10 squares across. Put in the letters and numbers along the edges to make the next step easier.

3. Use the art map to transfer the image

Now, still drawing very LIGHTLY with your pencil, copy the main contour lines of the object as shown in each square onto your working surface. It's not necessary to get every detail—just a simple line drawing will do. I recommend LIGHTLY and gently erasing the grid lines in the open, lighter areas before continuing.

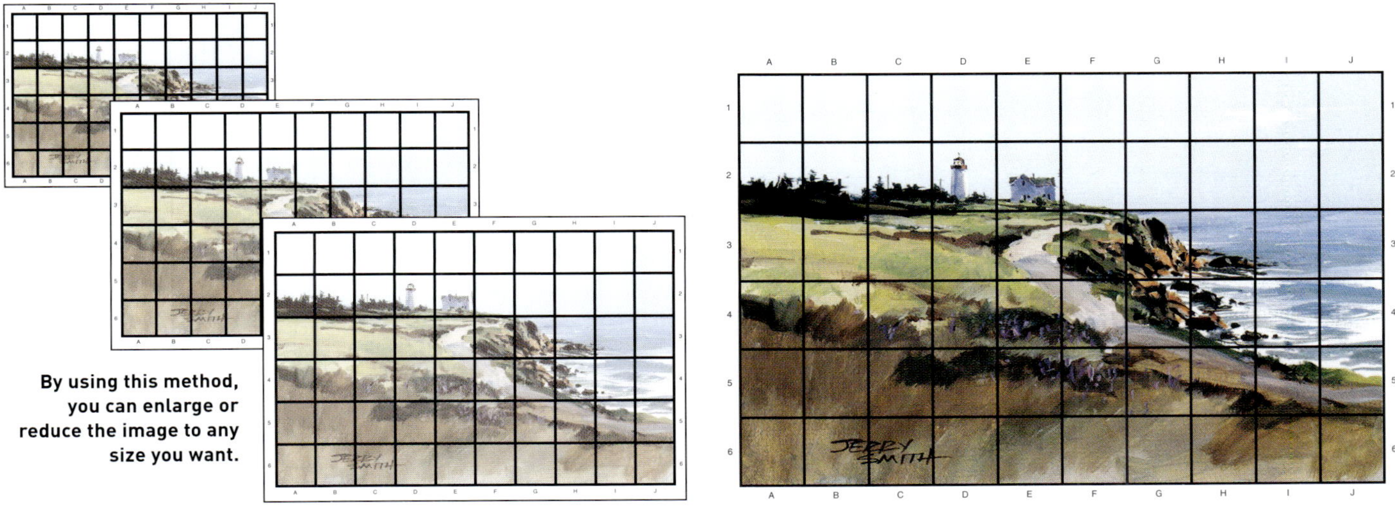

By using this method, you can enlarge or reduce the image to any size you want.

This is how your art map should look.

Here I've done the drawing in dark ink so you can see the idea, but you will do this lightly in pencil.

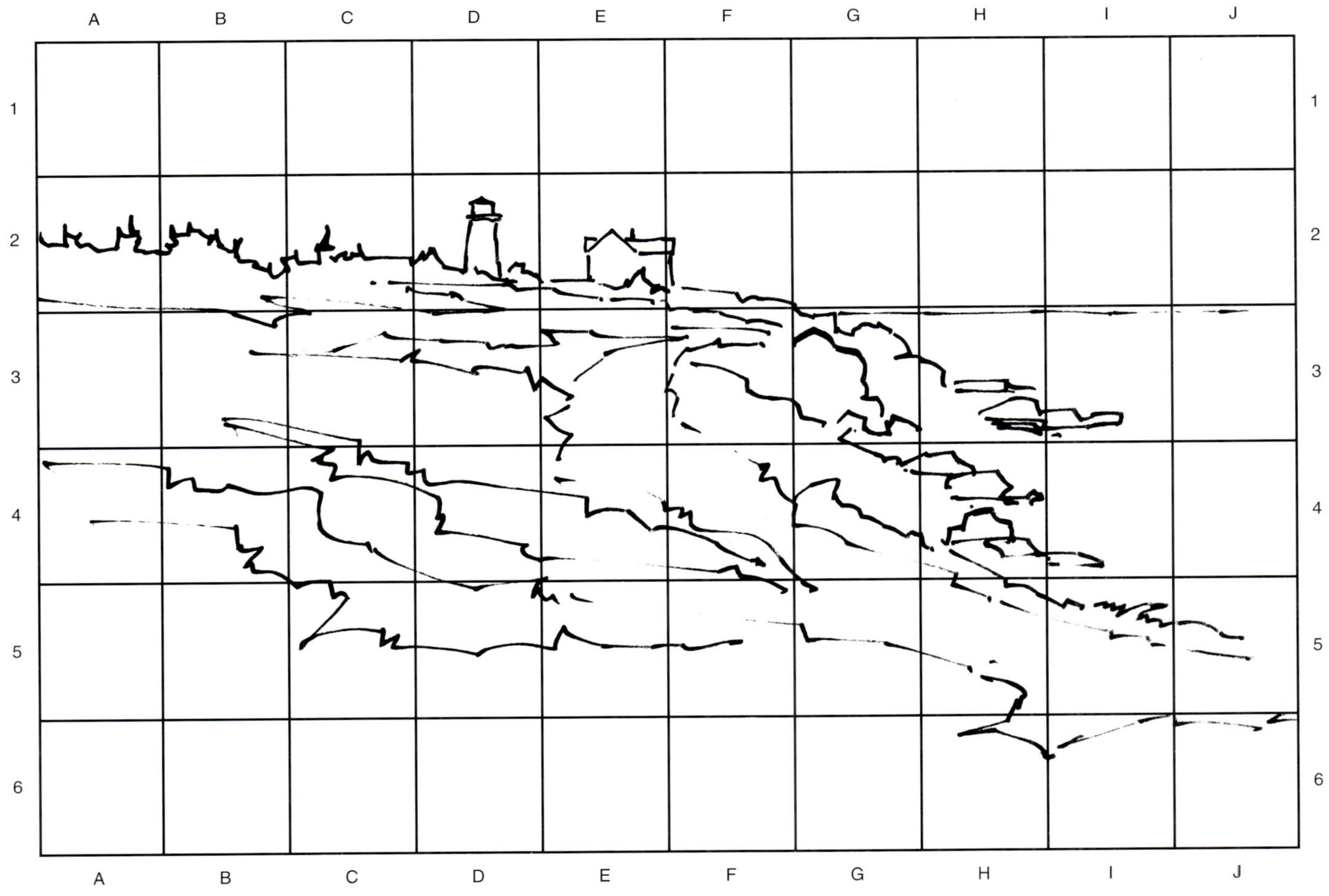

Study these pages before you start painting

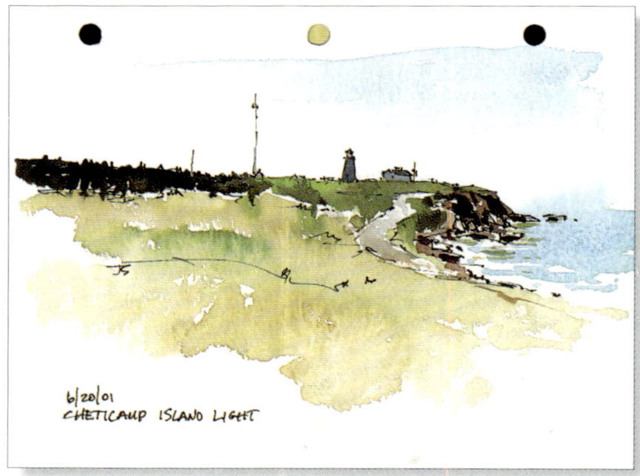

Sketches references
Quick sketches in either pen and pencil or ink and watercolor are a good way to work out the composition before starting to paint.

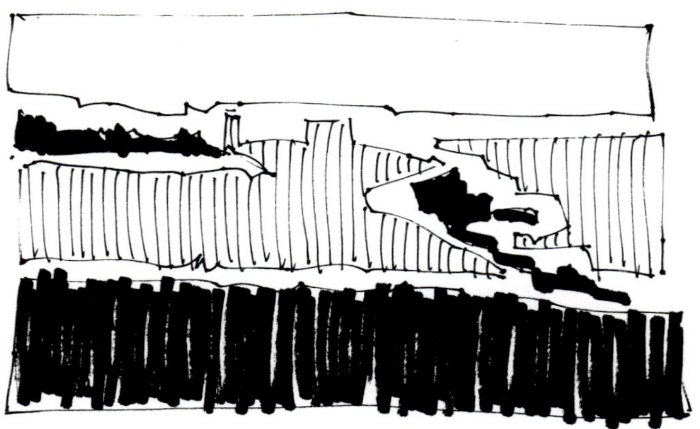

Shape map
With the exception of a few diagonals for conflict, you can see the predominance of horizontal shapes. The larger darks on the left are balanced by the smaller but more active darks on the right.

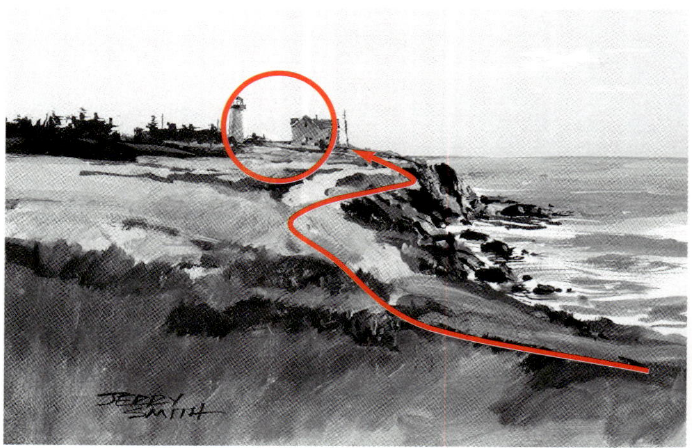

Design map
Horizontal and slightly oblique movement carry the design. The path leading to the lighthouse and into the painting is downplayed in the foreground to hold the viewer's eye in the painting. This is accomplished by integrating the path into the foreground with values and soft edges. The road nearly disappears to prevent it from taking the viewer's eye out of the painting. Also notice the lack of detail in the corners to keep the eye focused within.

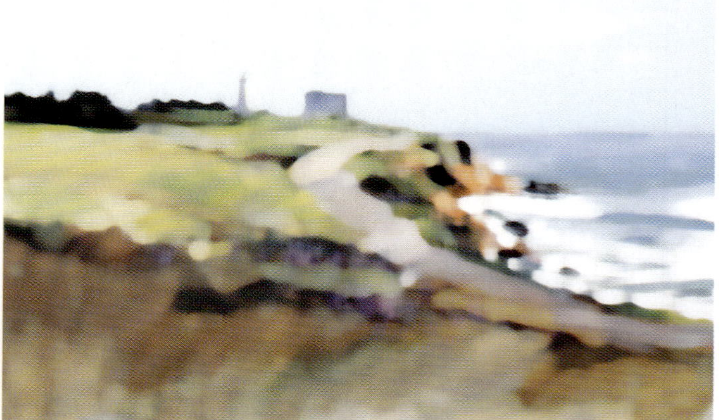

Color map (what you would see if you were to squint)

materials you'll need

painting surface
canvas, board or prepared paper

brushes
¼", ½" and 1" flats

nos. 4, 6 and 12 rounds

small rigger

other tools
2B pencil

ruler

palette

spray bottle to keep your palette moist

your acrylic palette for this painting

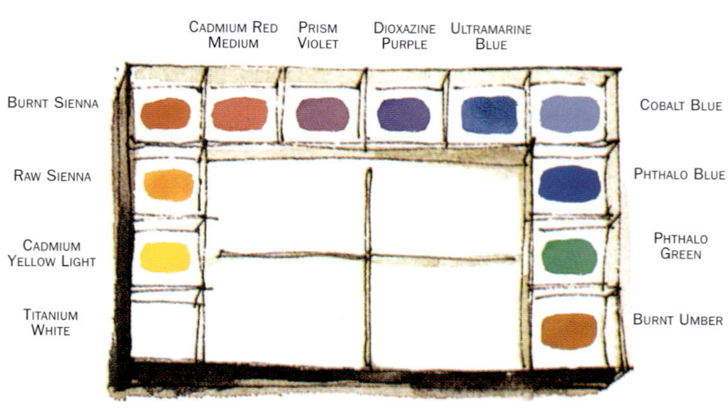

Consider the following elements

Light source

This is a backlit scene with the lighthouse catching a little light on the right side. Horizontal rock surfaces and patches of grass in the middle distance also catch sunlight.

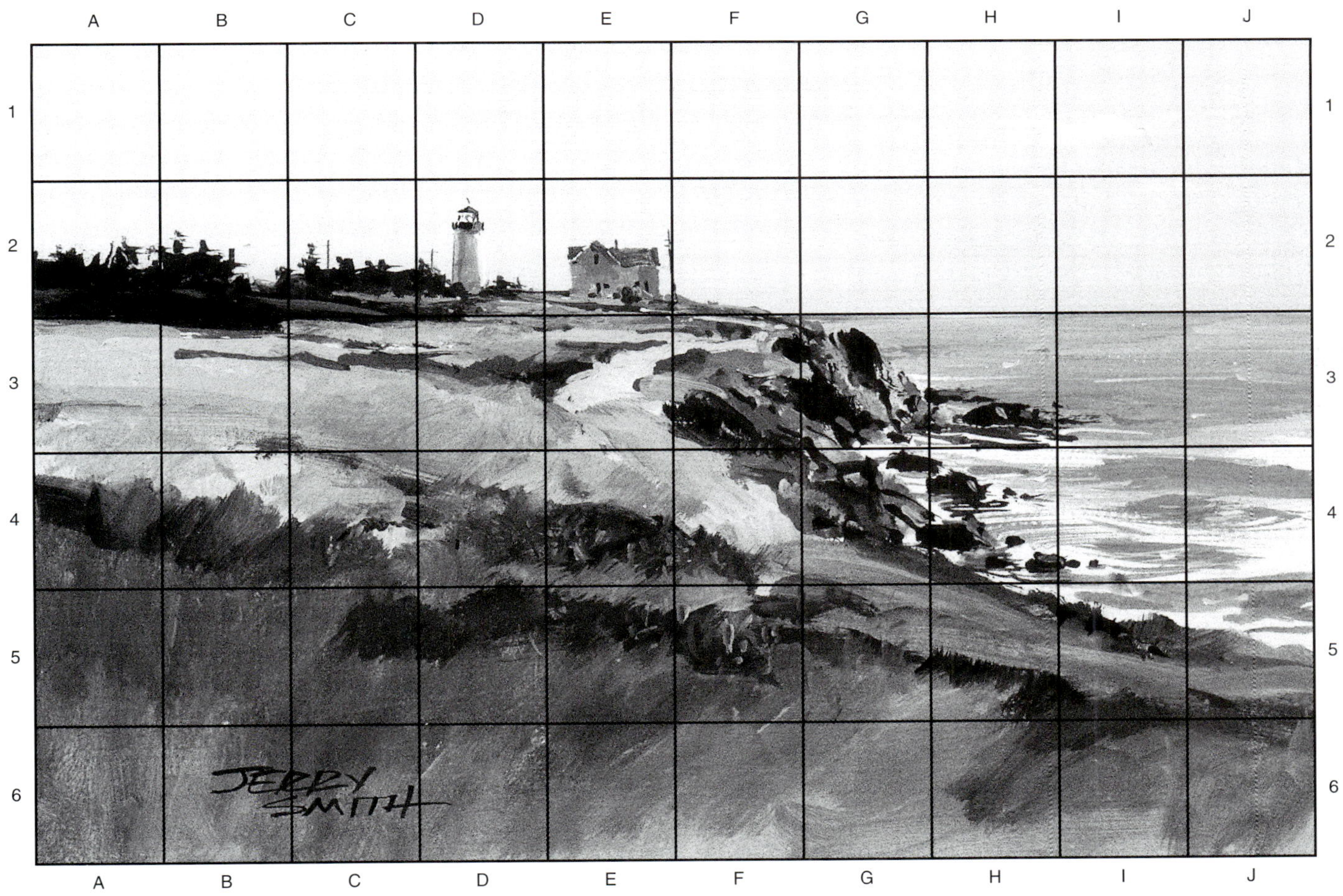

Bright idea

I cut and punch 6 x 8" (15 x 20cm) pieces of watercolor paper for small three-ring b nders to serve as my sketchbooks. I have filled many of the books over the years and find these quick-sketches superior to photos as references for paintings. My very compact kit is ideal for traveling.

Put it all together

4. Begin with the sky

Start with two coats of paint for the flat sky, then drybrush the wispy clouds on the dry surface.

5. Paint the foreground

Block in the dark horizontal shapes of the large foreground, using midtone values. Many of the brushstrokes from this initial scrub-in will remain visible in the completed painting.

6. Leave parts unpainted

While you're painting the darks in the rocky shore, leave white paper for the sunlit surfaces which are later glazed with warm color. Also leave unpainted the whites in the churning water.

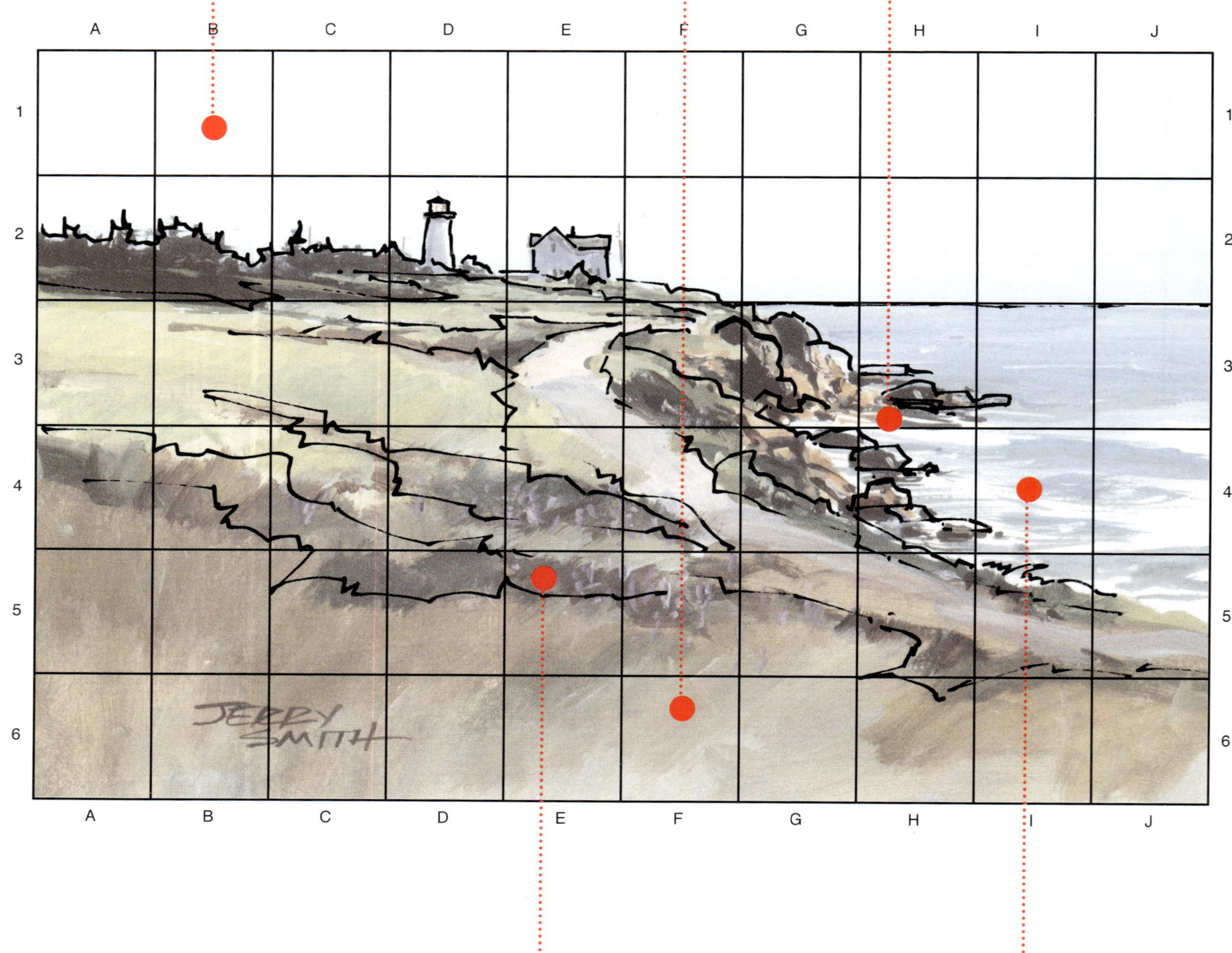

7. Paint the details

In the final stages use your rigger brush to touch in the details.

8. Add highlights

Enhance the unpainted whites in the water by thoughtfully placed opaque white paint. Add a warm color glaze to the unpainted parts of the dark rocks.

Learning points

- How to use horizontals to express tranquillity.
- How to put together a simple but efficient sketching kit.

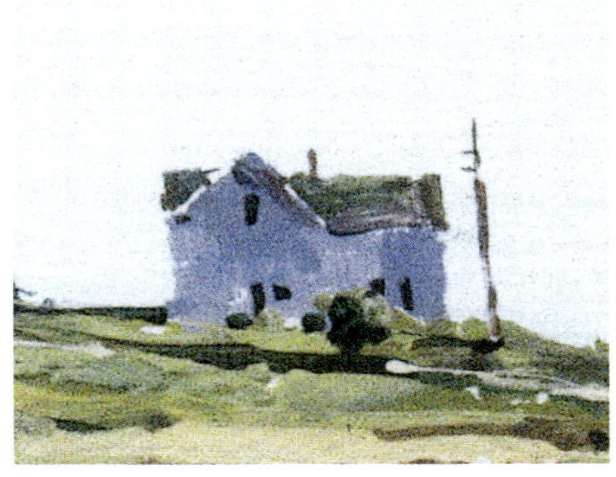

Detail

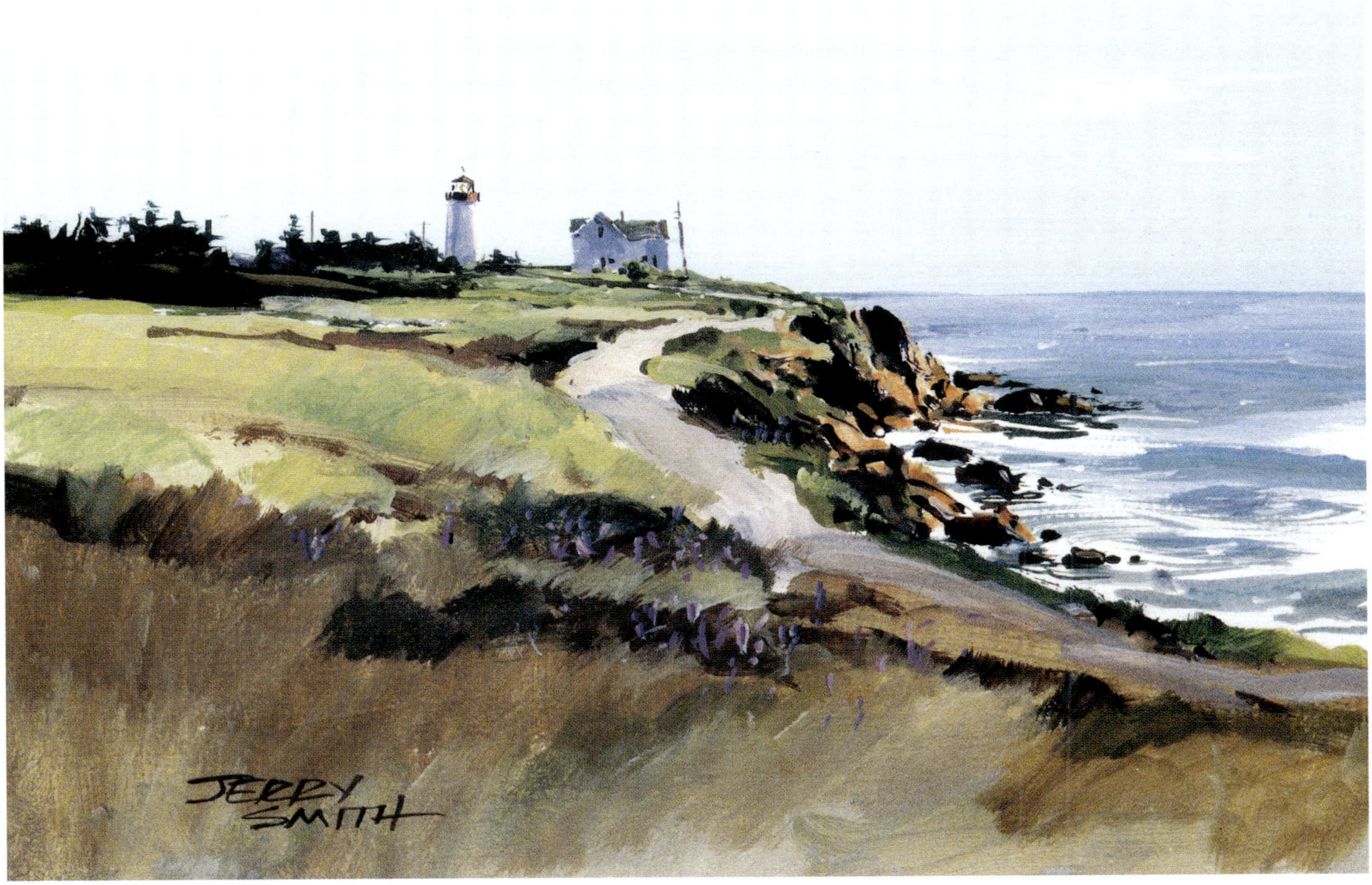

Cheticamp Light, **acrylic, 6 x 9" (15 x 23cm) by Jerry Smith ©**

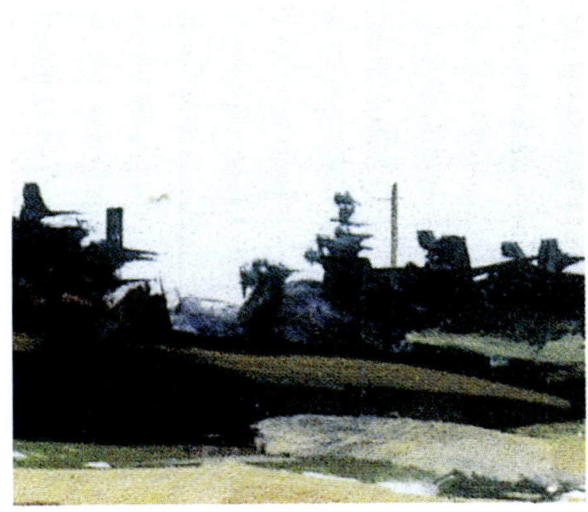

Detail

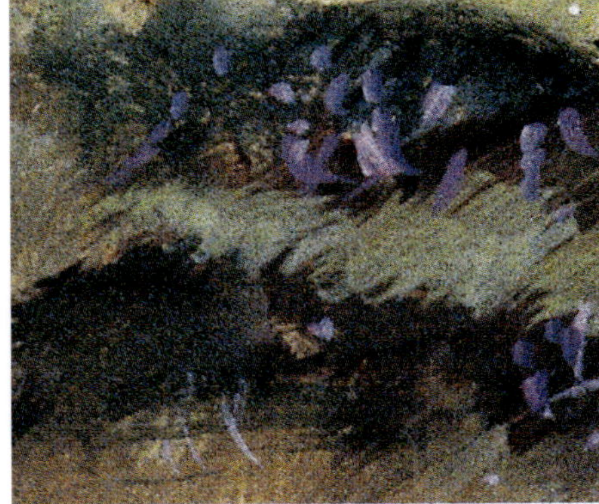

Detail

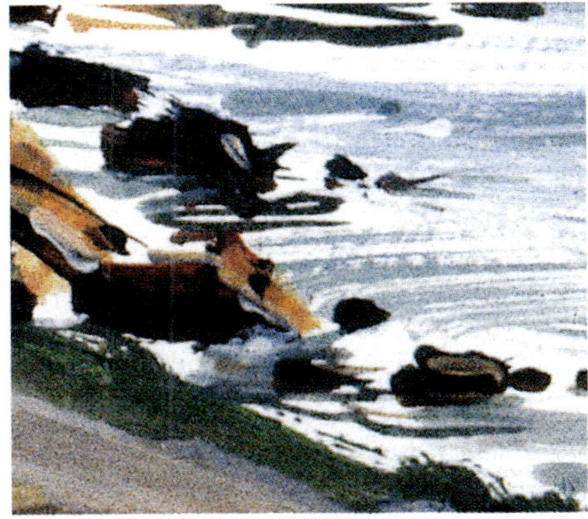

Detail

art map 7

Color toning for unity

Before you begin, read the entire project through so you know what's going to happen next.

A little freer, more impressionistic and color-driven, this painting presents a slight change in direction from the approach in previous projects.

1. The image to be transferred using the art map.

Read the instructions to see how to map this image across to your working surface.

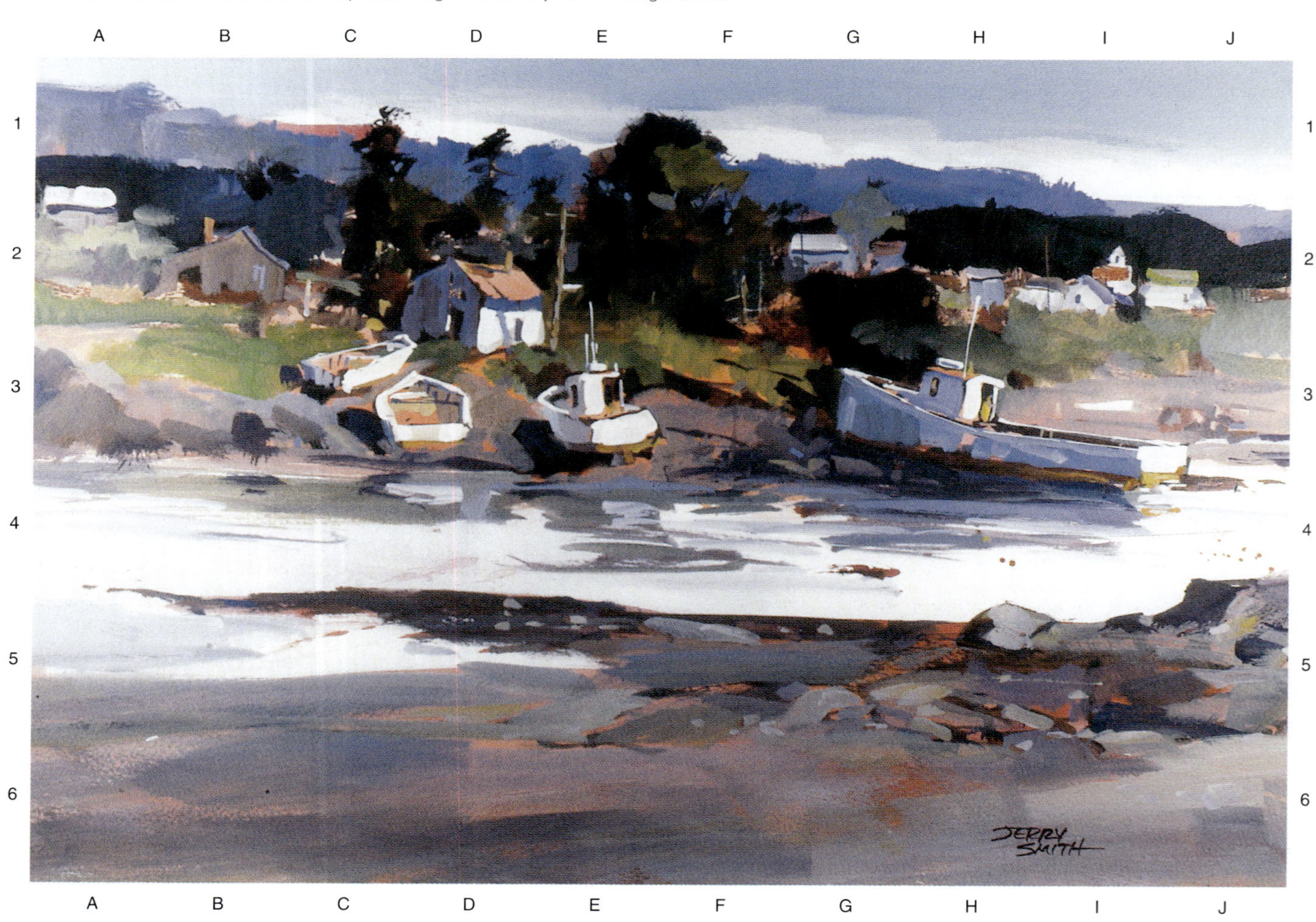

2. Map the image

With a 2B pencil, begin by LIGHTLY drawing a grid on your working surface that has the exact same number of squares as my grid. Your support can be the size of my original, or you can choose something proportionally larger or smaller. Your art map will be 6 squares down and 10 squares across. Put in the letters and numbers along the edges to make the next step easier.

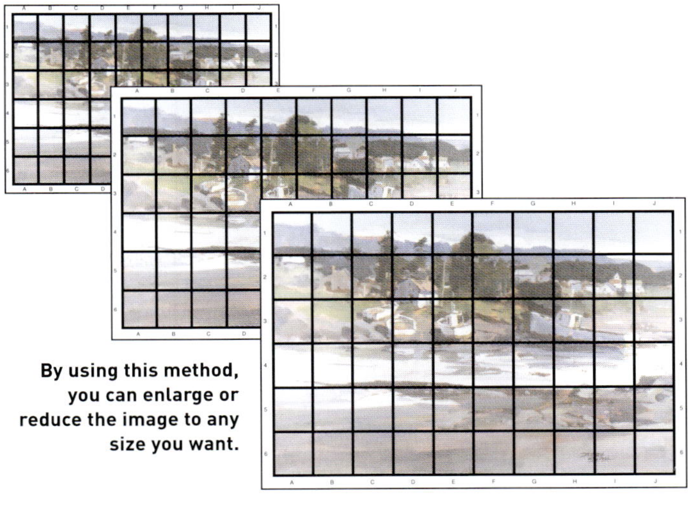

By using this method, you can enlarge or reduce the image to any size you want.

3. Use the art map to transfer the image

In this project you will be covering everything except the sky and water with a red wash. This underpainting will show through the finished painting. It may be better to rough in the wash, Let it dry, and then map the drawing.

Now, still drawing very LIGHTLY with your pencil, copy the main contour lines of the object as shown in each square onto your working surface. It's not necessary to get every detail—just a simple line drawing will do. I recommend LIGHTLY and gently erasing the grid lines in the open, lighter areas before continuing.

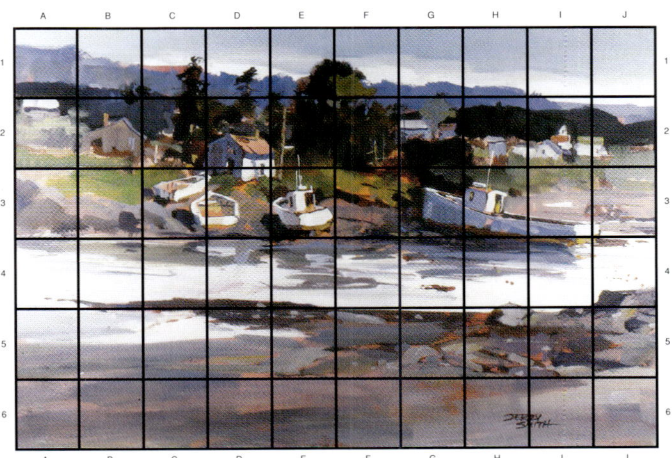

This is how your art map should look.

Here I've done the drawing in dark ink so you can see the idea, but you will do this lightly in pencil.

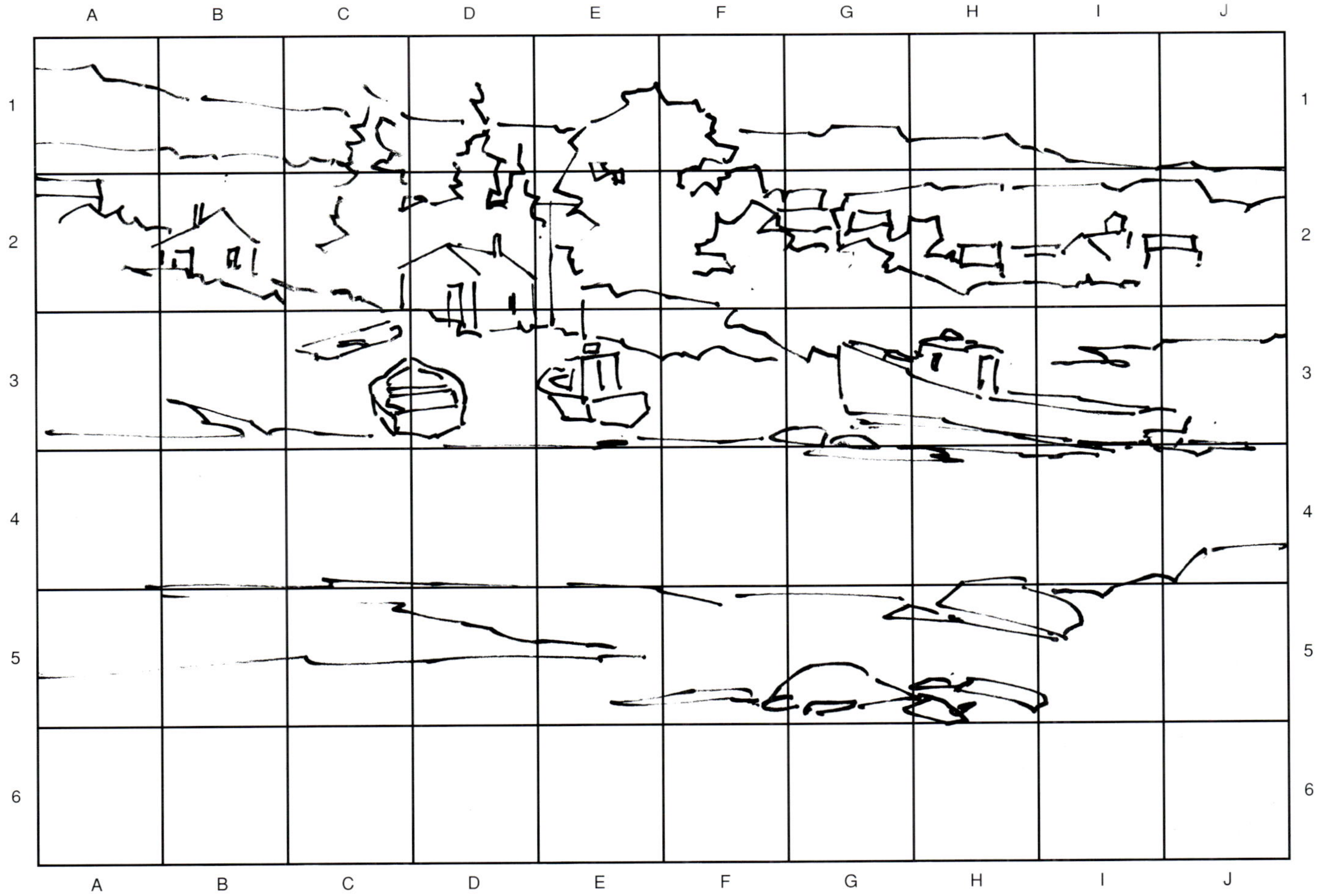

Study these pages before you start painting

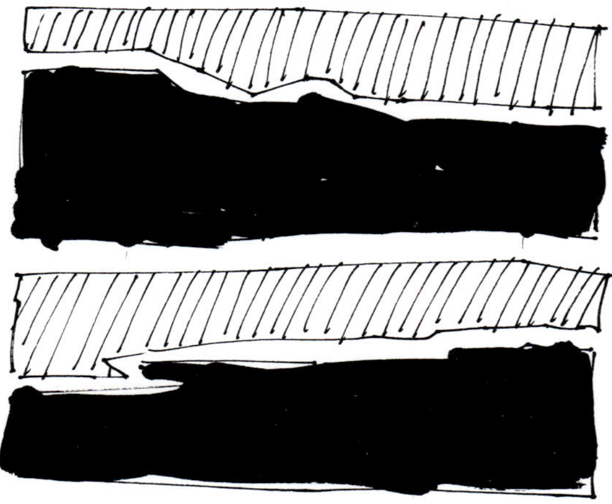

Shape map
The design plan is two big dark shapes and two light shapes. Note the big dark shape that ties the middle distance dark trees with the background. This entire shape provides a nice foil to highlight the brilliant white shapes. Detail in the corners is kept to a minimum.

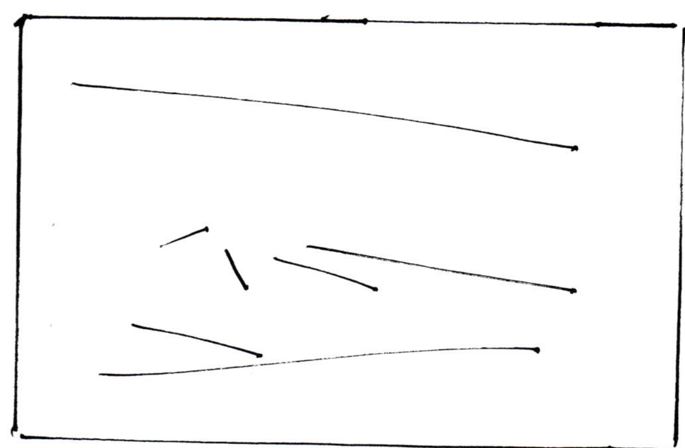

Design map
This composition relies on horizontal lines to convey the outgoing tide. Note the use of diagonals to create rhythm and tension as well as move the eye through the painting. The foreground beach area frames in the bottom of the painting and provides a directional entry into the painting. Reflections are used to pull the two large dark shapes together and vertical tree shapes tie picture planes together.

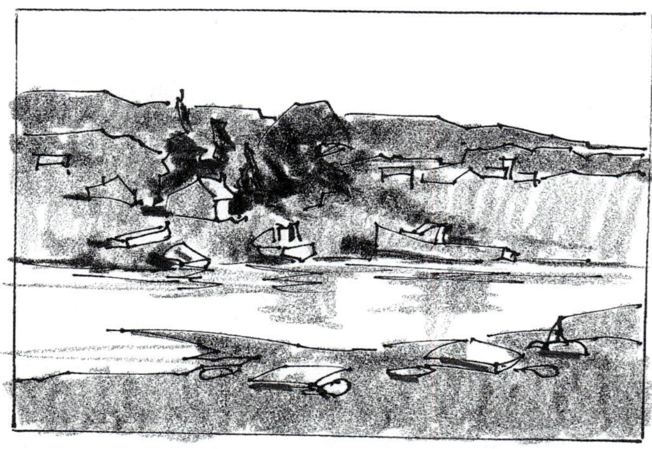

Thumbnail sketch
This photo reference is included to illustrate the many liberties that can be taken

Color map (what you would see if you were to squint)
The dominant red is enhanced and balanced by a variety of warm and cool greens. Spots of red were created throughout the painting by painting negatively around them.

materials you'll need

painting surface
15 x 22" (38 x 56cm) stretched 140lb (300 gsm) watercolor paper or canvas or board

brushes
¼", ½" and 1" flats

nos. 4, 6 and 12 rounds

small rigger

other tools
2B pencil

ruler

palette

spray bottle to keep your palette moist

your acrylic palette for this painting

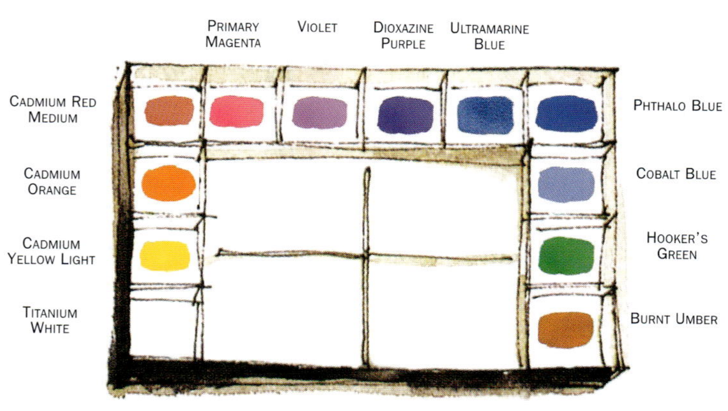

Consider the following elements

You can change what you see

This photo reference is included to illustrate the many liberties that can be taken to achieve the desired results.

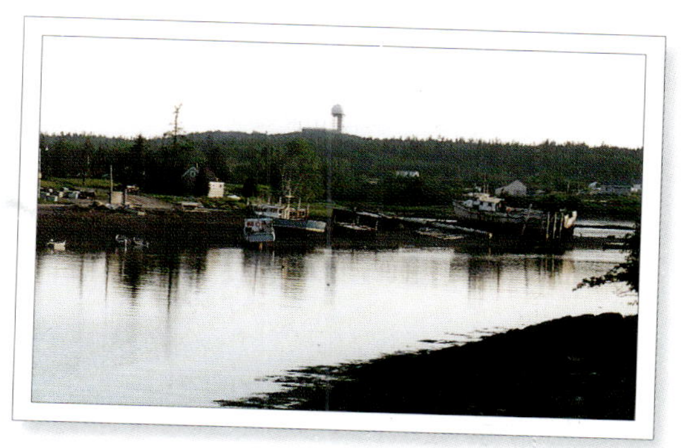

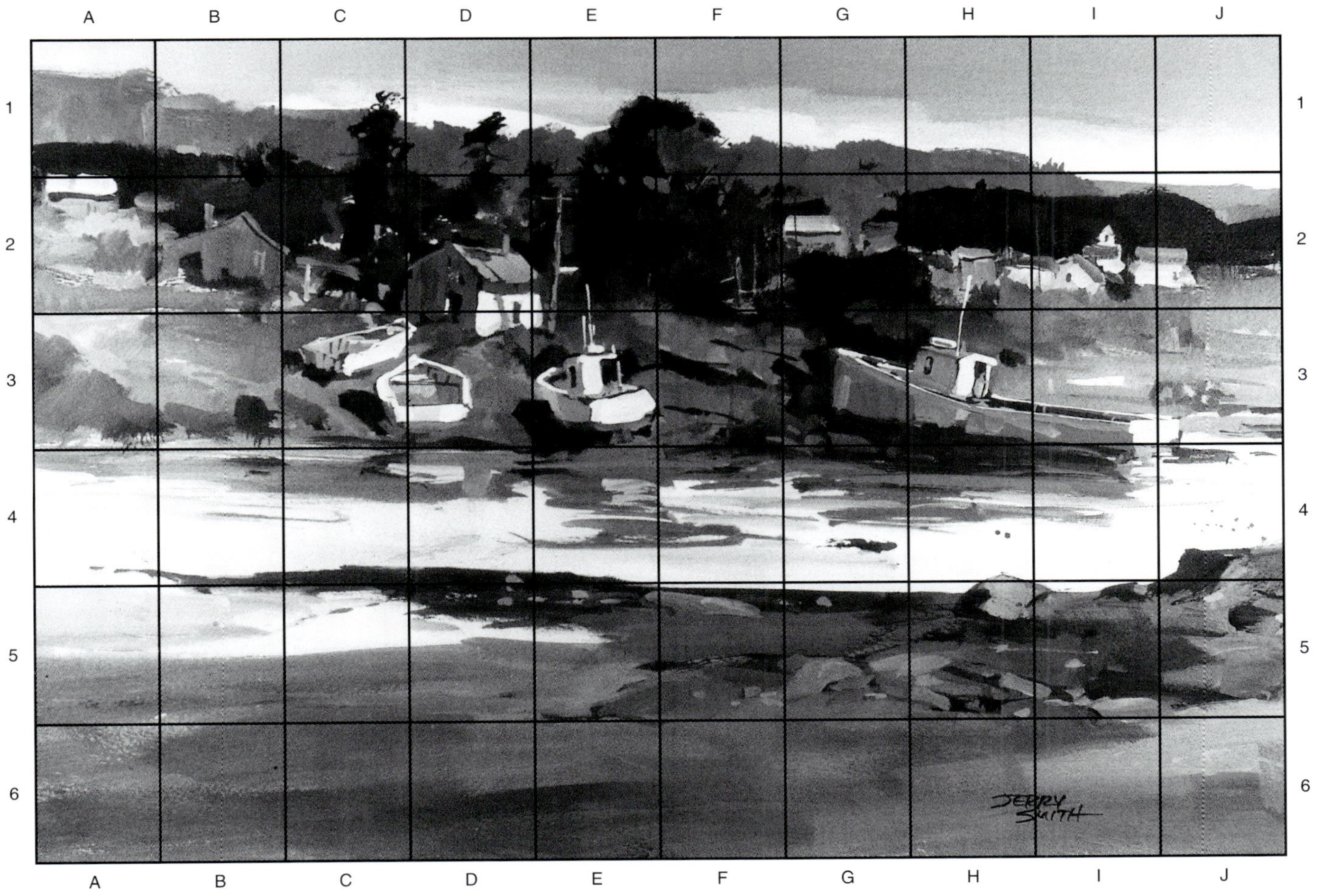

Positioning plan

The boats are somewhat scattered but positioned to lead the viewer into the painting.

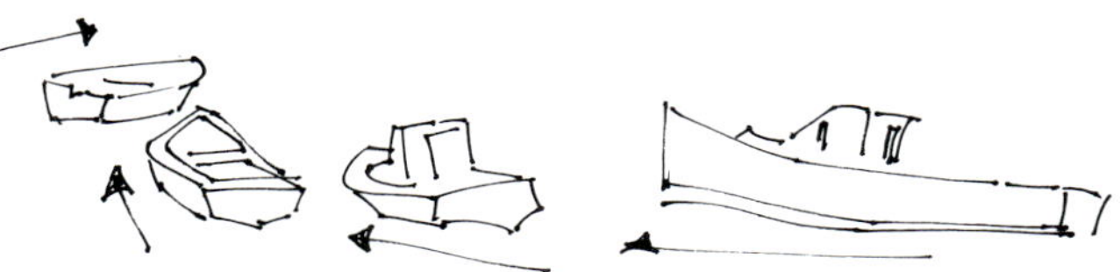

Put it all together

4. First lay in a red wash

Apply a wash of red paint covering everything except the sky and water shapes. Much of this underpainting will show through in the completed painting, and the influence of this color tone throughout will help unify the painting.

5. Put in your drawing

When the underpainting is completely dry, make your drawing with a #6 round brush and very dark (Cadmium Red and Phthalo Blue) acrylic paint.

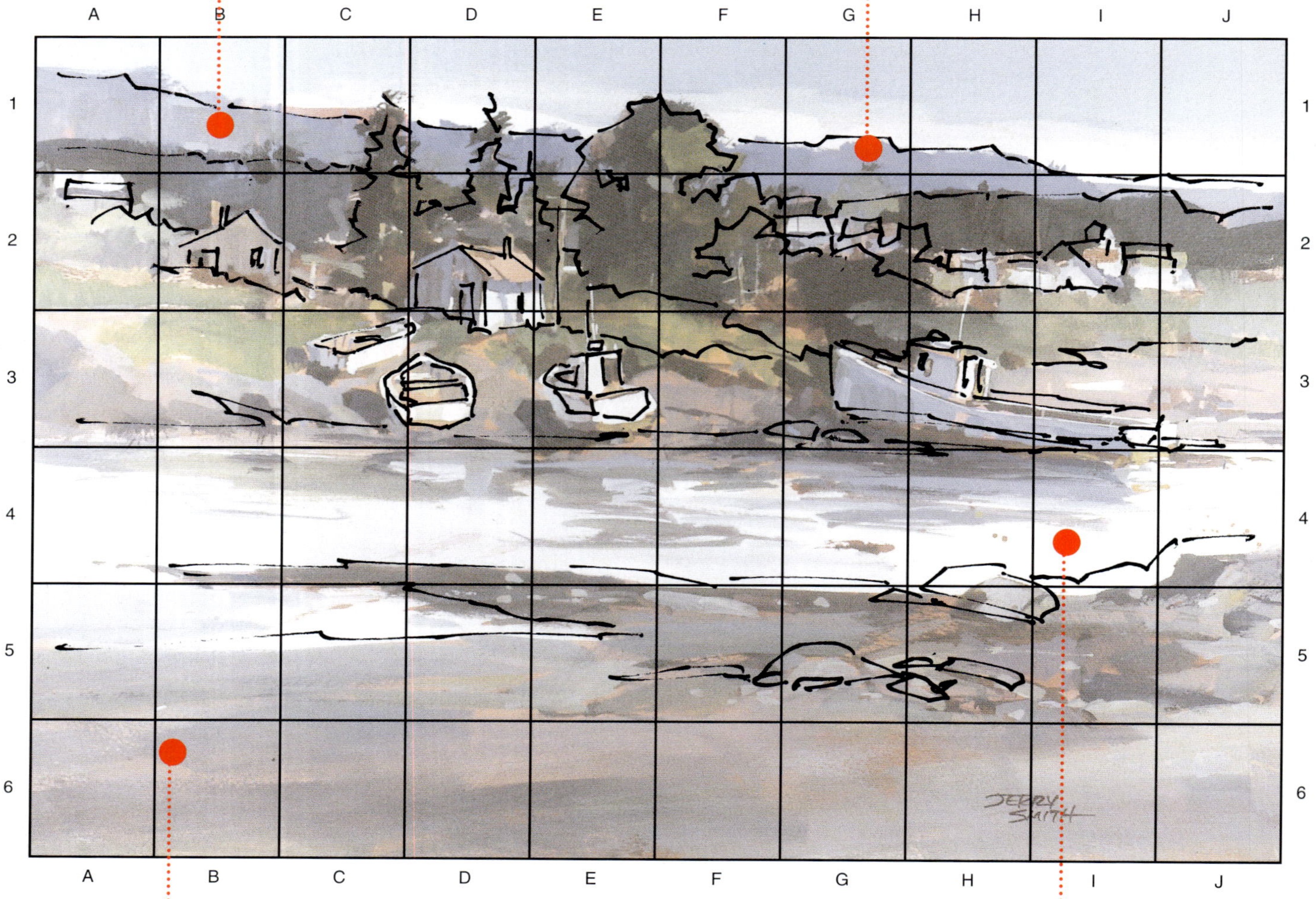

6. Now use bolder brushstrokes

Proceed with the painting using bold brushstrokes, leaving spots of the red underpainting showing throughout the painting.

7. Finish with bold touches

Finish the painting with bold touches of pure Titanium White slightly tinted with Diarylide Yellow.

Learning points

- Beginning a painting with color toning can be a useful tool in attaining color unity. The toned underpainting will provide a built-in color dominance that pulls the various parts of your painting together.
- Interesting results can be achieved when you break your painting routine and try a new approach.

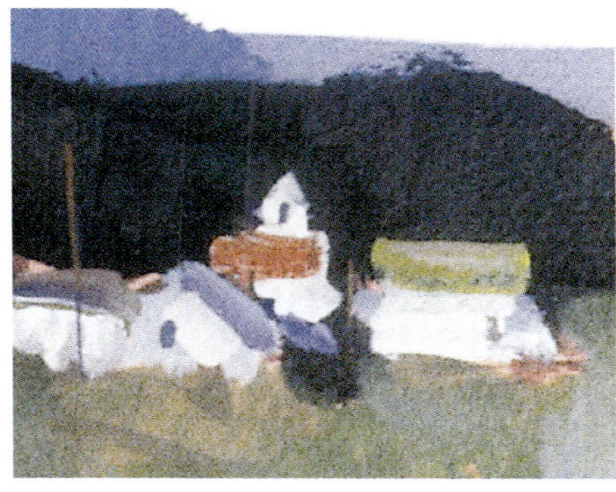

Detail

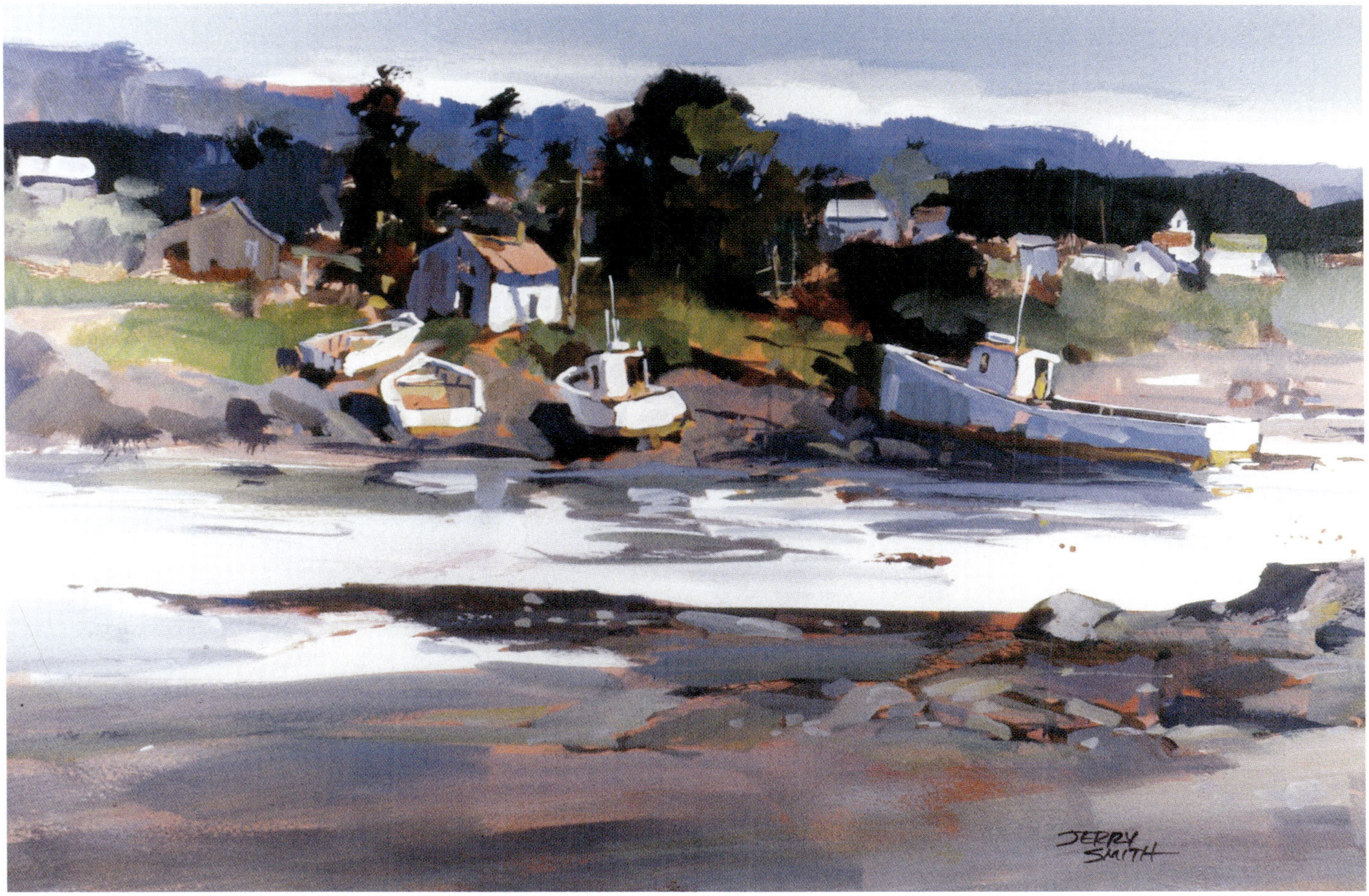

***Red Rock East*, acrylic, 15 x 21" (38 x 53cm) by Jerry Smith ©**

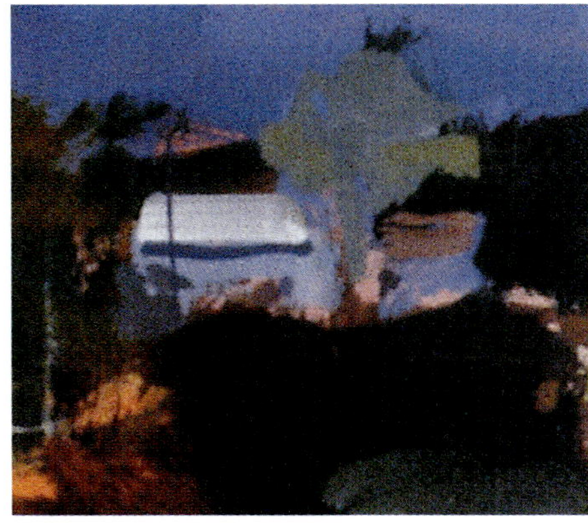

Detail

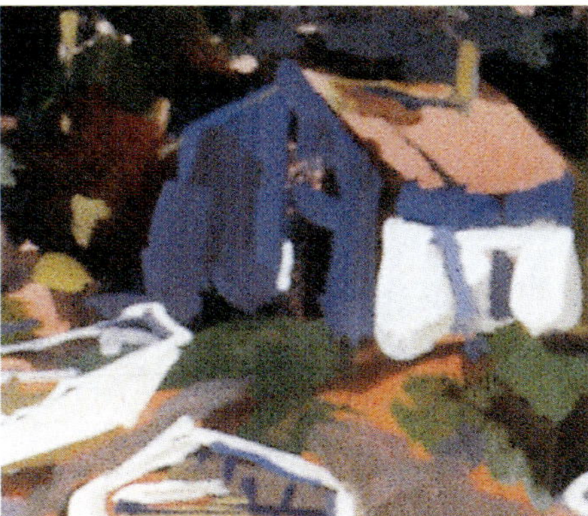

Detail

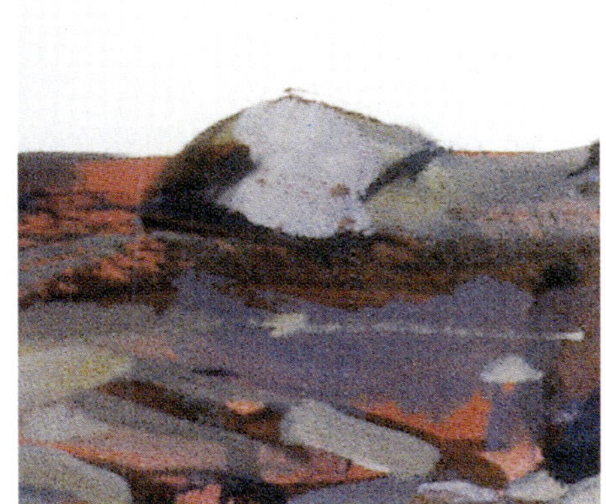

Detail

Before you begin, read the entire project through so you know what's going to happen next.

art map 8

Using expressive brushwork and color mixing

Lively brushwork and mixing paint with the brush as it is applied to the painting surface can imply a great deal of detail. This coastal setting was inspired by a few simple building shapes, illuminated by a colorful evening sky. Expressive brushwork and color blending is evident throughout the painting from the sky to the brushy foreground.

An additional challenge is presented by the fact that evening light is short-lived, changing the subtle landscape colors by the minute. A painting begun outside can sometimes be completed with sketch and photo references.

1. The image to be transferred using the art map.

Read the instructions to see how to map this image across to your working surface.

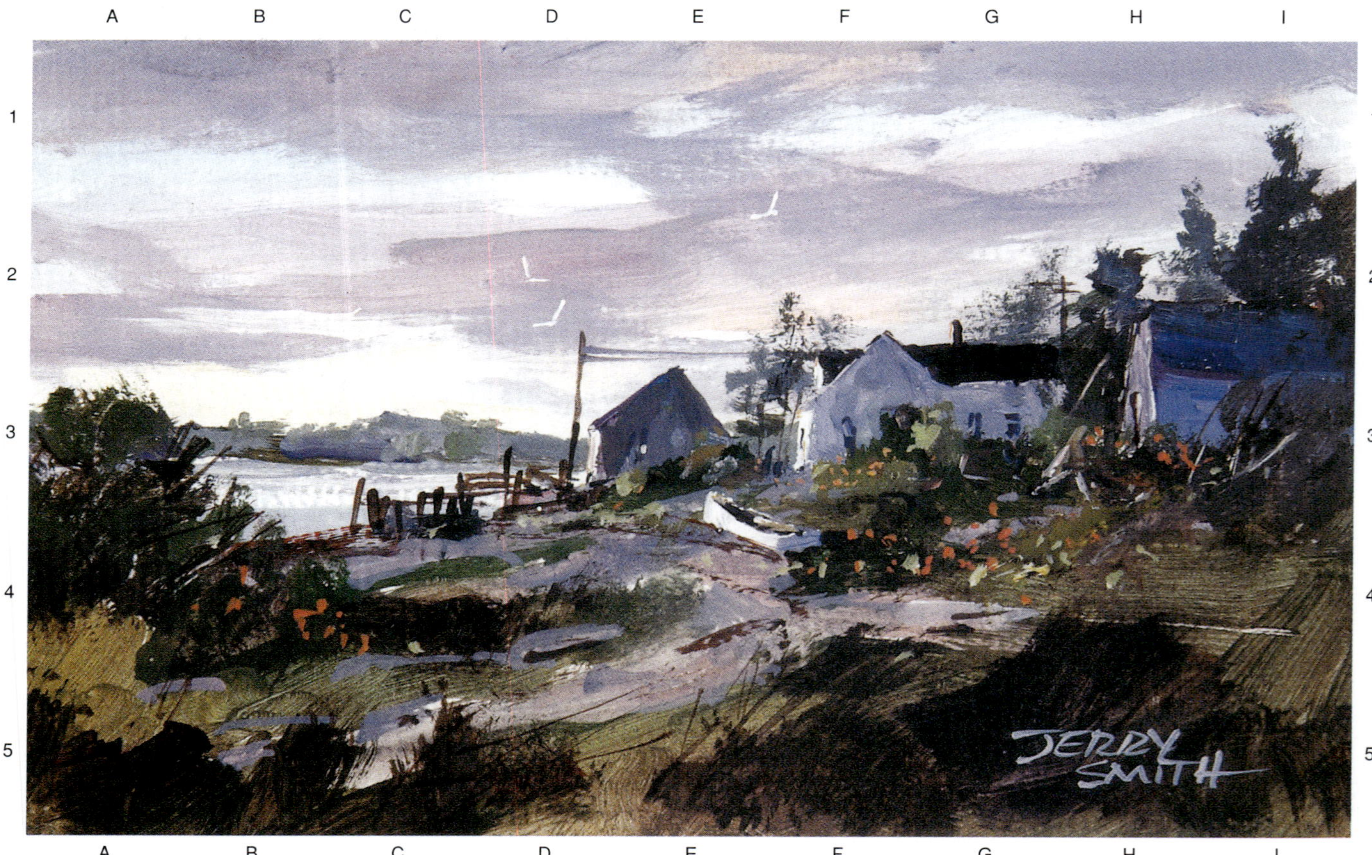

2. Map the image

With a 2B pencil, begin by LIGHTLY drawing a grid on your wroking surface that has the exact same number of squares as my grid. Your support can be the size of my original, or you can choose something proportionally larger or smaller. Your art map will be 5 squares down and 9 squares across. Put in the letters and numbers along the edges to make the next step easier.

3. Use the art map to transfer the image

Now, still drawing very LIGHTLY with your pencil, copy the main contour lines of the object as shown in each square onto your working surface. It's not necessary to get every detail—just a simple line drawing will do. I recommend LIGHTLY and gently erasing the grid lines in the open, lighter areas before continuing.

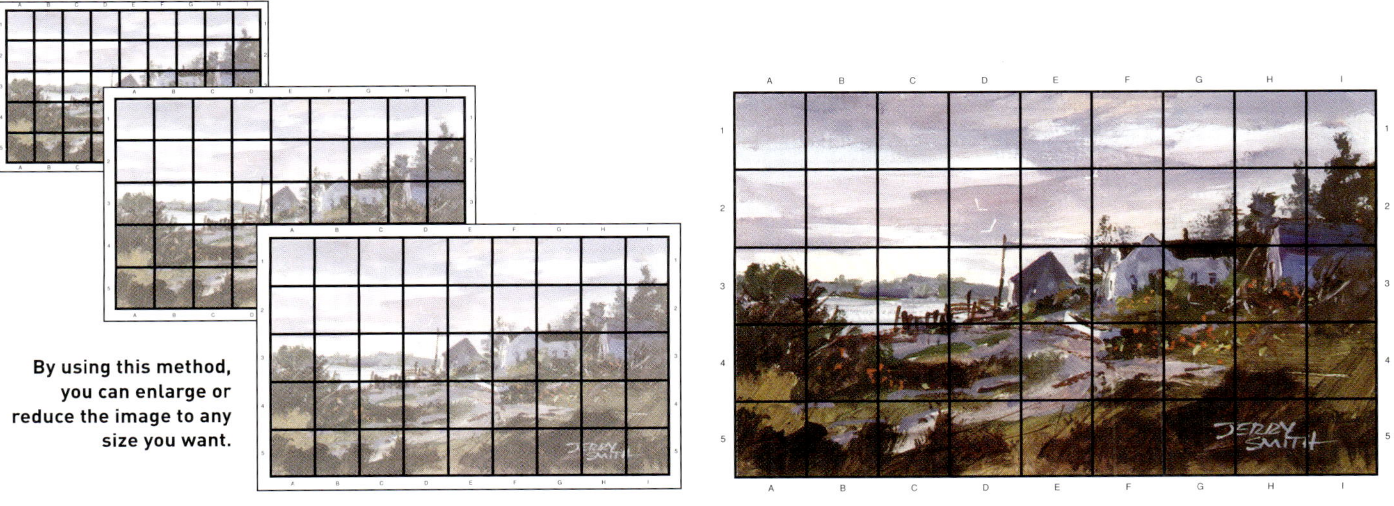

By using this method, you can enlarge or reduce the image to any size you want.

This is how your art map should look.

Here I've done the drawing in dark ink so you can see the idea, but you will do this lightly in pencil.

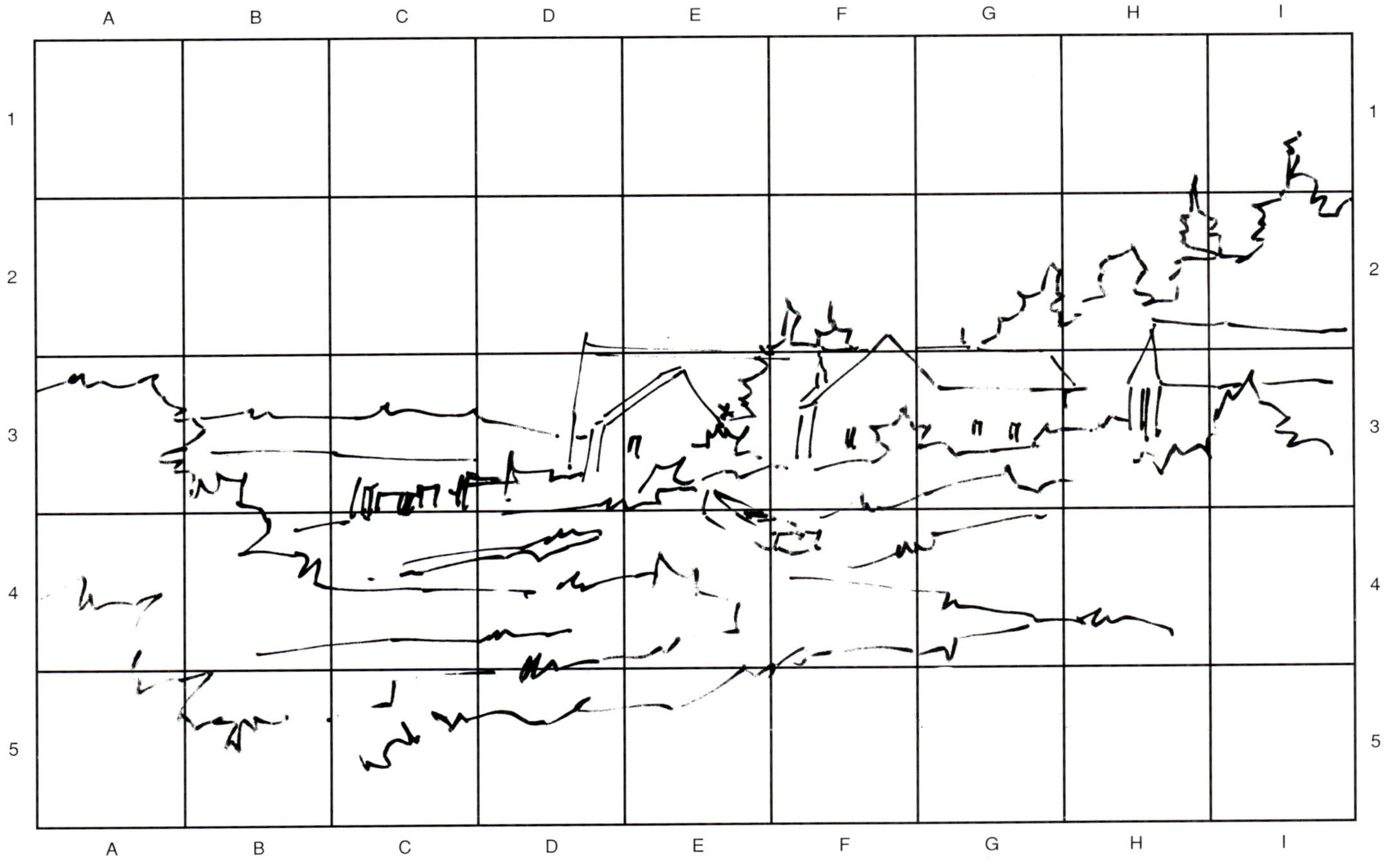

Study these pages before you start painting

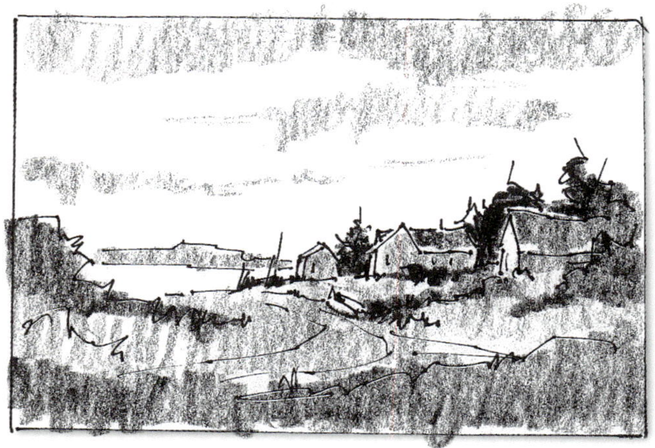

Thumbnail sketch
A quick thumbnail sketch helps organize thoughts and develop a painting plan.

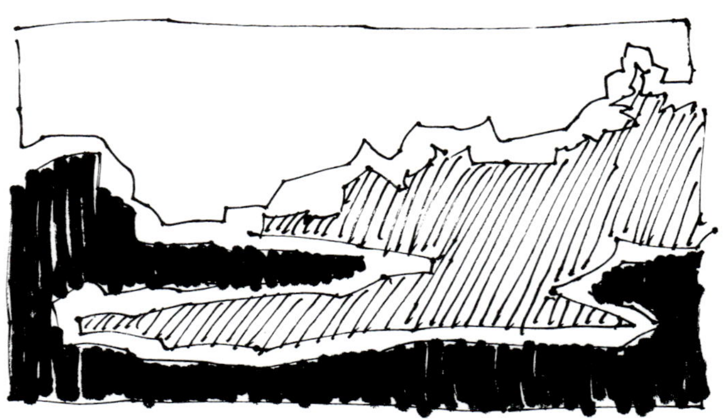

Shape map
The major shapes are defined by values and lead the viewer toward the focal area. The buildings and trees behind them interlock as one shape. Calligraphic rigger strokes provide contrast and pull the eye toward the center of interest.

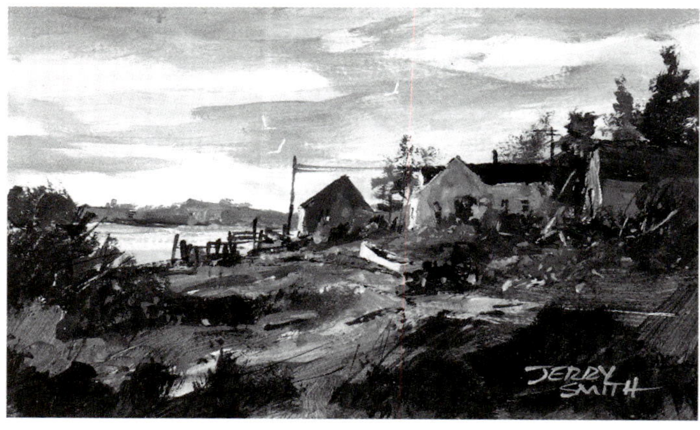

Tonal value map

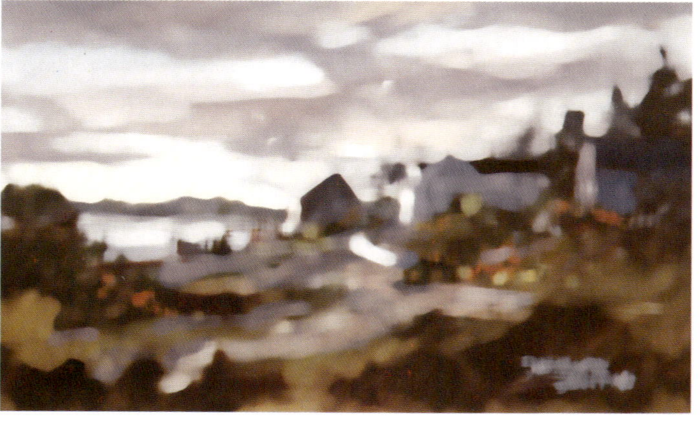

Color map (what you would see if you were to squint)
Squinting at the painting reveals a soft green/violet color harmony. The small rowboat provides a directional element as well as a repeat of the white accents on the buildings. Sky colors are repeated in foreground for color unity. Accents of bright color give life to the rich darks.

materials you'll need

painting surface
cold-press watercolor paper with one coat of gesso (either 140lb (300 gsm) or 300lb (638 gsm) paper could be used, but you'll find the 300lb a little more stable when applying washes), or canvas or board

brushes
¼", ½" and 1" flats
nos. 4, 6 and 12 rounds
rigger

other tools
2B pencil
ruler
palette
spray bottle to keep your palette moist

your acrylic palette for this painting

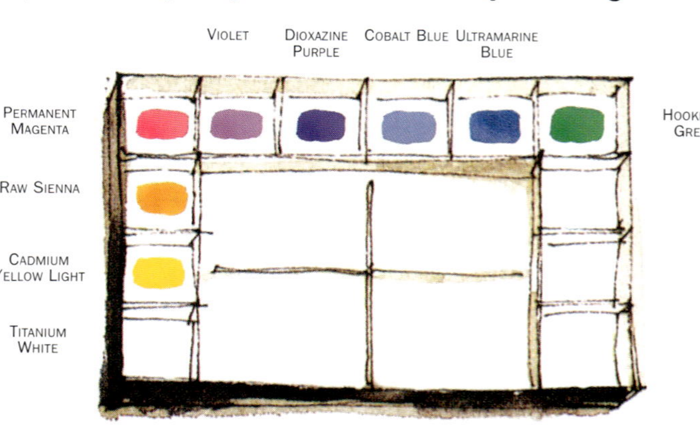

Consider the following elements

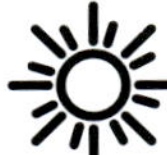

Light source

The low evening sun illuminates the water and perpendicular building planes. The tranquil mood is enhanced by placing the majority of the foreground and middle distance in shadow.

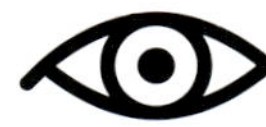

Viewpoint

The foreground pathway is an obvious entrance to the painting, but is intentionally kept somewhat obscured to keep it from being too dominant.

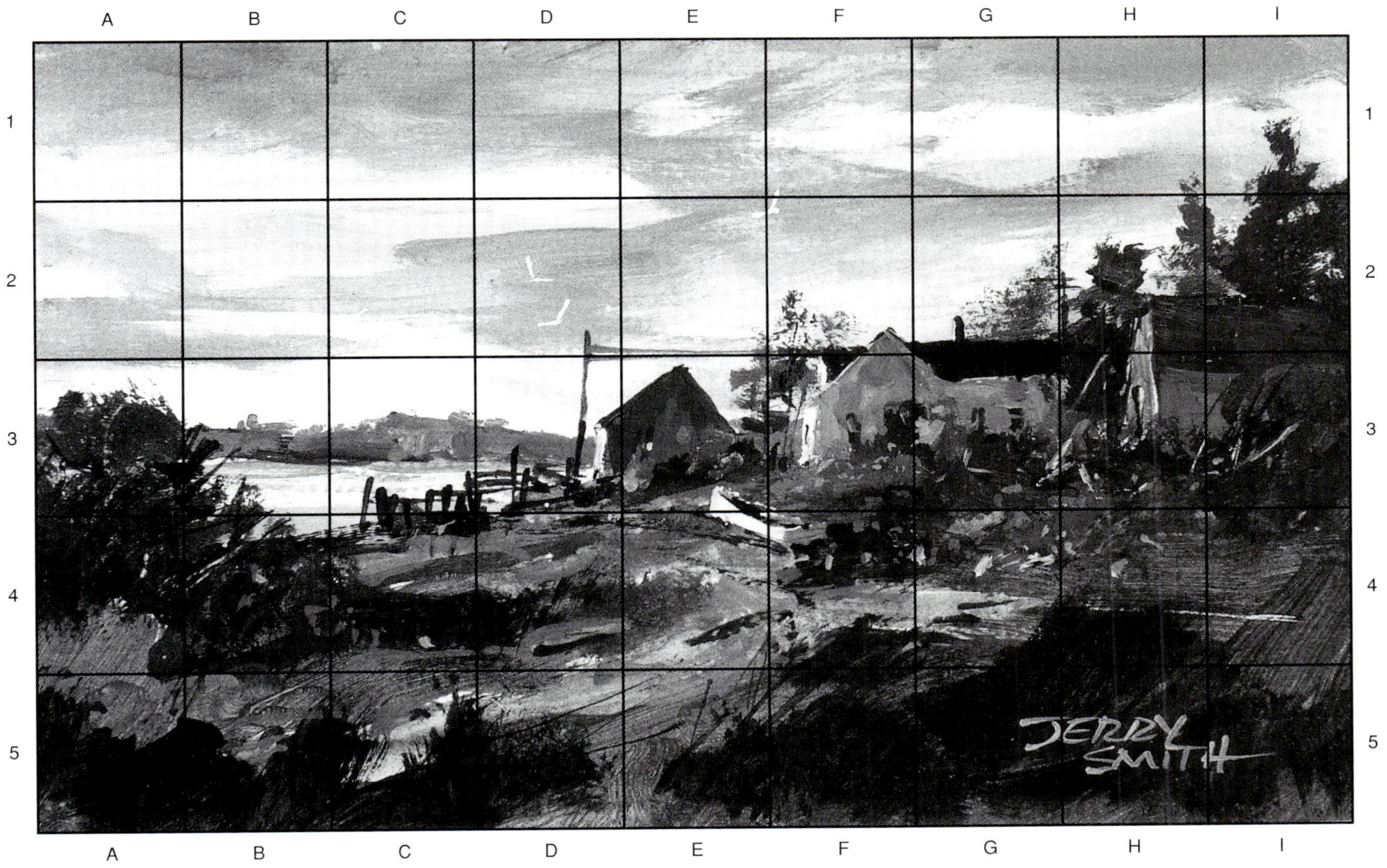

Make the most of your rigger brushes

Rigger brushes can be used to achieve loose, playful line work and brush strokes. They can be used for the drybrush technique as well as for linear work. Generally, more casual and interesting strokes are achieved by holding the brush high on the handle. The more pressure applied to the brush, the wider the brushstrokes.

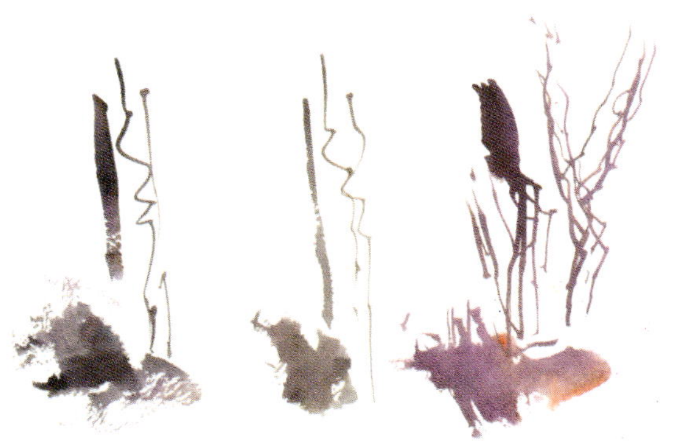

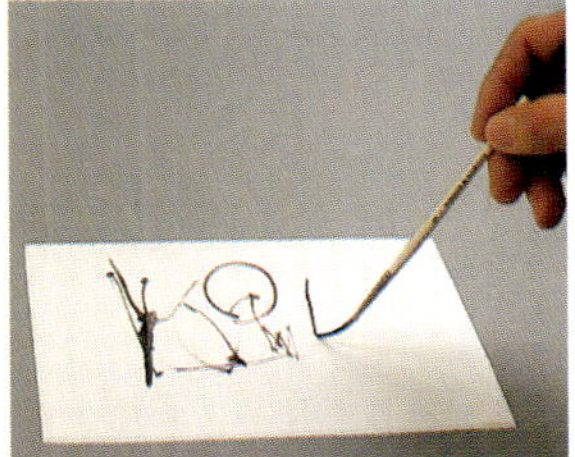

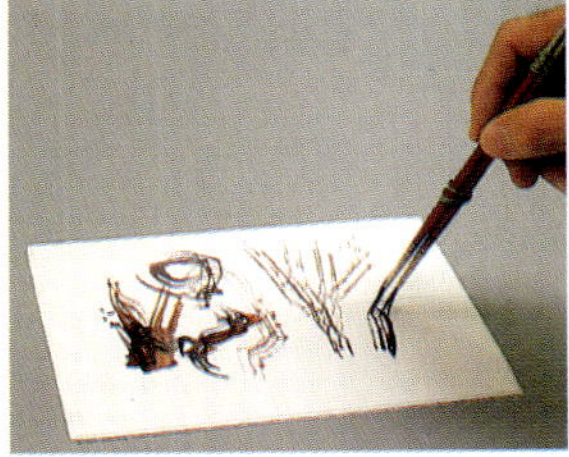

Put it all together

4. Block in the large shapes

Block in the large shapes with darks and midtones. Allow colors in this block-in stage to blend and mingle. The only edges that are carefully painted at this stage are those at the top of the distant tree line. Take care, because this section should be done in one pass and will be retained in the completed painting.

5. Overpaint boldly

When the initial washes have dried, overpaint them with bold brushstrokes of your half-inch flat brush. What you want is for these expressive brushstrokes to merely imply much of the foreground detail, leaving much of the initial undercoat to show through in the completed painting.

6. Let colors mingle

Allow your color to fuse and mingle as they are applied, creating a variety of edges and color variations.

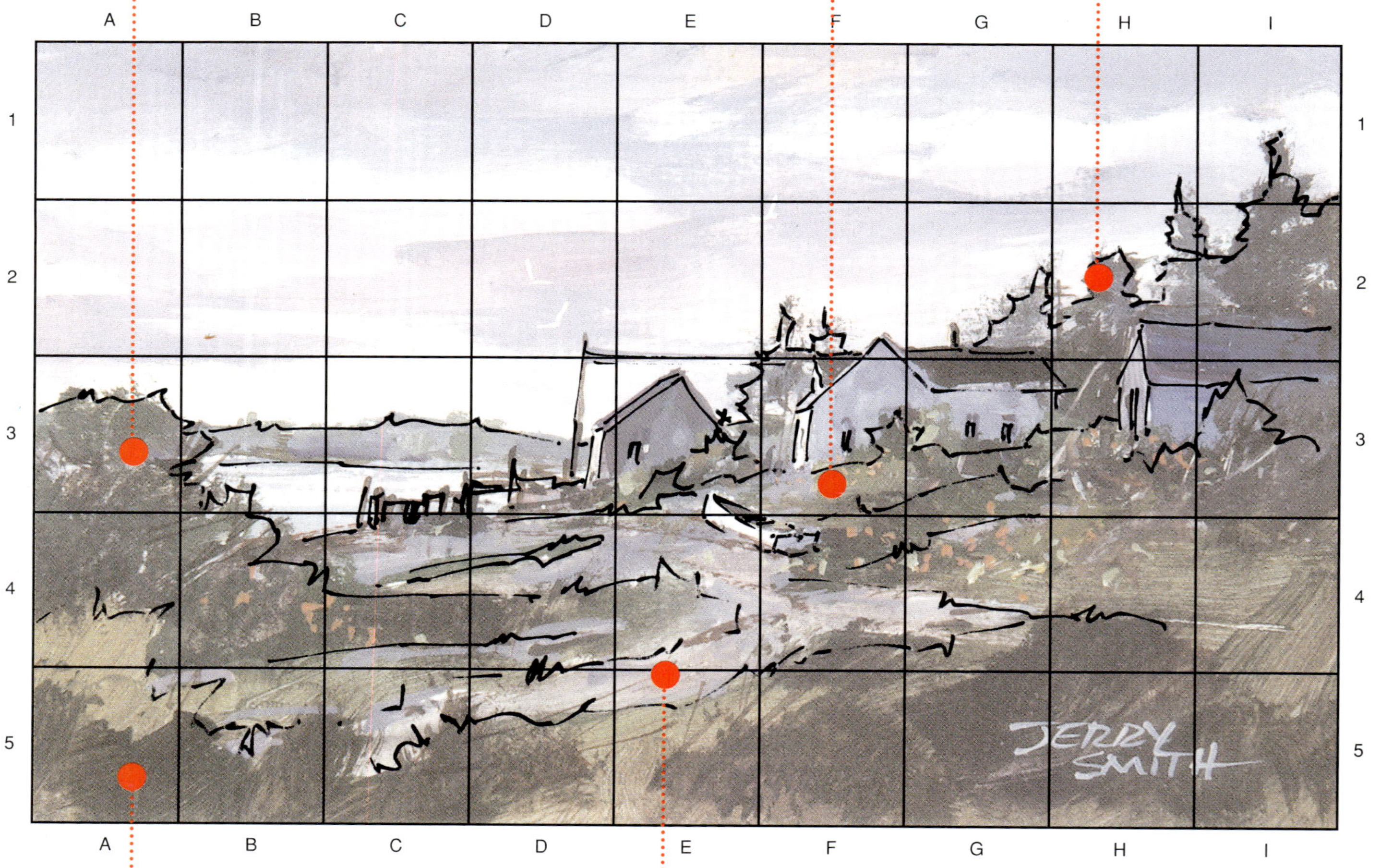

7. Paint the sky and grass

The sky is completed in two steps. The first layer is graded from a pale yellow at the horizon to a slightly darker blue/green at the top. After the first layer has thoroughly dried, the clouds are painted with various shades of violet blended on the paper. To give the impression of thick grass, drybrush over initial washes with a large brush. Just a few rigger strokes complete the effect.

8. Use gradations

Use either gradated color or gradated value to paint the gradual transitions.

9. Paint the water

Paint the water with a few horizontal strokes. To get the appearance of sparkle, drybrush on the textured watercolor paper. Repeat the sky colors in the water.

10. Refine elements

Using smaller brushes, refine the buildings and other focal elements.

11. Complete the painting

Complete the painting with bright highlights and rigger work.

Learning points

- Mixing and blending color directly on your painting surface can be more visually exciting than when it is thoroughly mixed on your palette.
- A great amount of detail can be implied with a few expressive brushstrokes. The rigger brush can be used to enhance the effect.

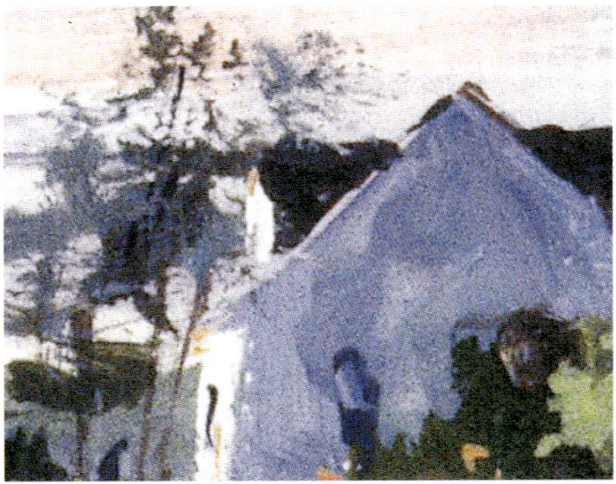

Detail

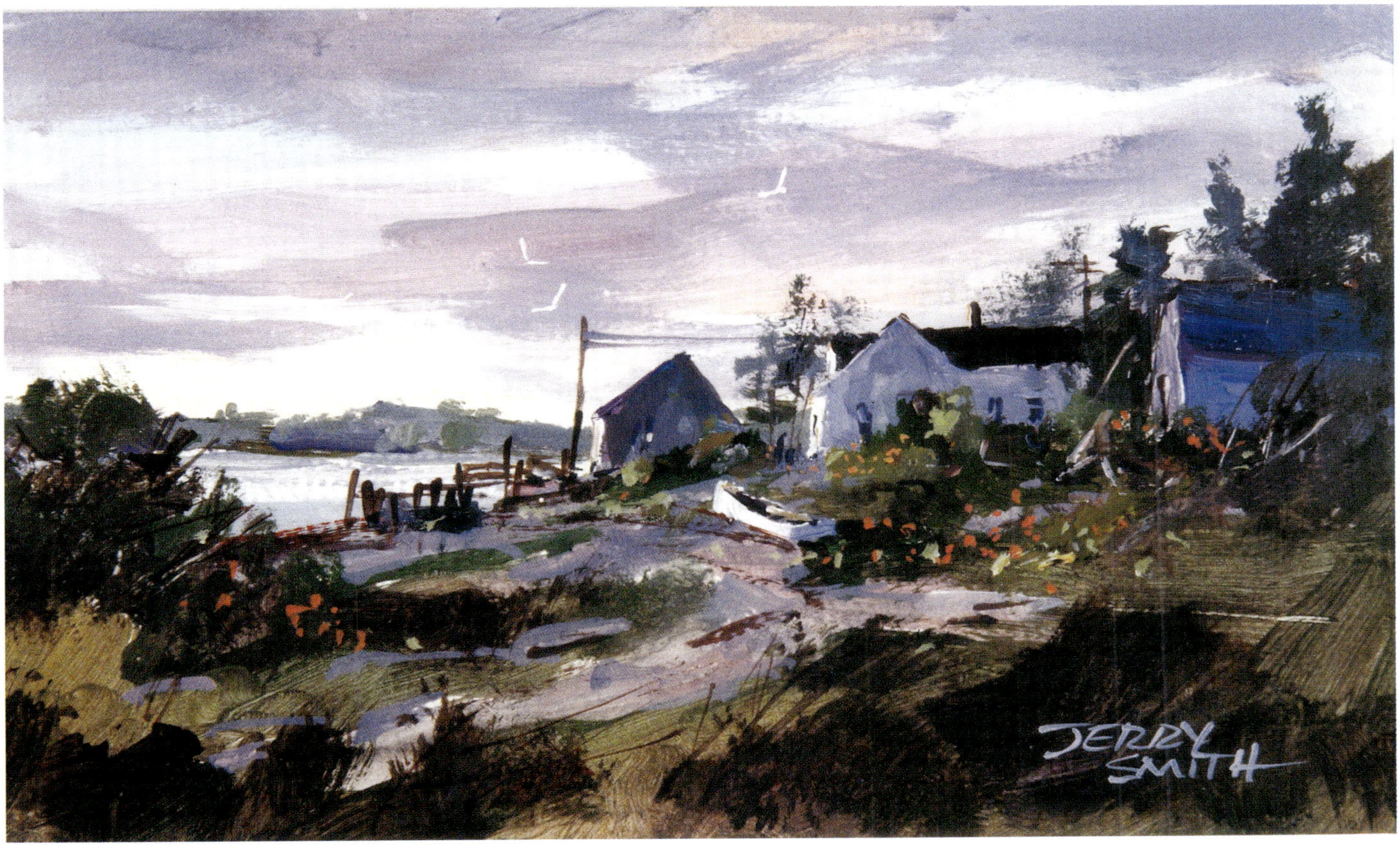

***Fleeting Light*, acrylic, 6 x 9" (15 x 23cm) by Jerry Smith ©**

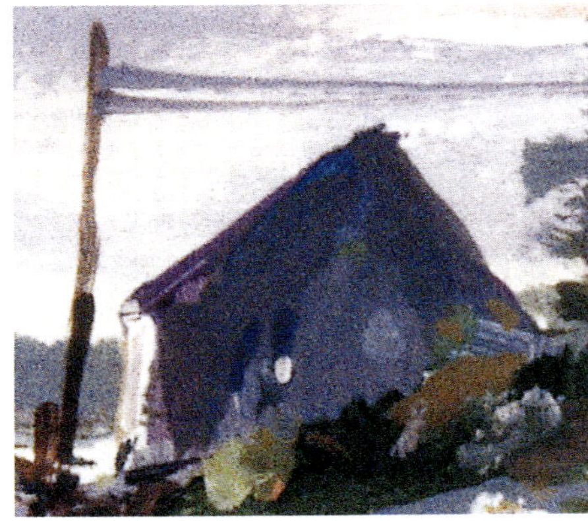

Detail

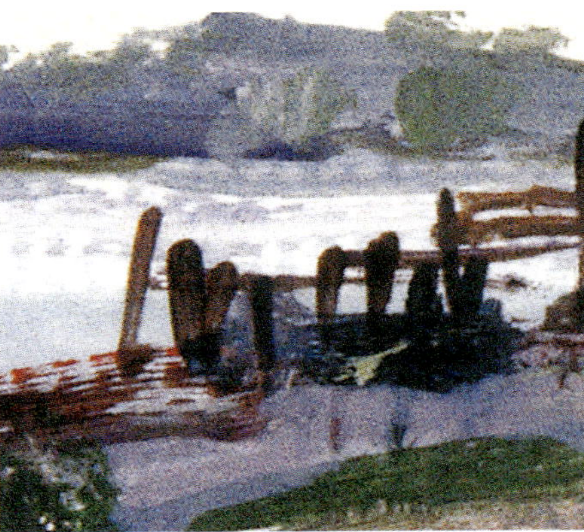

Detail

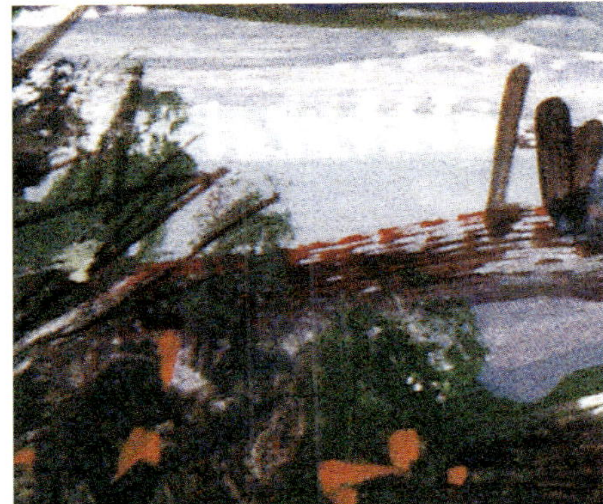

Detail

art map 9

Trying new approaches

Before you begin, read the entire project through so you know what's going to happen next.

Don't hesitate to take your paintings in a new direction if the spirit moves you. From time to time I will try to set aside periods of time for experimentation rather than production. Cultivating this attitude will help you expand your horizons and grow as an artist. The next few projects in this series are the results of such experimentation.

Over many years I accumulated a sizable stack of rejected and half-finished watercolors. In an experimental mode I began using the color and random shapes in these rejected watercolors as underpaintings for entirely different acrylic paintings. This was the way the painting in this exercise was developed. I'll try to explain my approach to painting this southern Indiana town.

1. The image to be transferred using the art map.

Read the instructions to see how to map this image across to your painting surface.

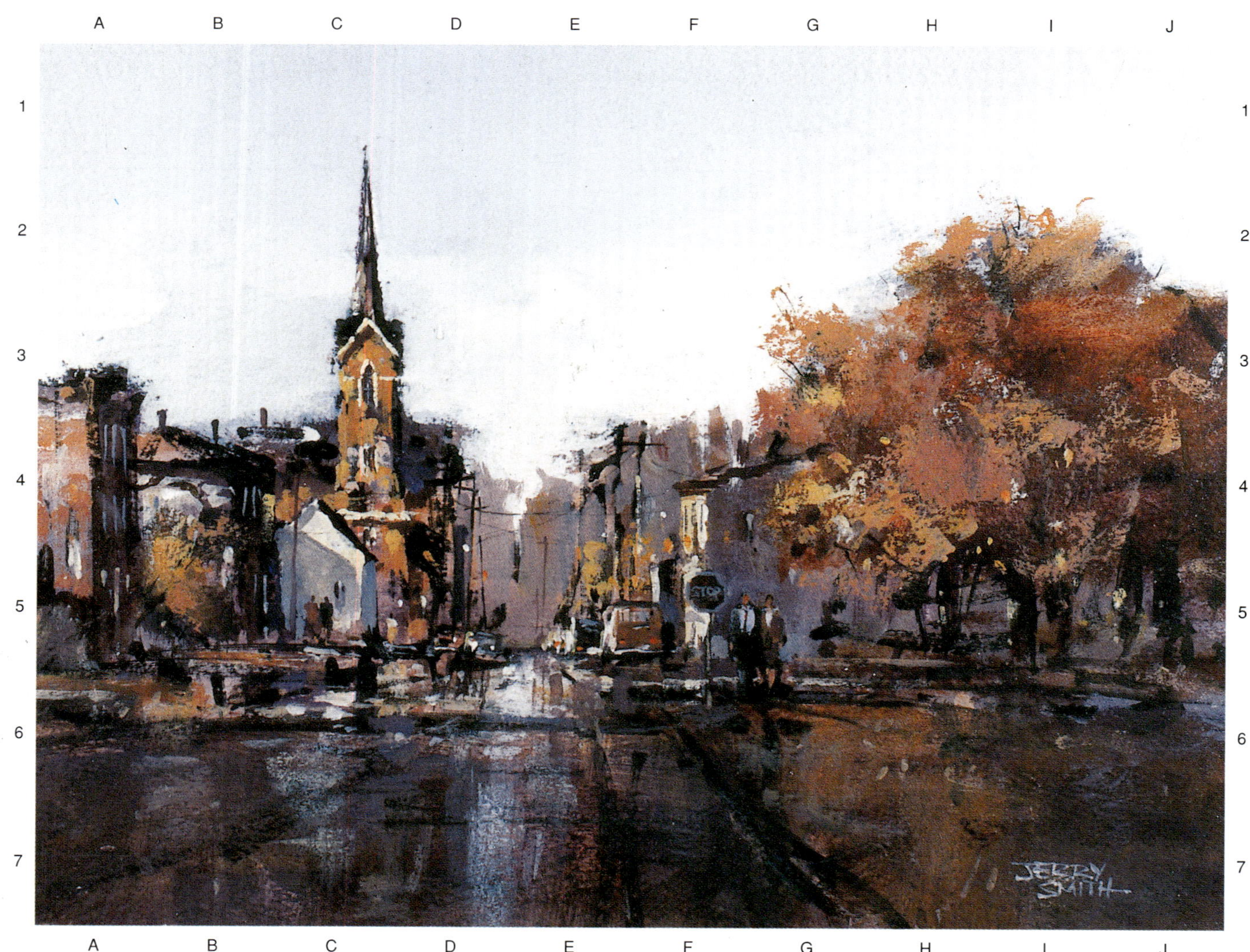

2. Map the image

With a 2B pencil, begin by LIGHTLY drawing a grid on your working surface that has the exact same number of squares as my grid. Your support can be the size of my original, or you can choose something proportionally larger or smaller. Your art map will be 7 squares down and 10 squares across. Put in the letters and numbers along the edges to make the next step easier.

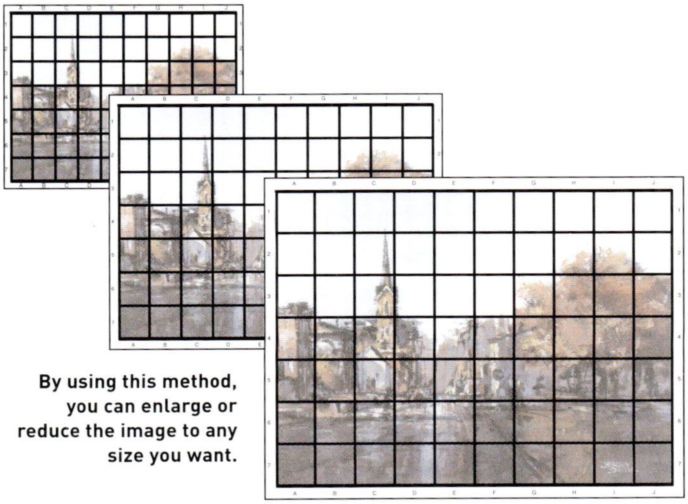

By using this method, you can enlarge or reduce the image to any size you want.

3. Use the art map to transfer the image

Now, still drawing very LIGHTLY with your pencil, copy the main contour lines of the object as shown in each square onto your working surface. It's not necessary to get every detail—just a simple line drawing will do. I recommend LIGHTLY and gently erasing the grid lines in the open, lighter areas before continuing.

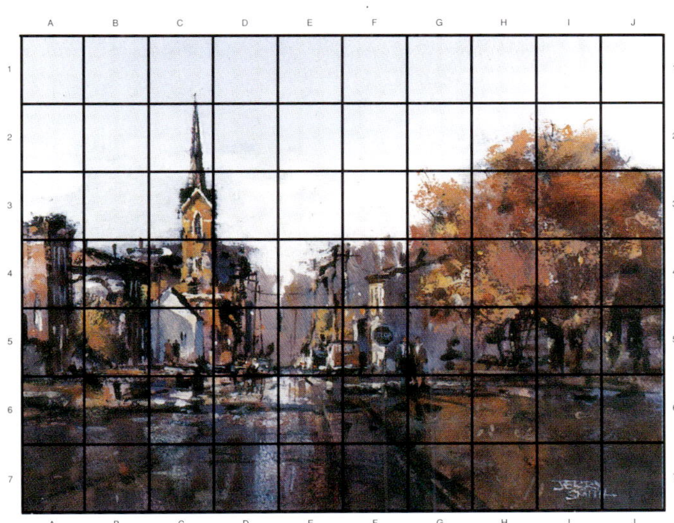

This is how your art map should look.

Here I've done the drawing in dark ink so you can see the idea, but you will do this lightly in pencil.

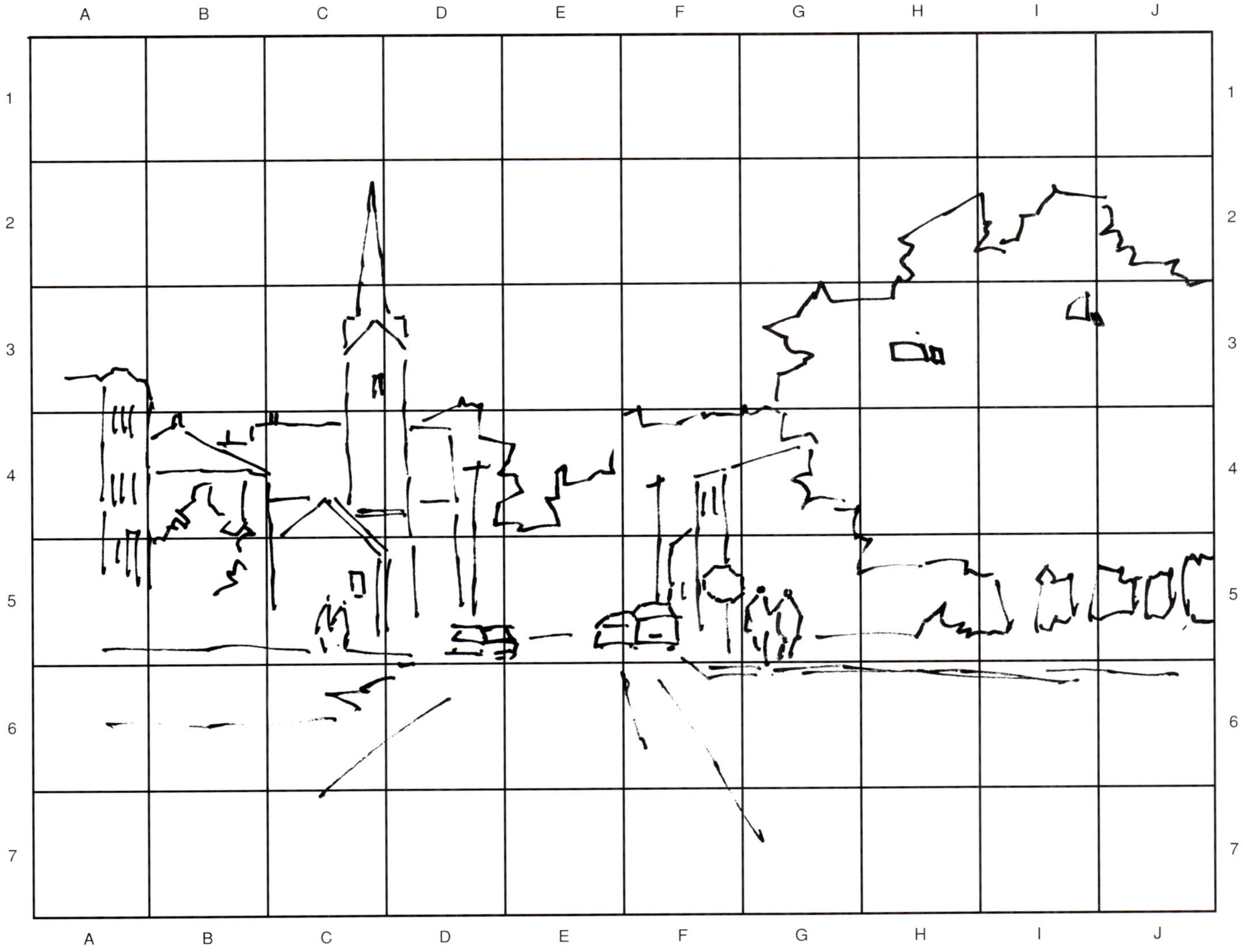

Study these pages before you start painting

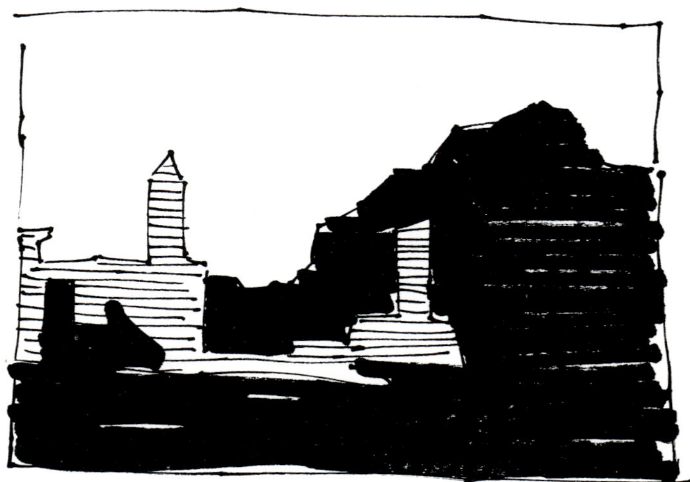

Shape map
Massed darks and mid tones focuses attention on sunlit passages. Notice the loose, abstract shapes and edges. This type of treatment should be consistent throughout the painting for the sake of unity.

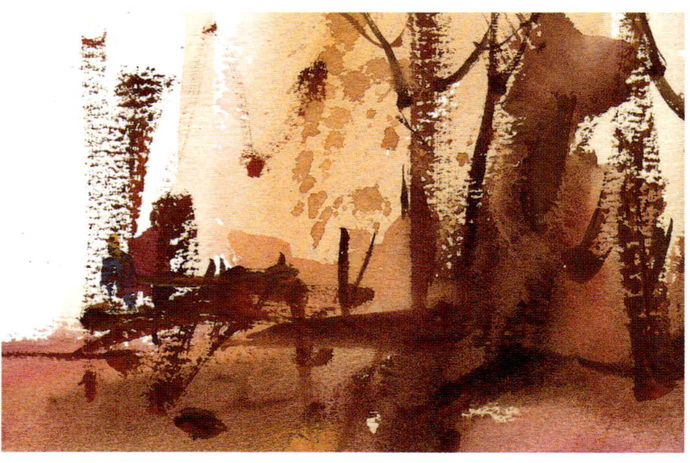

Texture
The texture of the cold press watercolor paper is used to advantage throughout the painting for texture and varied edges.

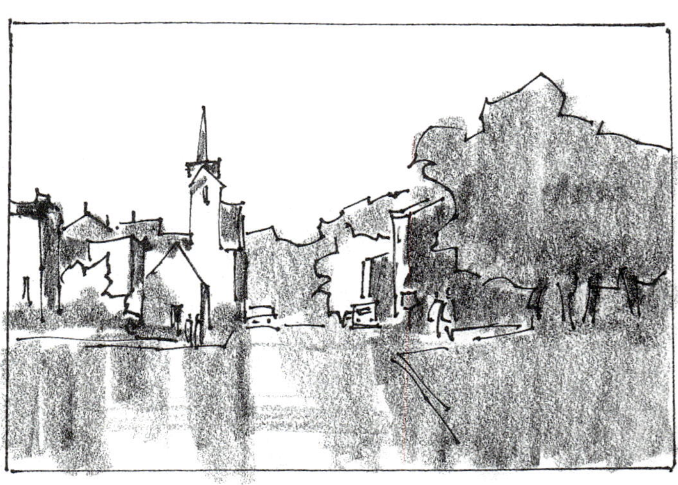

Thumbnail sketch
A quick thumbnail sketch in pencil and ink establishes your basic composition, light source and values.

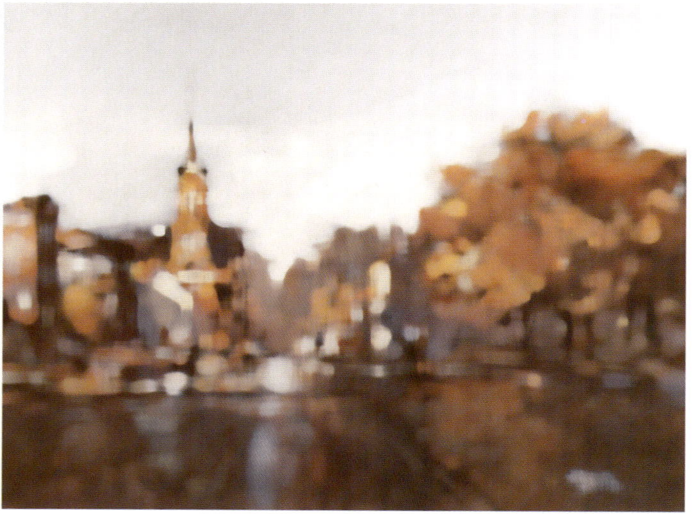

Color map (what you would see if you were to squint)

materials you'll need

painting surface
Use any rejected watercolor painting or a piece of watercolor paper with random watercolor washes and shapes. The colors in the underpainting do not really matter, except that some warm or earthy colors might be helpful. I will sometimes make extra slashes of color with acrylics on the paper to further obscure the images from the old painting.

brushes
¼", ½" and 1" flats
nos. 4, 6 and 12 rounds
rigger

other tools
2B pencil
ruler
palette
spray bottle to keep your palette moist
acrylic spray fixative

your acrylic palette for this painting

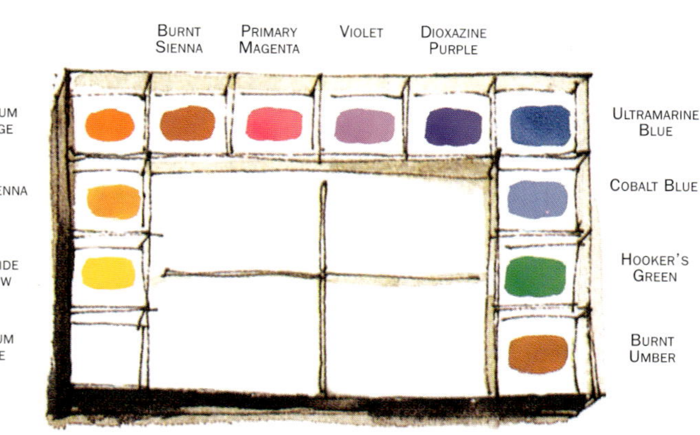

Consider the following elements

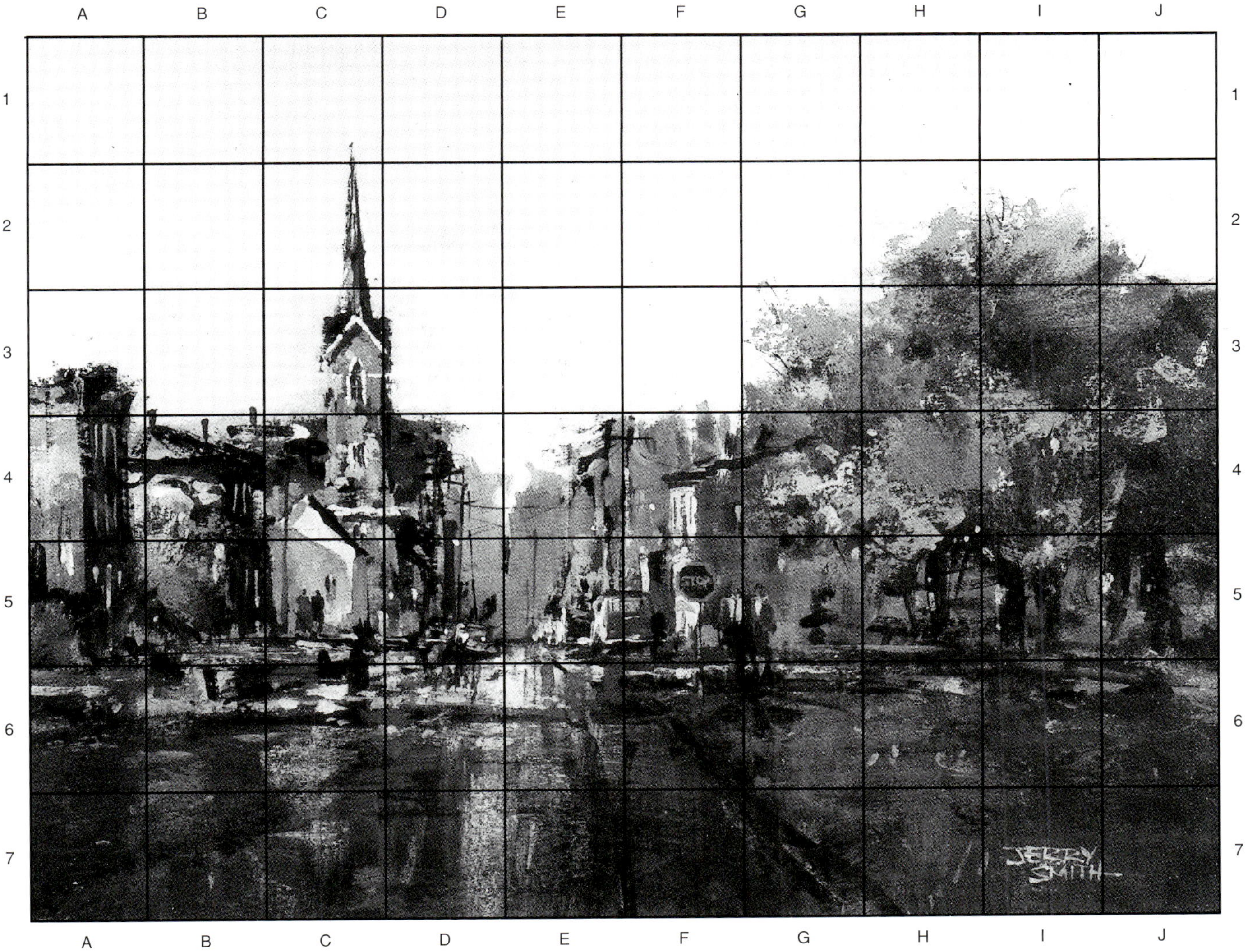

4. Begin with black lines

Begin by making a linear drawing with thinned black acrylic and a #6 round brush. Lively blacks can be made by mixing any of the dark colors on your palette. Mixing Ultramarine Blue and Burnt Umber makes a good black. Pay no regard to the underpainting at that stage.

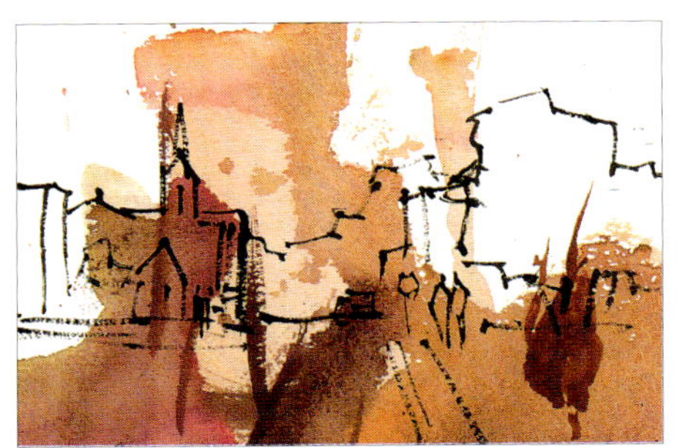

Put it all together

5. Apply color

With the line drawing loosely completed, begin applying new color while attempting to be sensitive to the useful color and shapes that could be retained from the underpainting.

6. Use negative space

The sky is negatively painted around the positive shapes in the painting.

7. Overpaint sparingly

You should overpaint and refine several times. In other areas leave the initial washes visible.

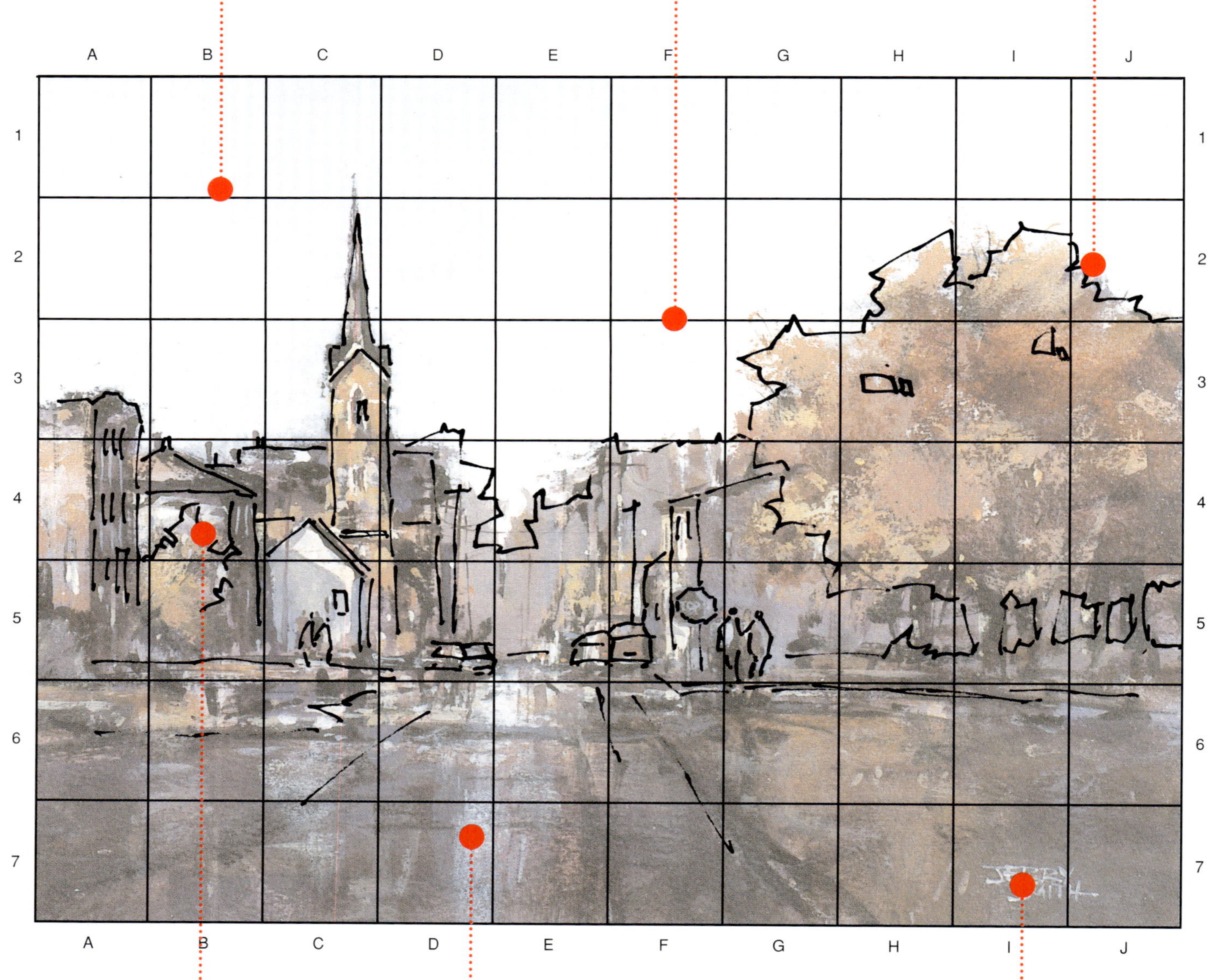

8. Paint the brights

The final steps include painting the brightest sunlit areas.

9. Paint key details

To provide scale and add life to the scene, paint merely suggestions of figures and vehicles. To liven the foreground, put just a hint of sky color in the street.

10. Spray and coat

When it's completed, spray the painting with acrylic spray fixative, then brush the final varnish on. The fixative prevents the remaining watercolor from being smeared by the varnish coat.

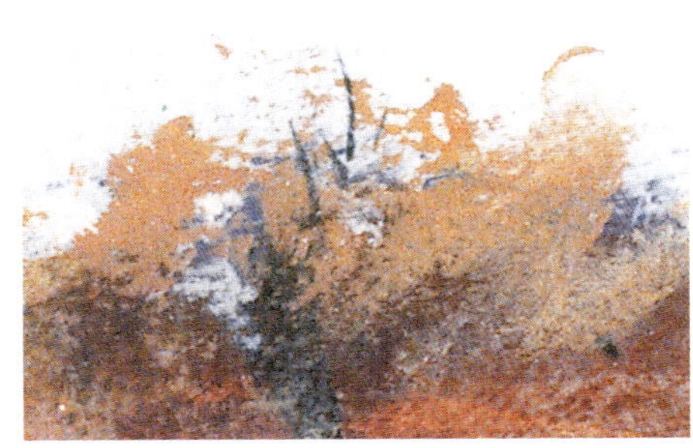
Detail

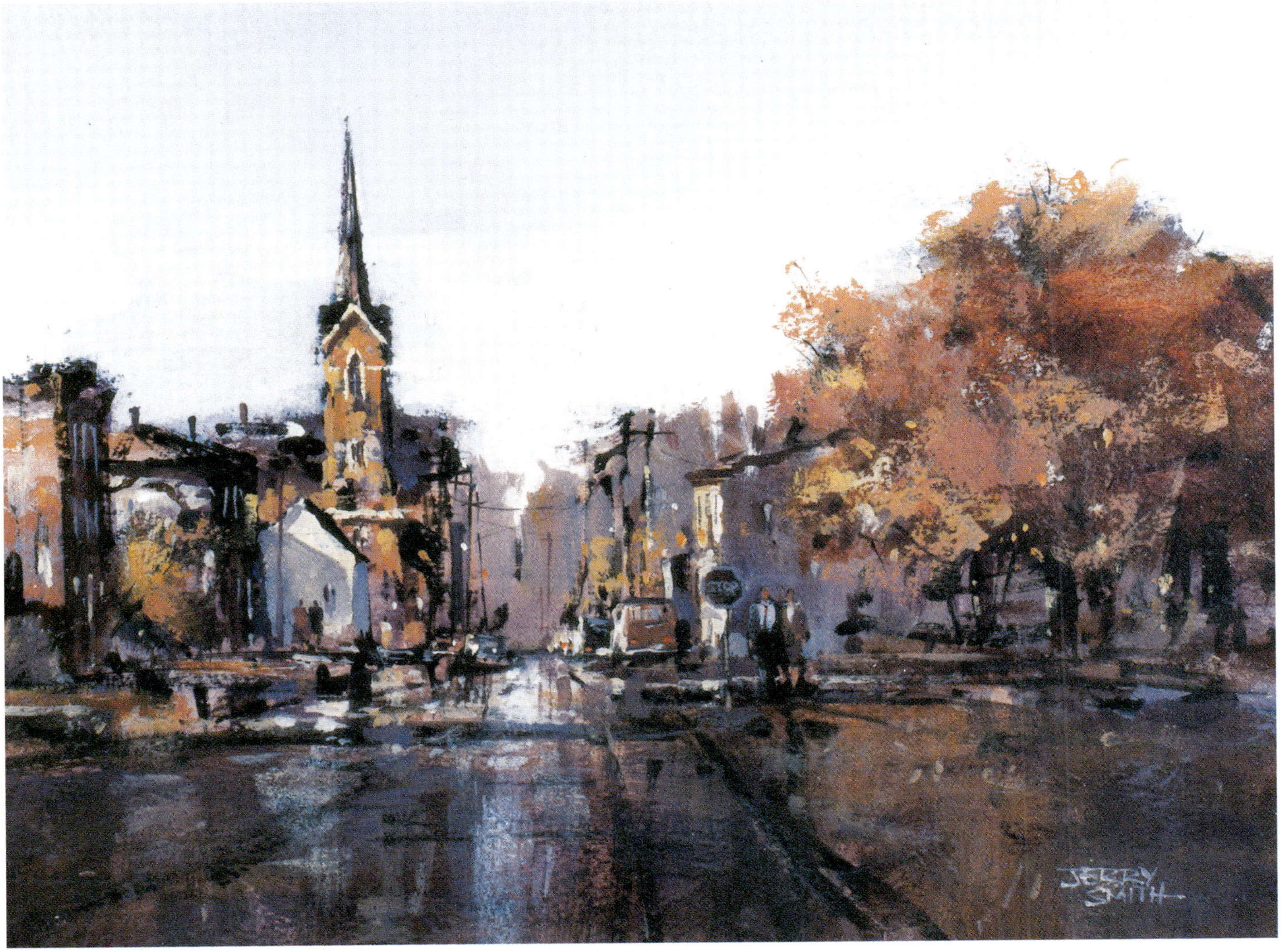

Village Texture, acrylic, 11 x 15" (28 x 38cm) by Jerry Smith ©

Detail

Detail

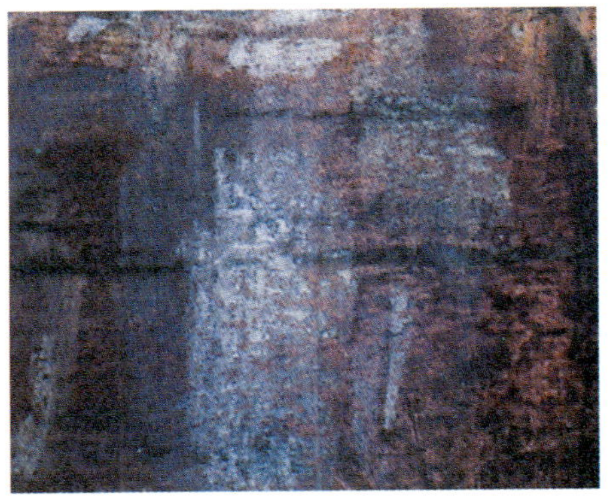
Detail

art map 10

Using lines and textures expressively

For many years my wife and I have made annual trips to the Maine coast. I return to Indiana not only with completed paintings, but also with a large number of sketches and photos. I use this reference material to do more expressive and interpretive paintings in the studio. **Like art map 9, this painting was worked over the top of a rejected watercolor.** You may transfer the drawing as in the previous exercises, although my painting was started with only a loose drawing in acrylic paint. Even if you take a similar approach you will still find the grid system useful in getting objects positioned on your paper.

The approach in this project capitalizes on the texture of the watercolor paper. With this approach you don't paint the entire surface. Let some of the underpainting work for you. You'll be pleasantly surprised by the exciting shapes and textures that emerge from the underpainting.

1. The image to be transferred using the art map.

Read the instructions to see how to map this image across to your working surface.

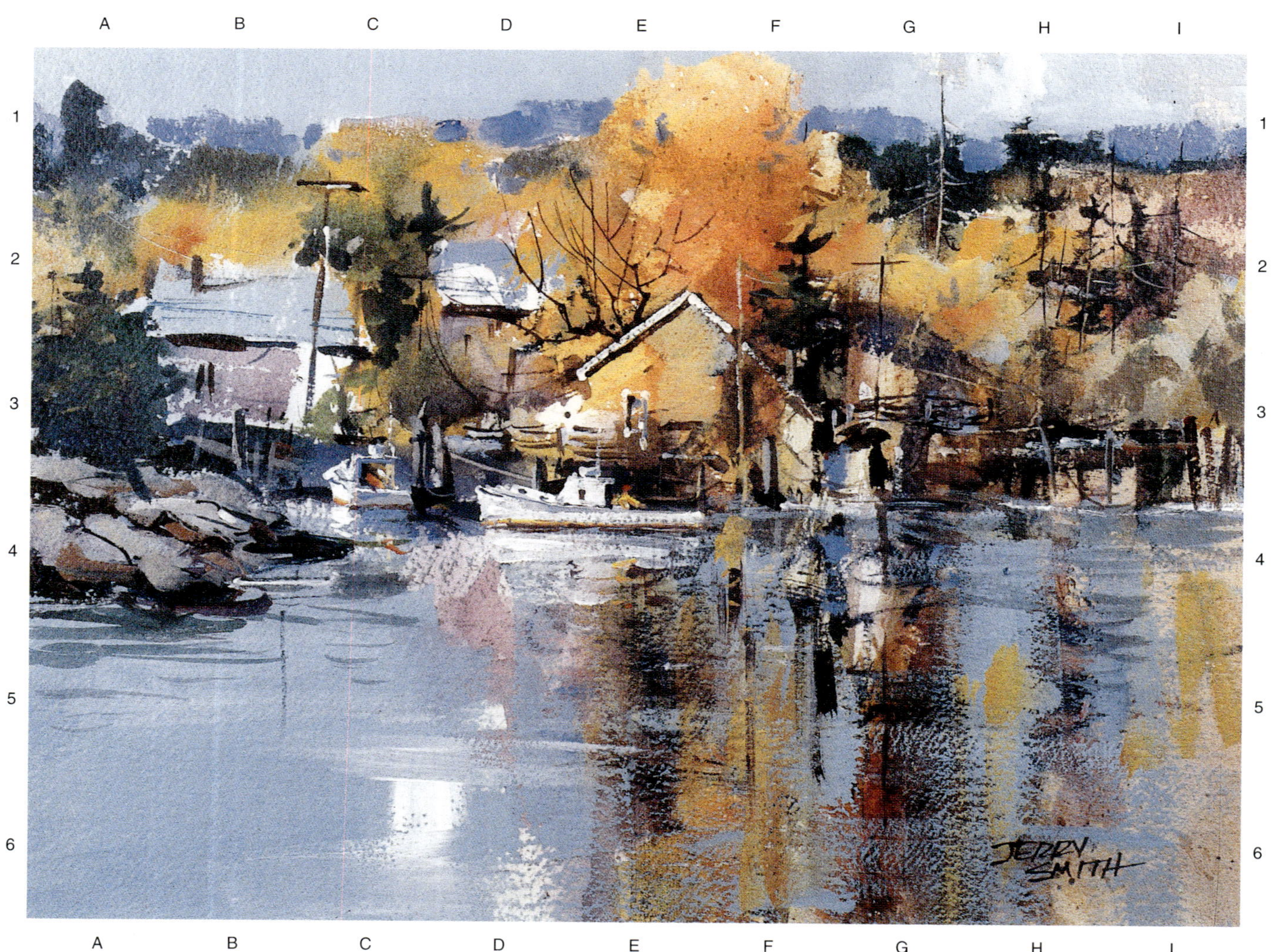

2. Map the image

With a 2B pencil, begin by LIGHTLY drawing a grid on your working surface that has the exact same number of squares as my grid. Your support can be the size of my original, or you can choose something proportionally larger or smaller. Your art map will be 6 squares down and 9 squares across. Put in the letters and numbers along the edges to make the next step easier.

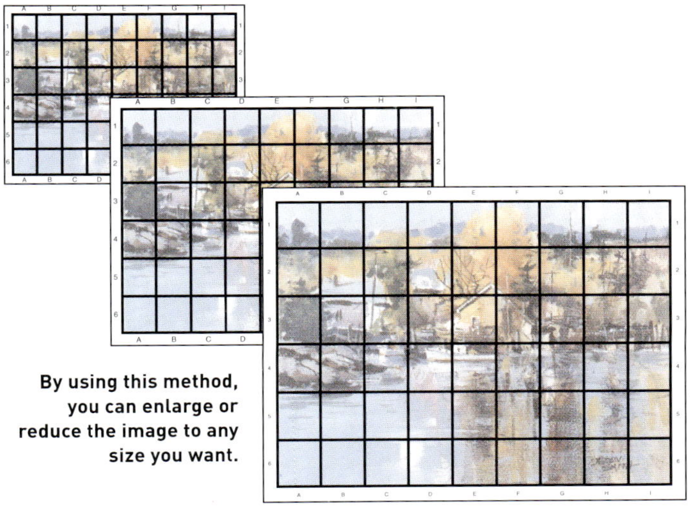

By using this method, you can enlarge or reduce the image to any size you want.

3. Use the art map to transfer the image

Now, still drawing very LIGHTLY with your pencil, copy the main contour lines of the object as shown in each square onto your working surface. It's not necessary to get every detail—just a simple line drawing will do. I recommend LIGHTLY and gently erasing the grid lines in the open, lighter areas before continuing.

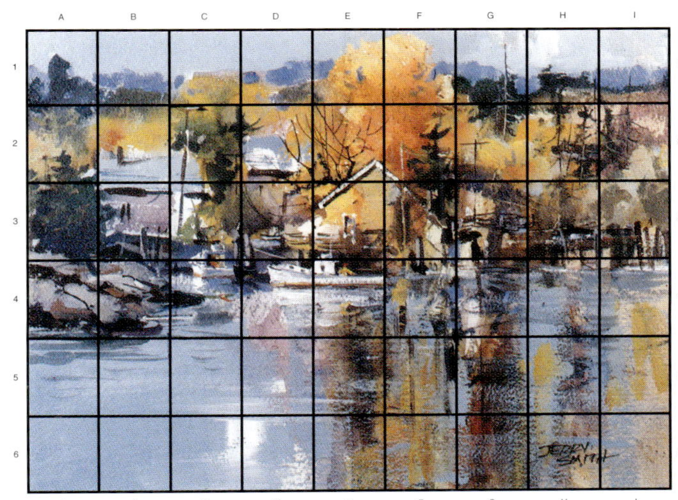

This is how your art map should look.

Here I've done the drawing in dark ink so you can see the idea, but you will do this lightly in pencil.

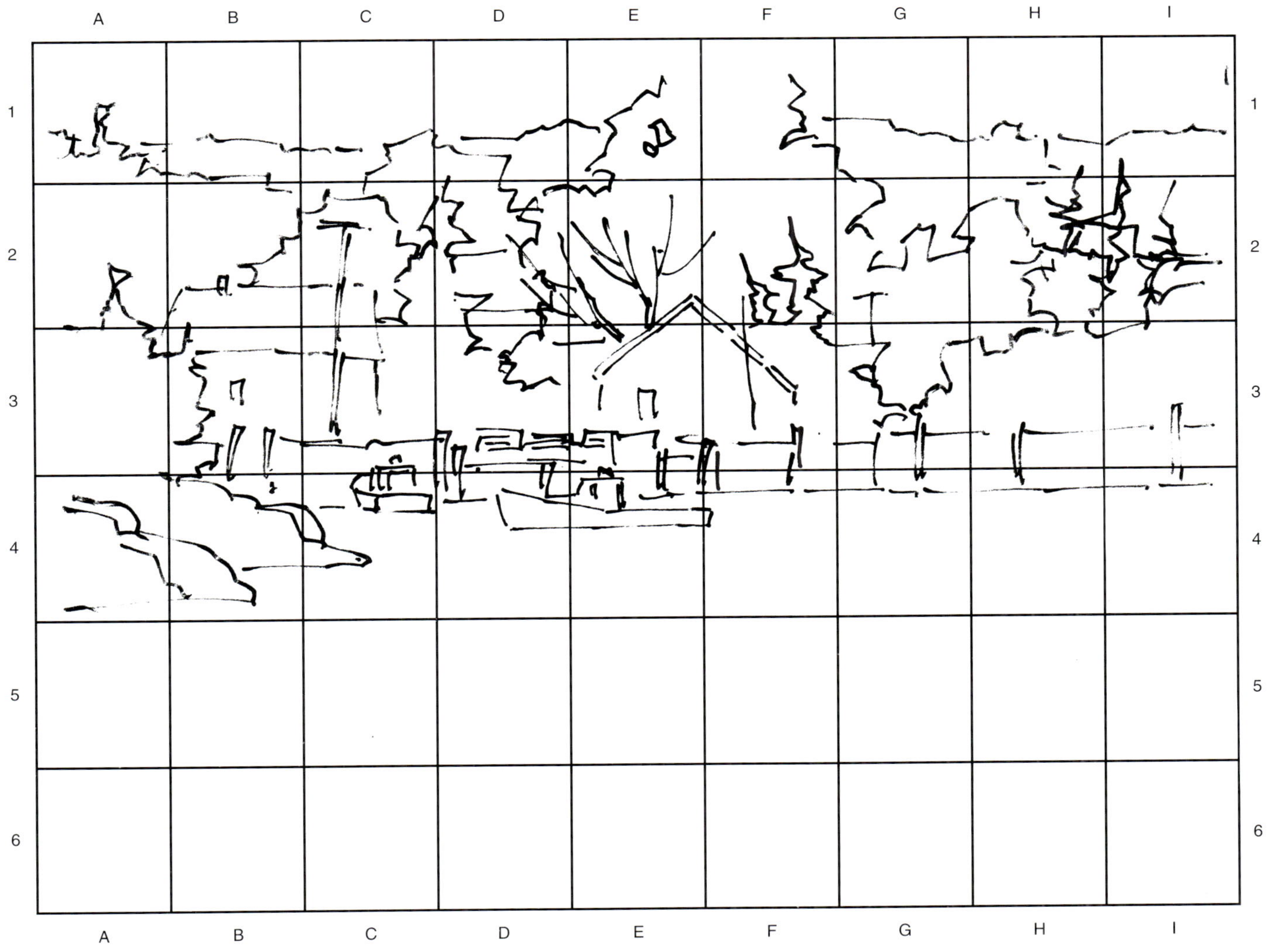

A B C D E F G H I

1 2 3 4 5 6

Study these pages before you start painting

Opaque vs. Transparent
An important property of acrylic paints is the ability to use them either opaquely or as transparent washes. While some colors are more transparent than others, any color can be made opaque by layering on enough paint.

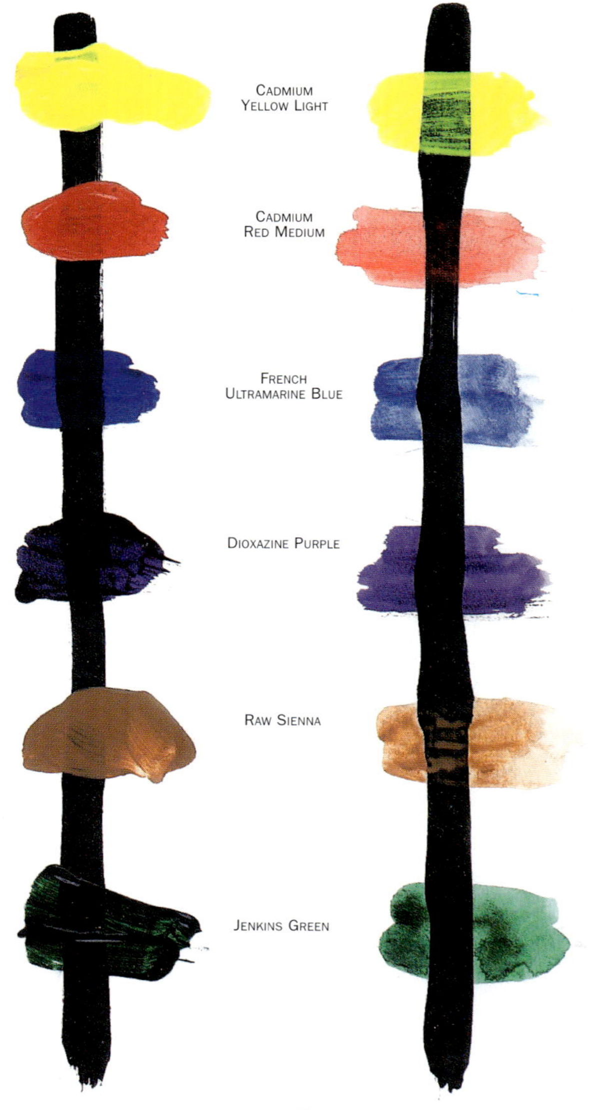

Opaque
Layers of color can obliterate even a black line.

Transparent
Here's what happens when you paint thin color over a black line.

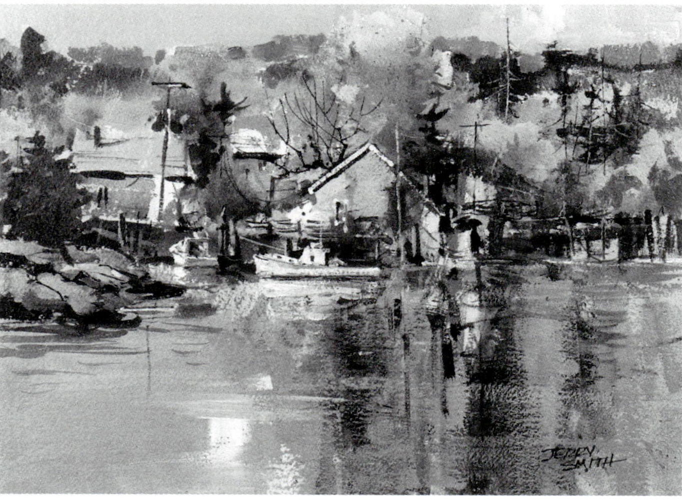

Tonal value map
The tonal revision of this painting indicates that it is color- rather than value-dominated. Values are within a narrow range, colors provide the impact.

Color map (what you would see if you were to squint)
Note that the color plan is a complementary blue/orange plan with green and violet accents. Many of the exciting elements of this painting are derived from the original watercolor washes. Shapes and colors are nicely repeated in foreground water reflections without being presented as mirror images.

materials you'll need

painting surface
discarded watercolor made on heavy paper

brushes
1/4", 1/2" and 1" flats
nos. 4, 6 and 12 rounds
small rigger 1 or 2

other tools
2B pencil
ruler
palette
spray bottle to keep your palette moist
acrylic spray fixative

your acrylic palette for this painting

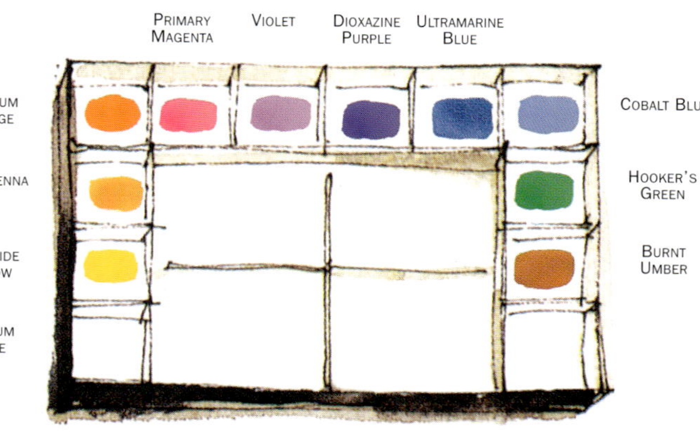

Consider the following elements

Light source

Here the strong light is coming from the left, indicated by the bright highlights. When your intent is to paint reflections in water, strong bright light is best.

Bright idea

A degree of rhythm is achieved through the repetition of darks in various sizes and shapes throughout. Some are placed at the center of interest for contrast and focus.

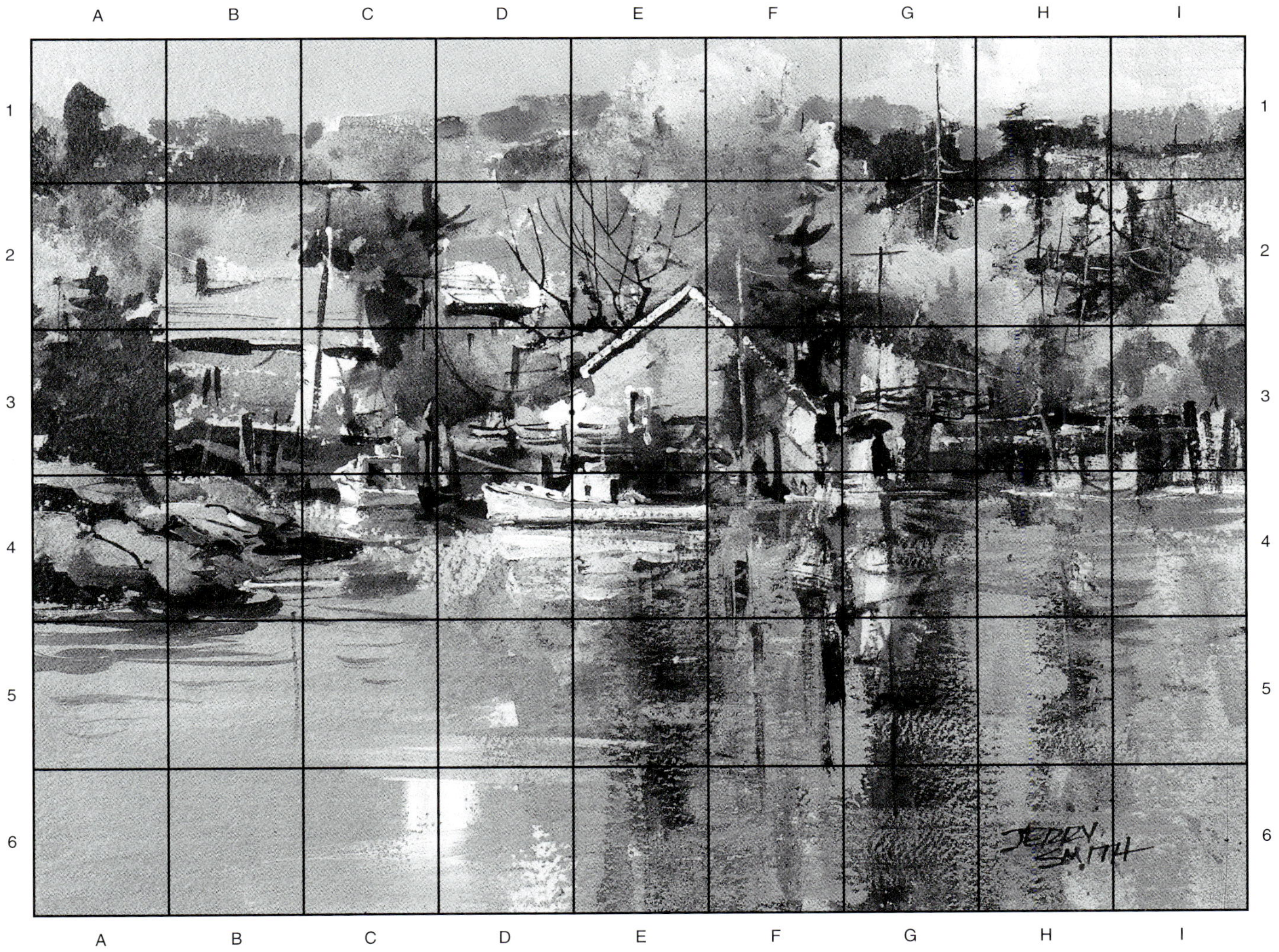

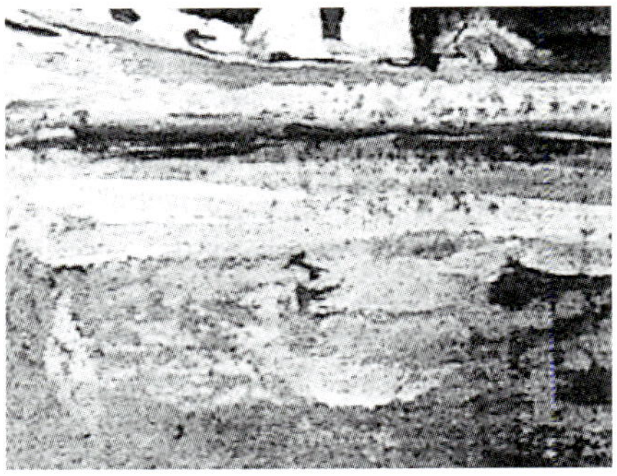

detail

Put it all together

4. Start with the lines

From the outset keep in mind that lines play an important role in this painting, because they tie shapes together from background to foreground.

5. Draw loosely

Loosely draw the major elements (buildings, boats, piers, and rocks) over the watercolor washes. Remember, some of this drawing will remain in the completed painting, but with acrylics you have the advantage of being able to repaint anything you wish. It relieves a lot of the pressure.

6. Apply color

Apply color as desired, with consideration given to how much of the underpainting you want exposed. Be constantly on the alert for exciting surprises.

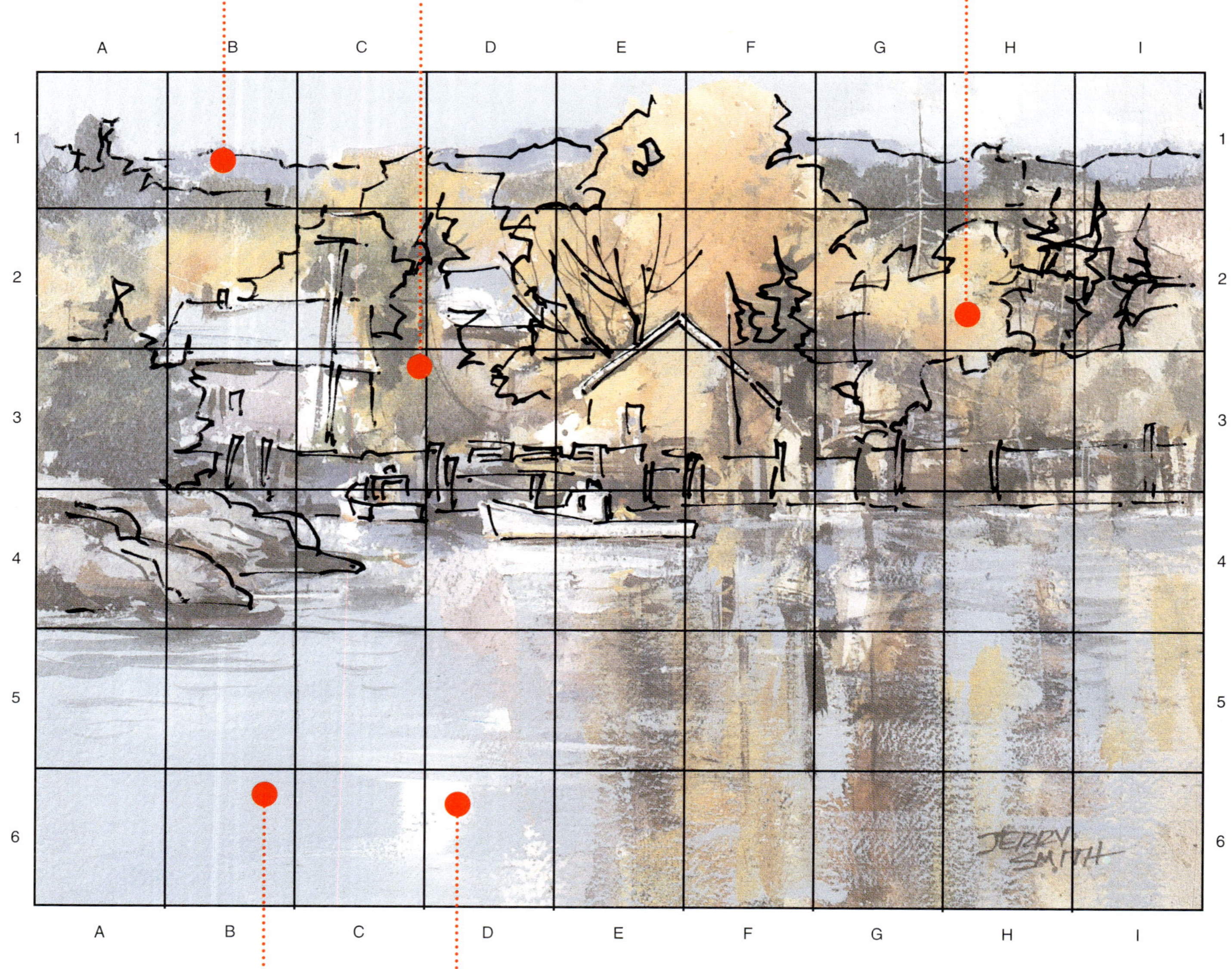

7. Use your drybrush

Throughout your painting use a drybrush freely to enhance texture.

Textural interest is increased through a wide variation in edges and textures. Soft watercolor textures will contrast nicely with harder edged textures.

8. Complete with highlights

Complete the painting with bright highlights and additional line work to pull it together. For some highlighted areas, such as the white boats, add acrylic paint. For other highlights, leave the pure, untouched watercolor paper.

Learning points

- Plan ahead, but interpret as you go. Be on the lookout for those exciting developments that just happen.
- Line work can unify, separate, move the eye and add punch to your paintings.
- Let the texture of your paper work for you.

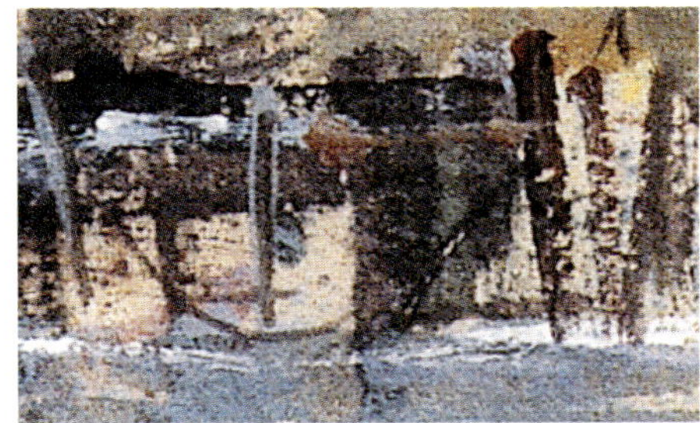

Detail

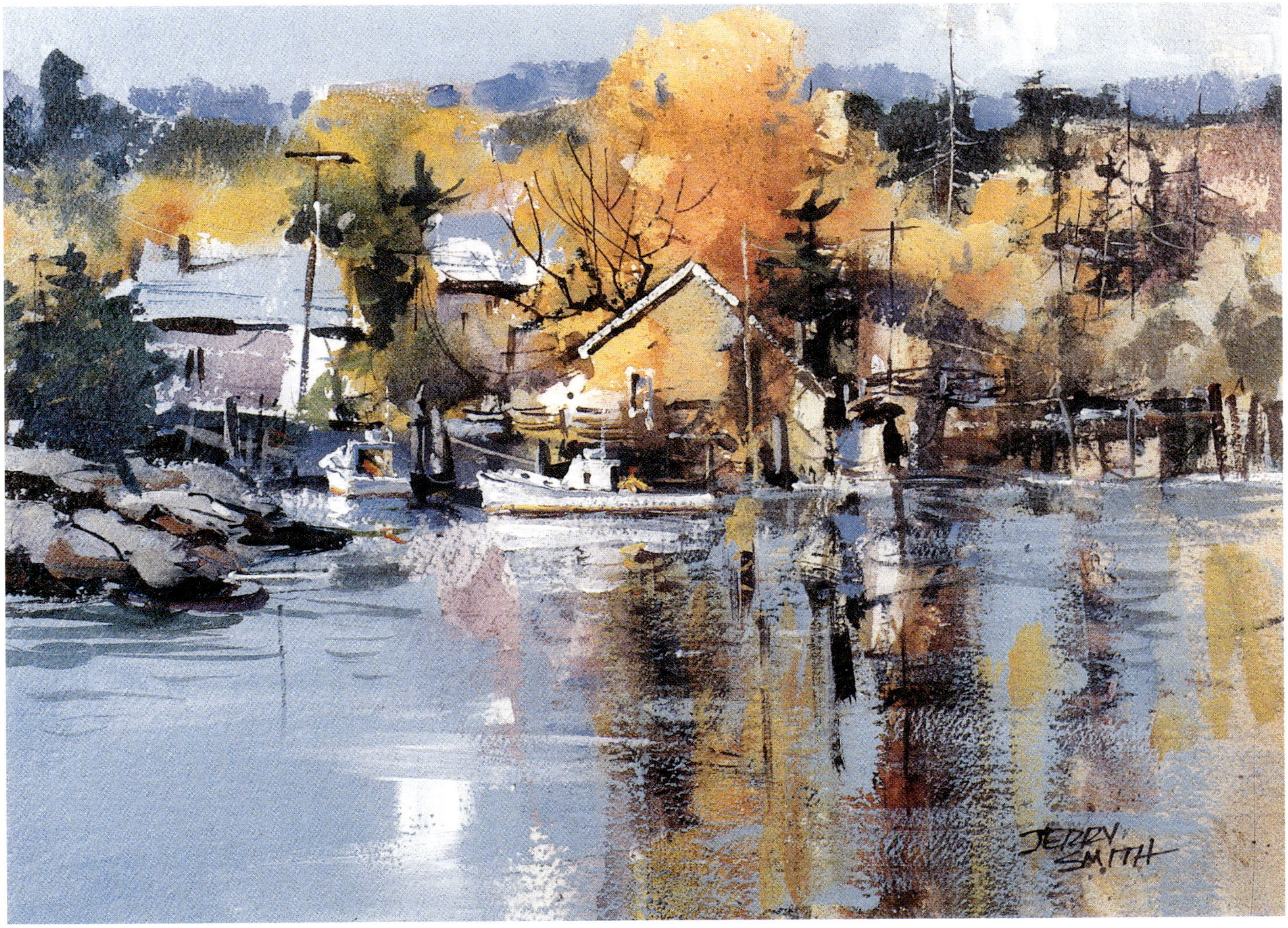

***Harbor Reflections*, acrylic, 11 x 15" (28 x 38cm) by Jerry Smith ©**

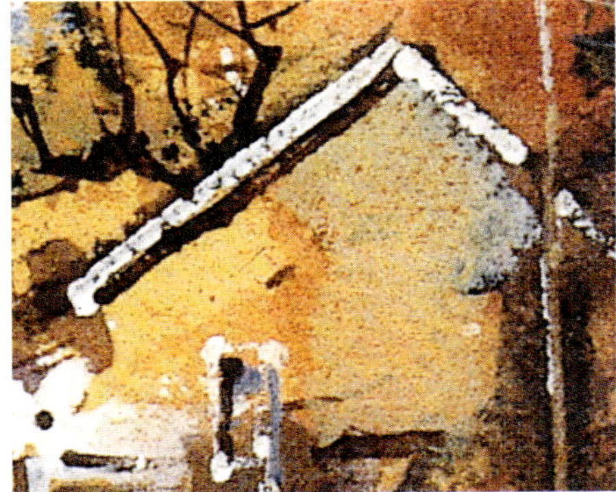

Detail

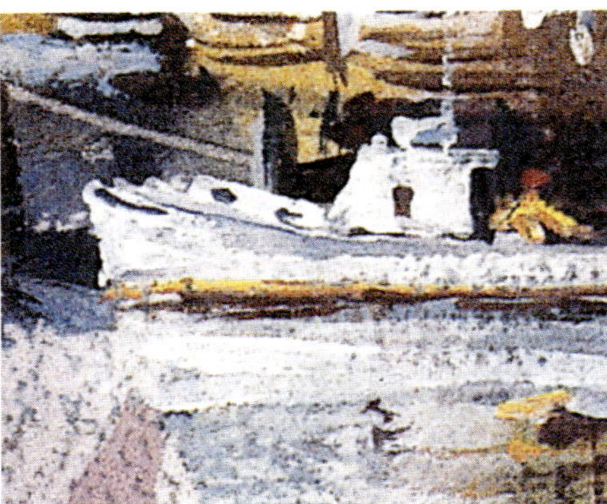

Detail

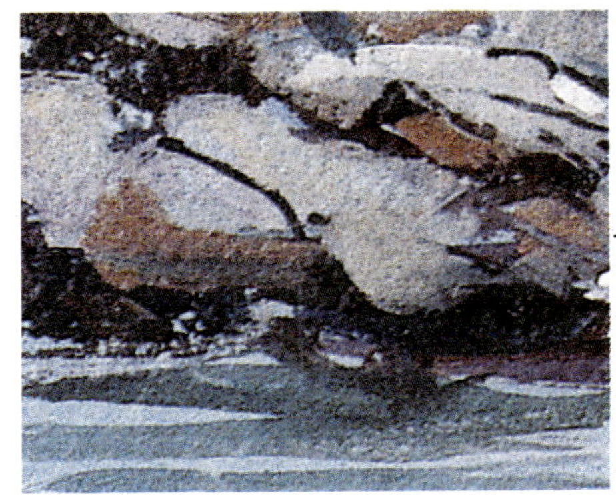

Detail

Before you begin, read the entire project through so you know what's going to happen next.

art map 11

Adding collage for texture and expression

Once again I'd like to make a slight shift in direction. This project and the following two incorporate collage material into acrylic painting. While the technique may at first seem a little complicated, you might find that collage elements are worth the effort when they add a whole new dimension to your work.

While the full spectrum of collage painting has an infinite range of technique and potential materials, the exercises presented here are limited to a narrow range of collage techniques. These paintings involved only tissue paper as collage material to enhance the texture in the paintings. You'll find that collage and acrylic painting are very compatible.

1. The image to be transferred using the art map.

Read the instructions to see how to map this image across to your working surface.

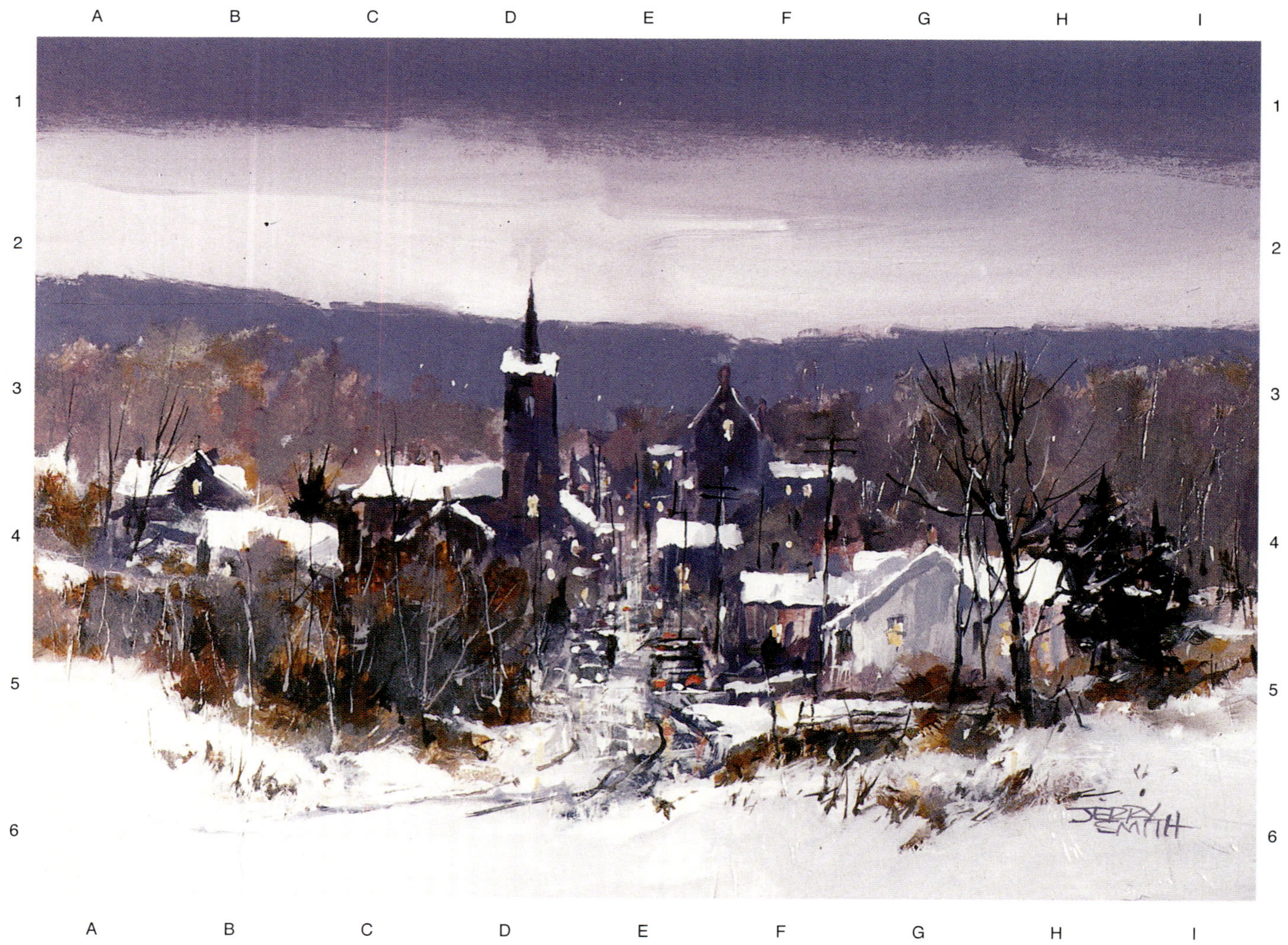

2. Map the image

With a 2B pencil, begin by LIGHTLY drawing a grid on your working surface that has the exact same number of squares as my grid. Your support can be the size of my original, or you can choose something proportionally larger or smaller. Your art map will be 6 squares down and 9 squares across. Put in the letters and numbers along the edges to make the next step easier.

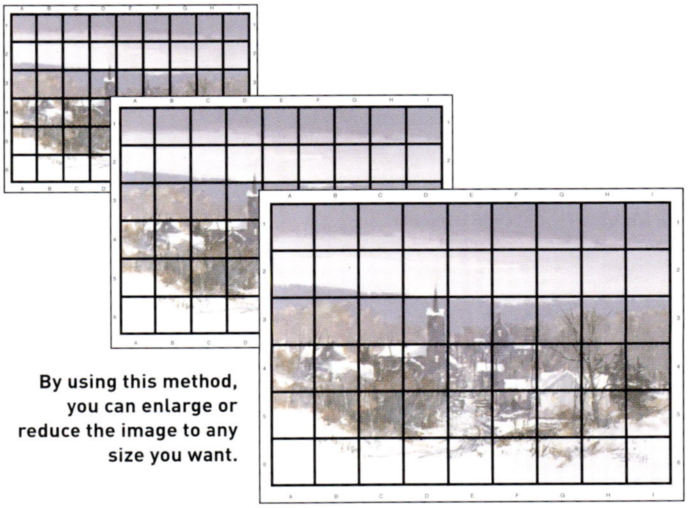

By using this method, you can enlarge or reduce the image to any size you want.

3. Use the art map to transfer the image

Now, still drawing very LIGHTLY with your pencil, copy the main contour lines of the object as shown in each square onto your working surfacce. It's not necessary to get every detail—just a simple line drawing will do. I recommend LIGHTLY and gently erasing the grid lines in the open, lighter areas before continuing.

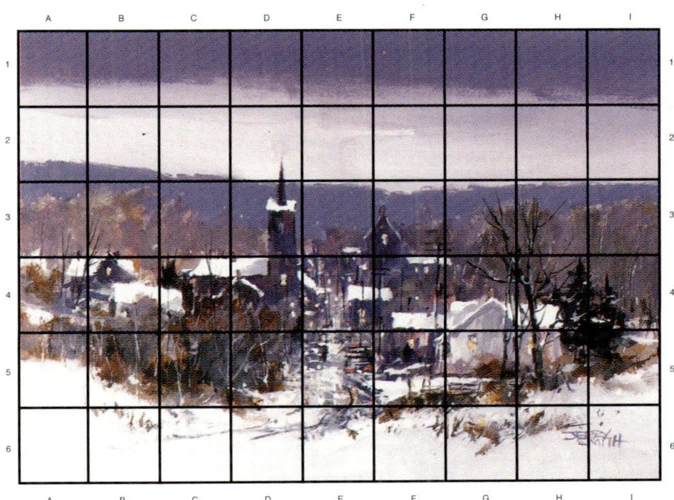

This is how your art map should look.

Here I've done the drawing in dark ink so you can see the idea, but you will do this lightly in pencil.

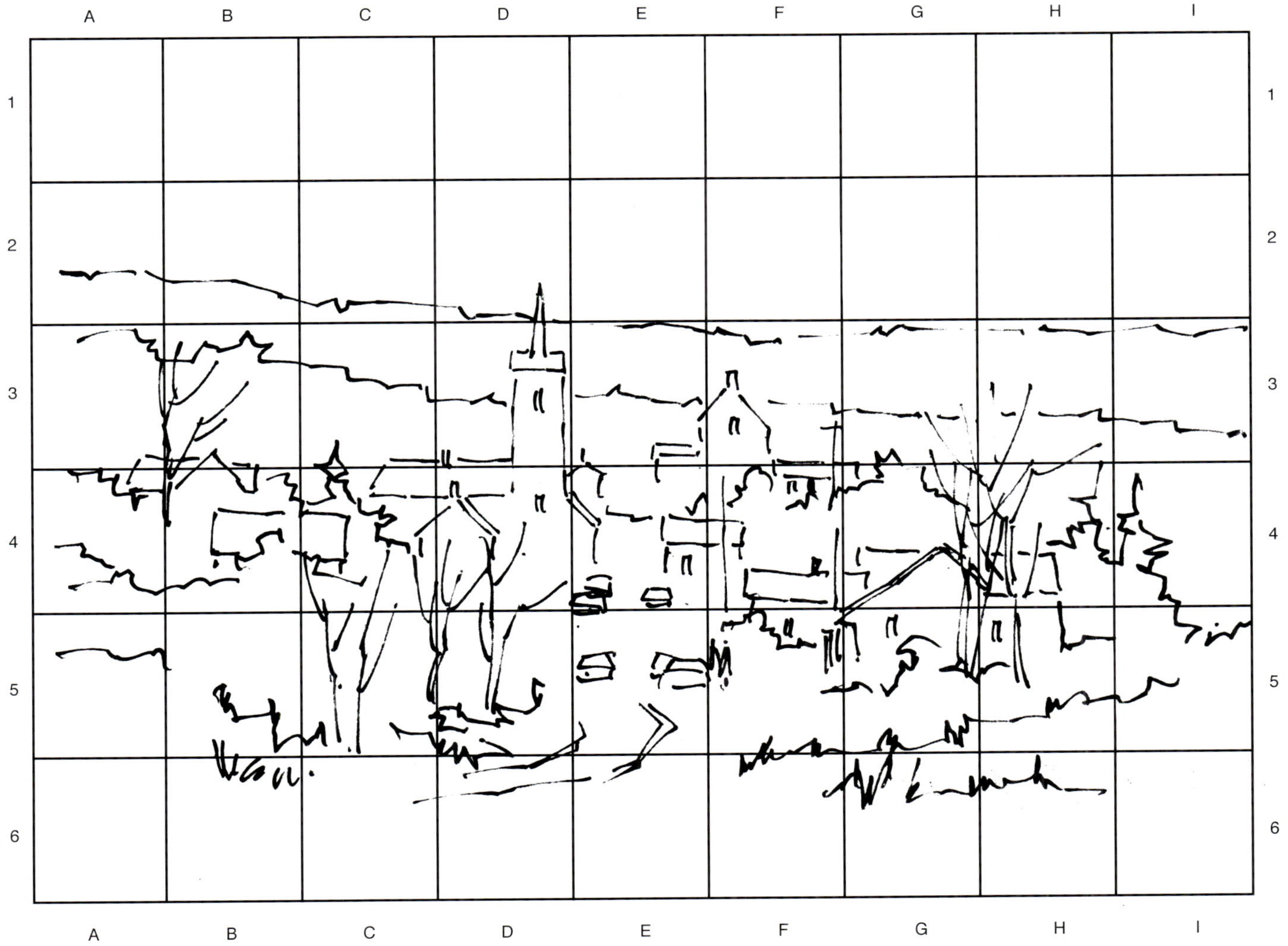

Study these pages before you start painting

The planning and design process is always important regardless of the medium. However, the use of collage material in the painting process requires some flexibility in our thinking as we proceed. The painting sometimes takes its own direction.

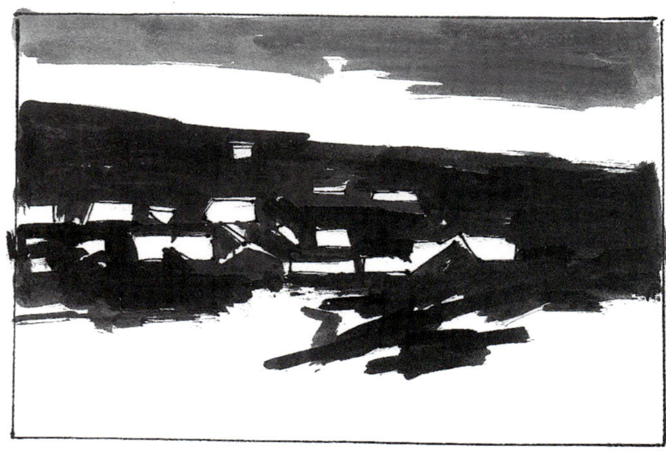

Shape map
Buildings and trees are loosely rendered and tied together in one large shape broken up by a pattern of snow-covered rooftops. Usually what appears to be a rather complex drawing can be broken down into simple geometric shapes. Note how calligraphy lines, including both painted and collaged, pull the shapes together.

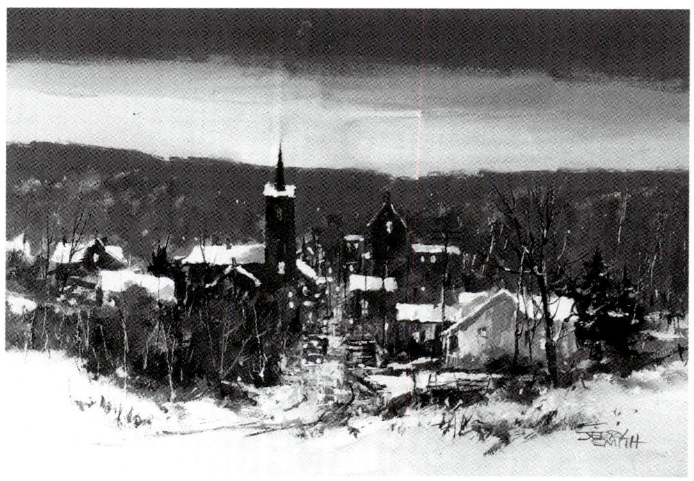

Highlights and contrasts
A few cool, dark greens provide a color accent. Other highlighted areas, such as the white boats, are added with acrylic paint. Automobiles provide scale. Spots of light such as windows add life and provide bright color contrasts.

Color map (what you would see if you were to squint)

materials you'll need

painting surface
canvas, board or paper

brushes
¼", ½" and 1" flats
nos. 4, 6 and 12 rounds
small rigger 1 or 2

other tools
2B pencil
ruler
palette
spray bottle to keep your palette moist
white tissue paper (the thinner the better)
acrylic gloss medium

your acrylic palette for this painting

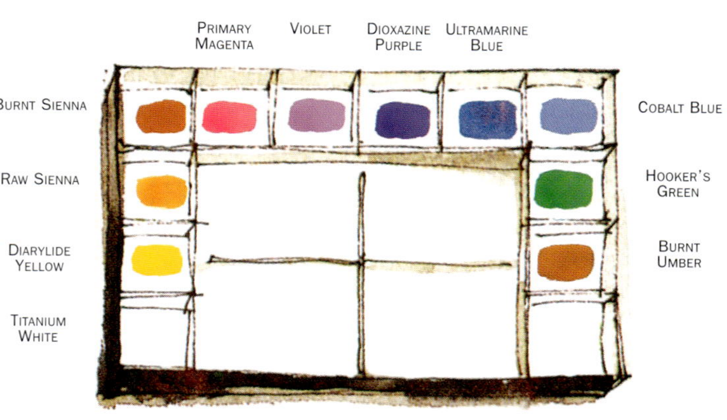

Consider the following elements

4. Block in large shapes

Loosely block in large shapes on your working surface. It's not necessary to save windows and white rooftops at this point since they will be added in final stages.

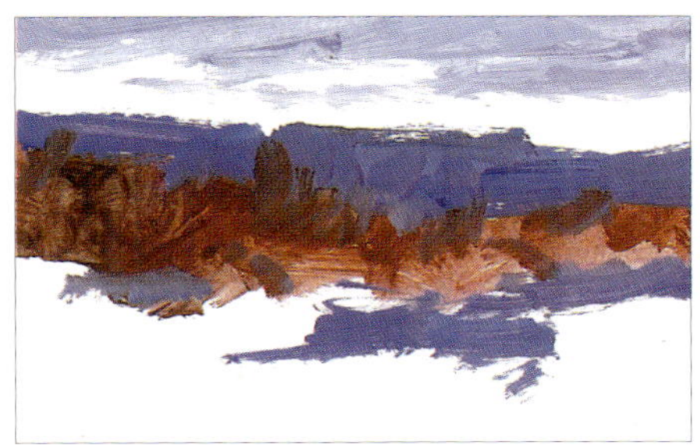

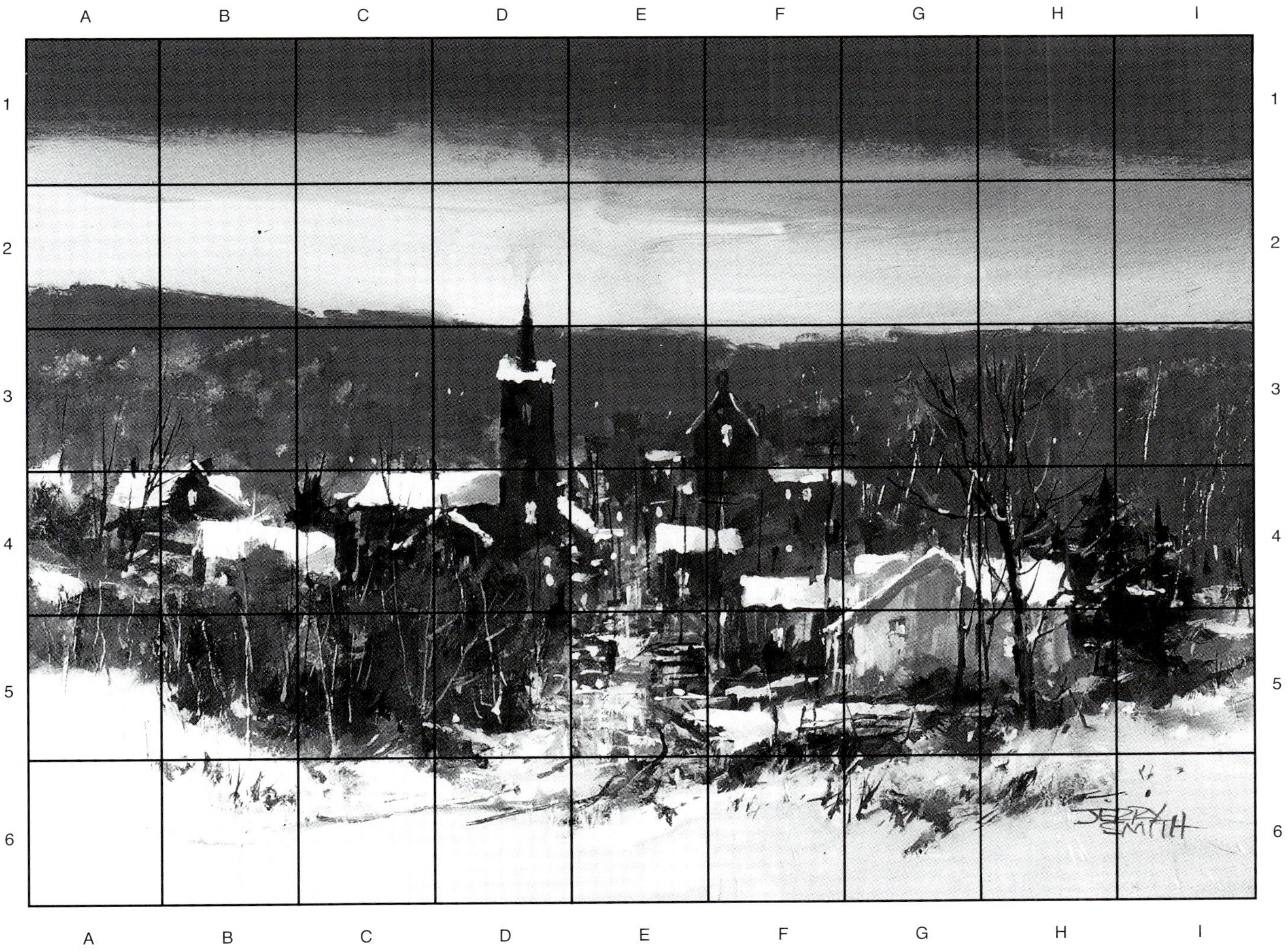

5. Prepare the collage tissue paper

Randomly apply acrylic paint to the tissue paper. Use the colors you intend to use in the painting and allow them to blend and fuse on the tissue. Use random lines and shapes. Hang the tissue sheets to dry. When dry the tissue can be torn into smaller pieces to be applied with acrylic medium wherever you wish to add color and texture. Texture can be further enhanced by crushing and crinkling the tissue before applying. In this case I applied collage paper over much, but not all, of the middle distance and background. You may leave some of the blocked in color to show through the openings.

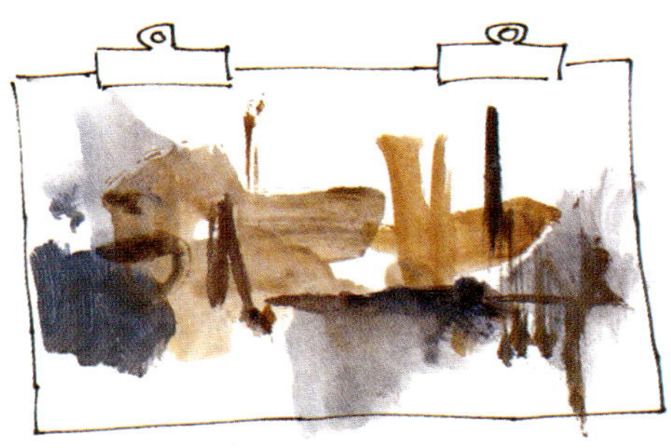

Put it all together

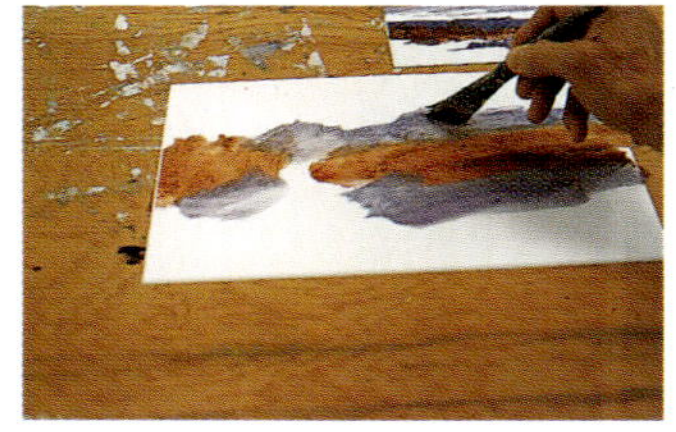

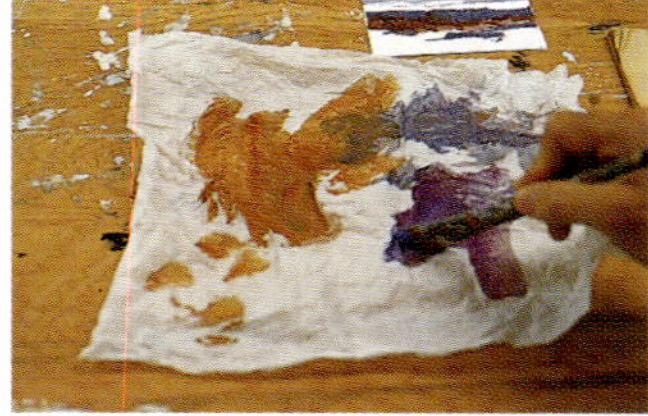

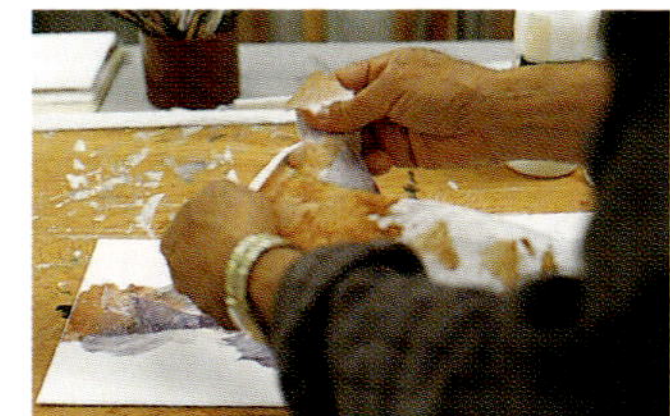

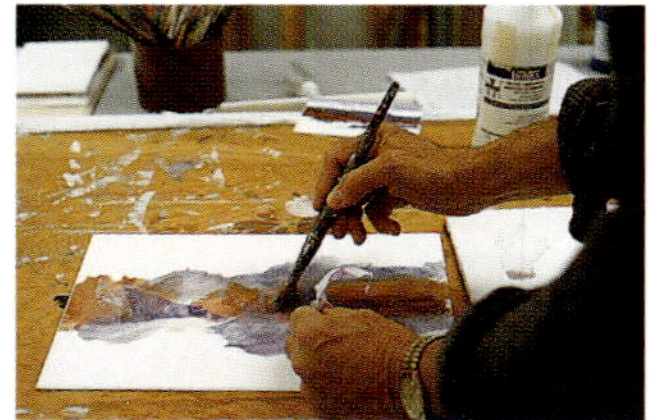

6. Apply the tissue paper

First apply acrylic medium thinned with water to the support board. Next apply the pieces of tissue as desired. Then apply another coat of thinned medium, using a large soft brush to avoid moving the tissue as the medium is applied.

7. Start painting

When the collage application has thoroughly dried you can begin painting with acrylic paints. You can take advantage of the collage texture and shapes to take your painting to a new level.

8. Let textures work for you

Many of the tree trunks and branches were made by drybrushing over crinkled tissue.

9. Finish with sealing

When completed, give the entire painting another coat of thinned acrylic medium. This will unify the various textures in the painting and seal everything under a layer of polymer film.

Learning points

- Plan ahead, but interpret as you go. Be on the lookout for those exciting developments that "just happen."
- Line work can unify, separate, move the eye and add punch to your paintings.
- Let the texture of your paper work for you.

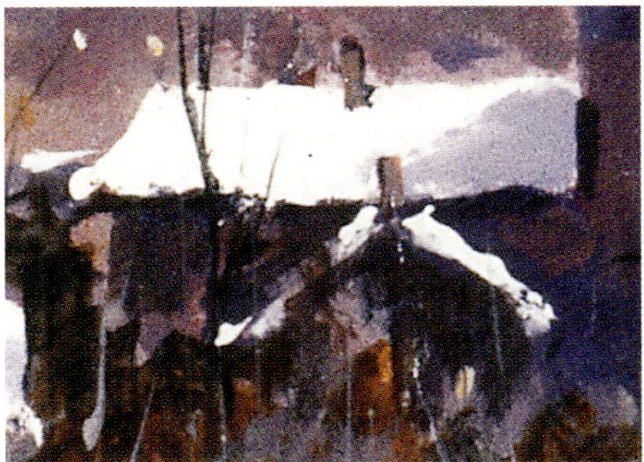

Detail

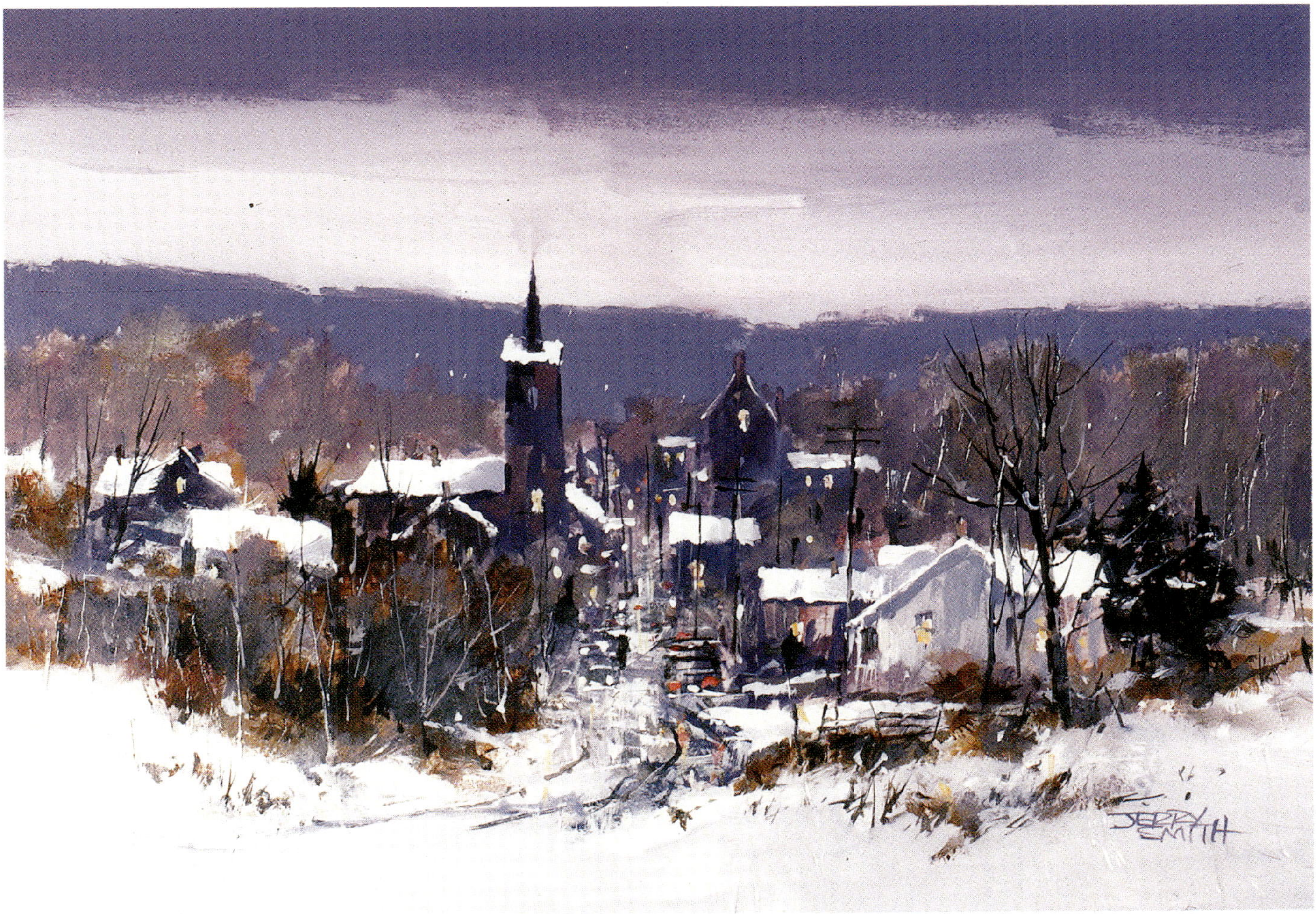

***Rooftop Patterns*, acrylic, 11 x 15" (28 x 30cm) by Jerry Smith ©**

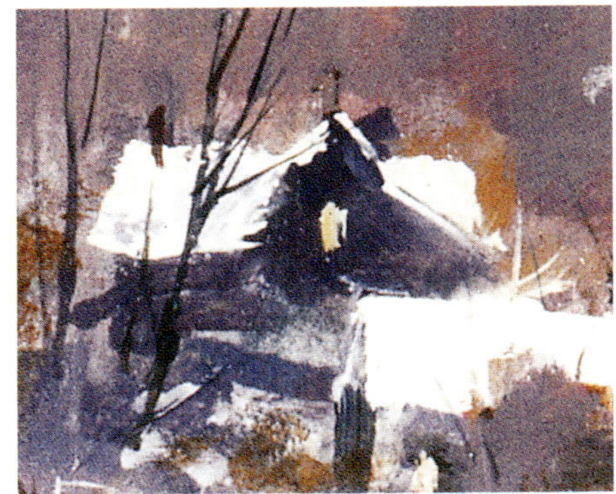

Detail

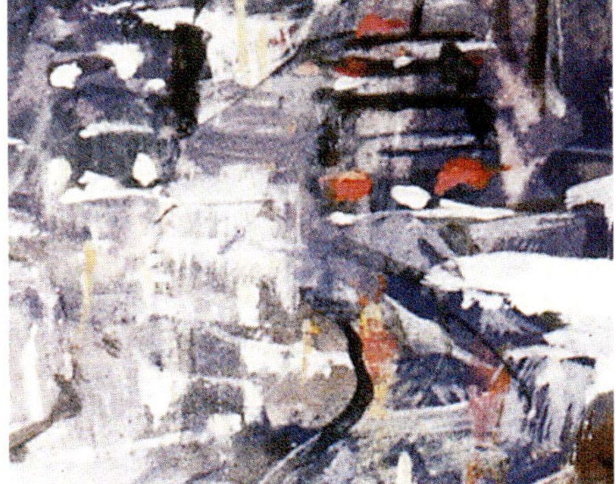

Detail

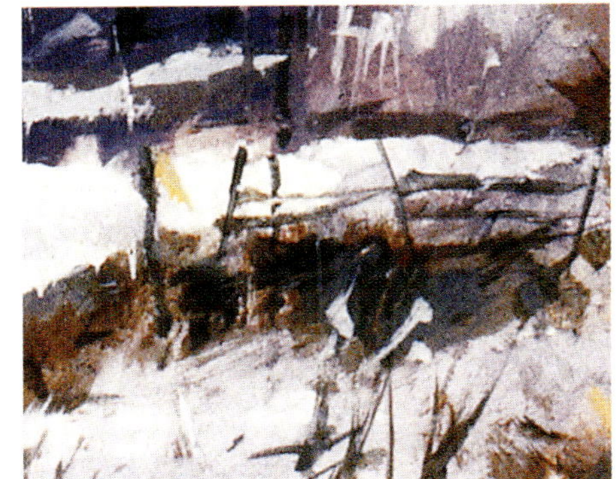

Detail

Before you begin, read the entire project through so you know what's going to happen next.

art map 12

Painting a wet street scene using collage

Urban paintings and street scenes can be challenging, but adding them to your repertoire can open up new avenues for painting expression. With so much activity and detail in a cityscape, I find it necessary to simplify shapes and detail as much as possible.

This painting project incorporates a little of everything covered in the previous projects. **The surface was a discarded watercolor painting**, and all of the collage and painting techniques presented in previous project were brought into play.

The painting process itself is basically the same as in the previous exercise, with two exceptions. First, there is less collage tissue used here in order to take better advantage of the texture of the watercolor paper. Second, before starting the discarded watercolor is coated with a spray fixative so that the watercolor paint won't dissolve and smear when the acrylic medium is applied.

1. The image to be transferred using the art map.

Read the instructions to see how to map this image across to your working surface.

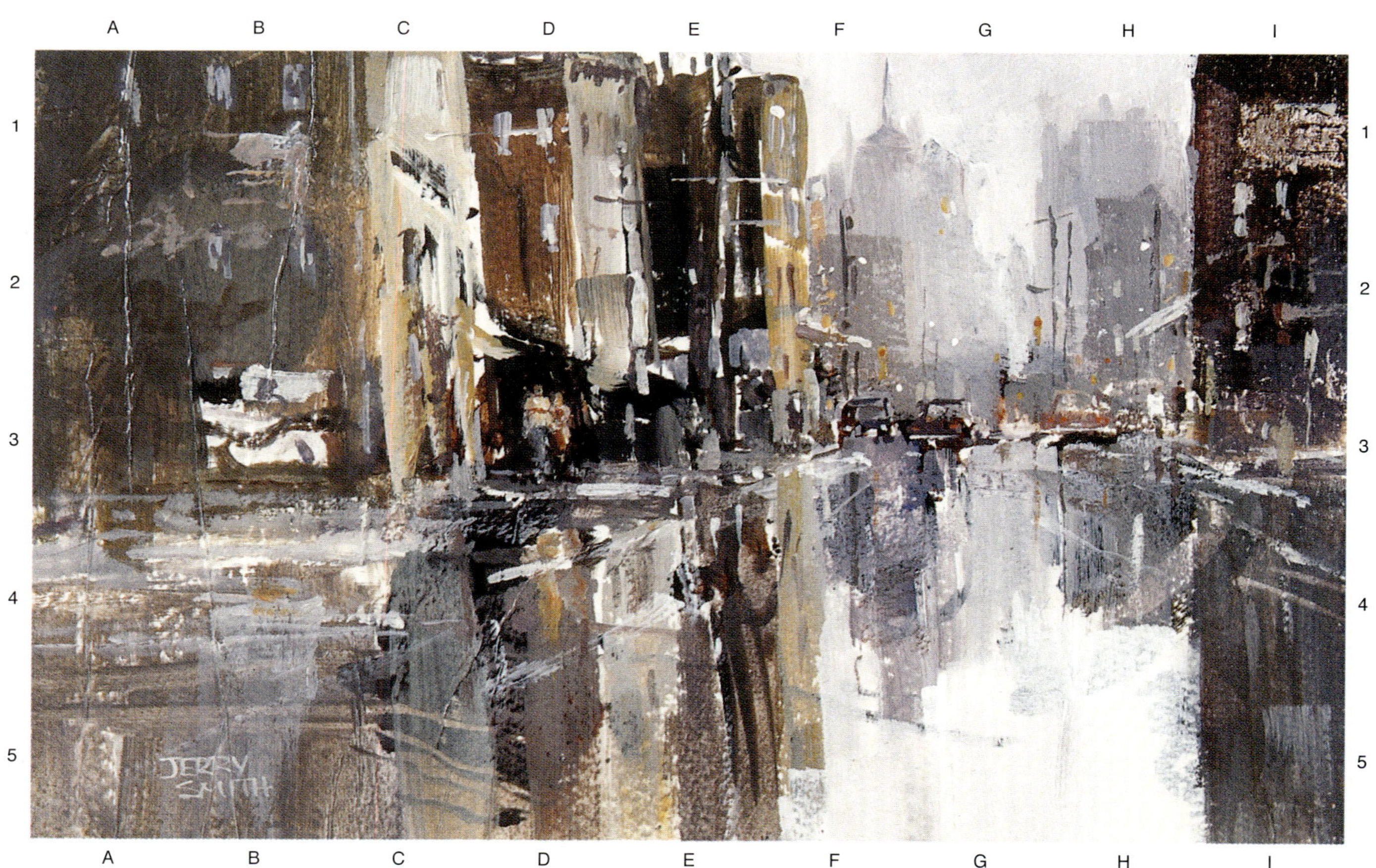

2. Map the image

With a 2B pencil, begin by LIGHTLY drawing a grid on your working surface that has the exact same number of squares as my grid. Your support can be the size of my original, or you can choose something proportionally larger or smaller. Your art map will be 6 squares down and 9 squares across. Put in the letters and numbers along the edges to make the next step easier.

3. Use the art map to transfer the image

Now, still drawing very LIGHTLY with your pencil, copy the main contour lines of the object as shown in each square onto your working surface. It's not necessary to get every detail—just a simple line drawing will do. I recommend LIGHTLY and gently erasing the grid lines in the open, lighter areas before continuing.

Note that it would be best to transfer the drawing after the collage material has been applied and has had time to dry. It will probably take 30 minutes or so to dry sufficiently.

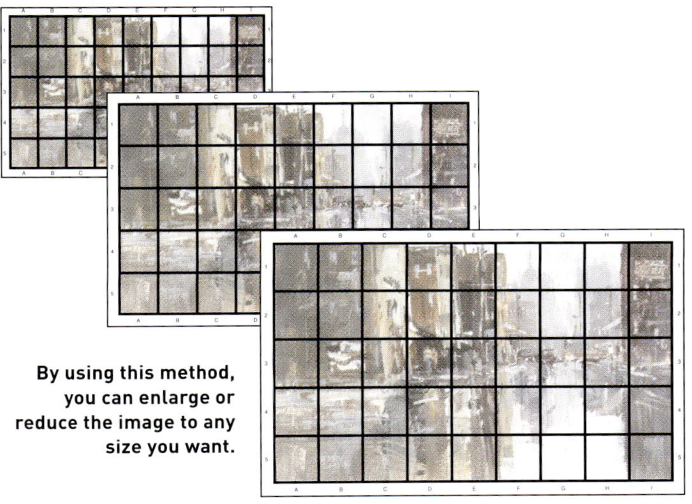

By using this method, you can enlarge or reduce the image to any size you want.

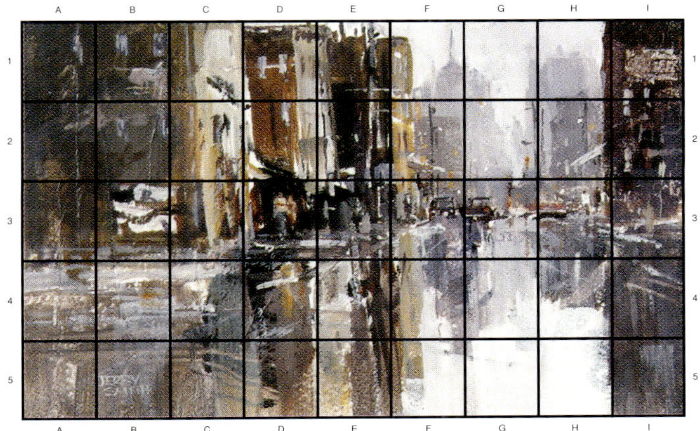

This is how your art map should look.

Here I've done the drawing in dark ink so you can see the idea, but you will do this lightly in pencil.

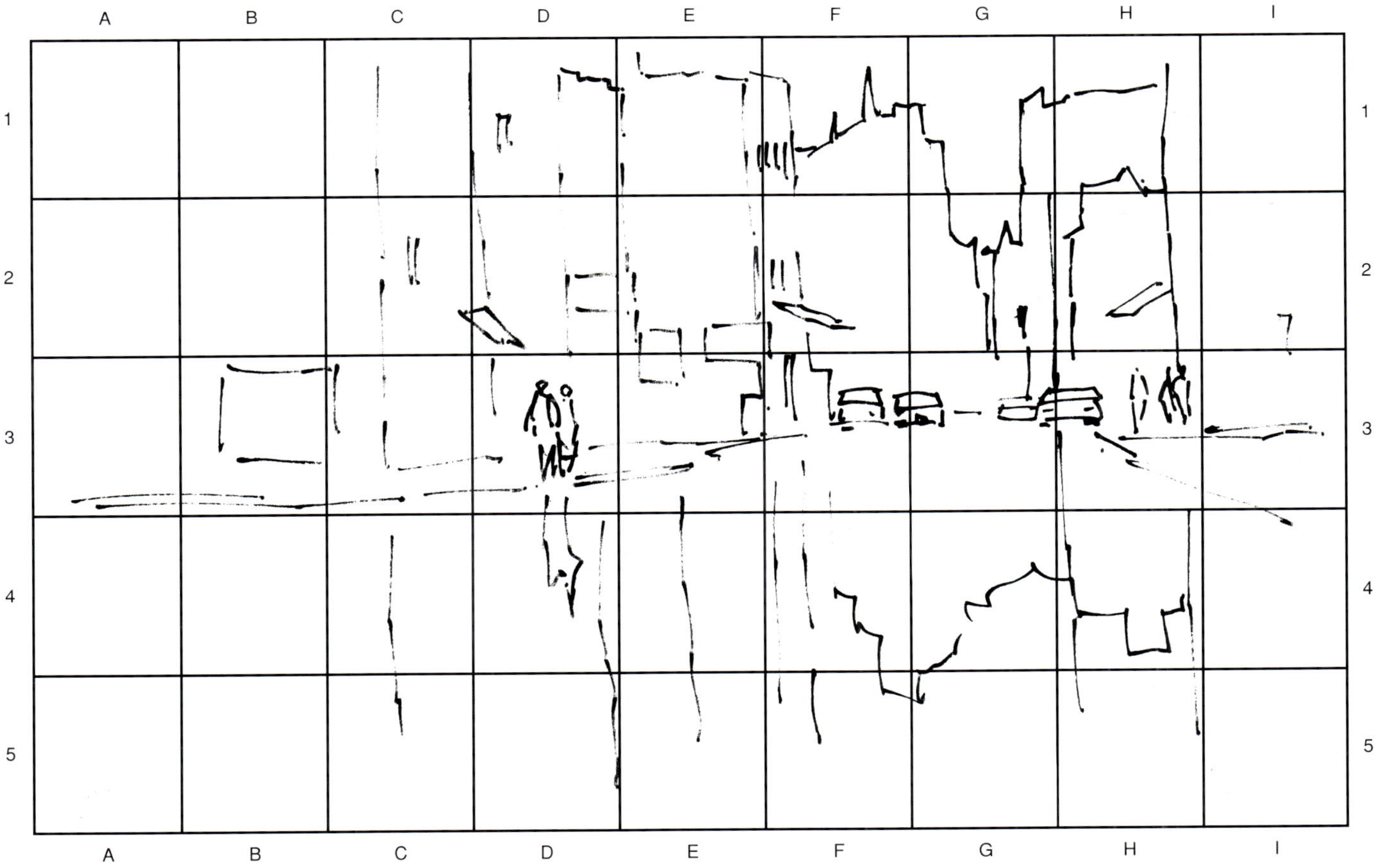

Study these pages before you start painting

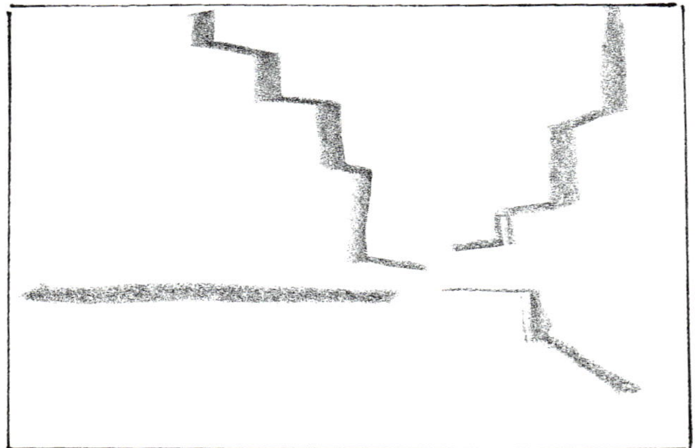

Design plan
The perspective of the street and rectangular buildings leads the eye to the center of interest. Many small shapes such as signs, poles, awnings, figures, and automobiles are scattered throughout to add life and provide scale. Concentrated darks and a variety of edges pull the eye into the painting. Spots of color and traffic activity complete the painting.

Shape plan
The mood is that of a brightening day after a shower. The wet, reflective street helps convey the mood and contributes to the design by pulling the foreground and background together into one long shape.

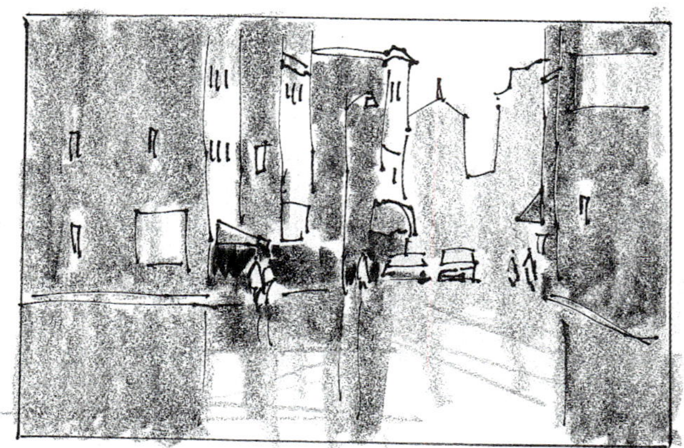

Thumbnail sketch

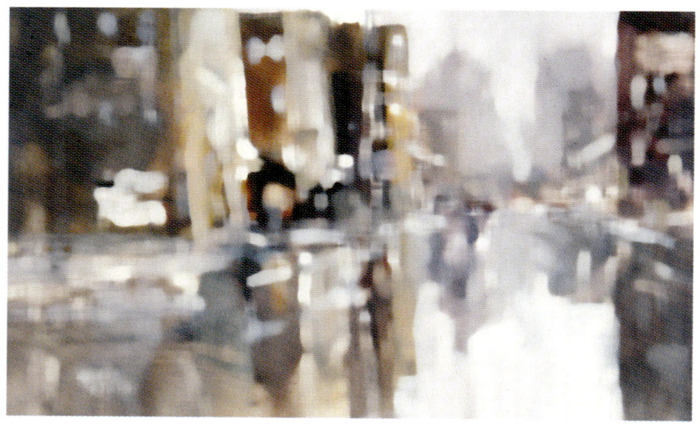

Color map (what you would see if you were to squint)
Squinting at the painting reveals a soft green/violet color harmony. The small rowboat provides a directional element as well as a repeat of the white accents on the buildings. Sky colors are repeated in foreground for color unity. Accents of bright color give life to the rich darks.

materials you'll need

painting surface
discarded 300lb (638 gsm) watercolor painting or paper toned with random colors and shapes

brushes
¼", ½" and 1" flats
nos. 4, 6 and 12 rounds
small rigger 1 or 2

other tools
2B pencil
ruler
palette
spray bottle to keep your palette moist
white tissue paper (the thinner the better)
acrylic gloss medium
acrylic spray fixative
satin polymer varnish

your acrylic palette for this painting

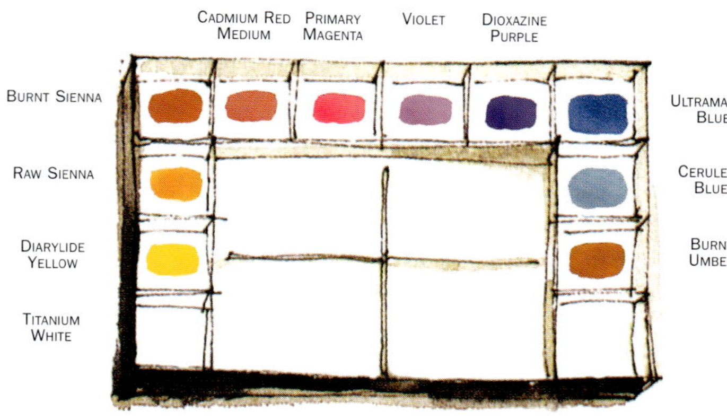

Consider the following elements

Light source

Though the mood is subdued, the light source is evident.

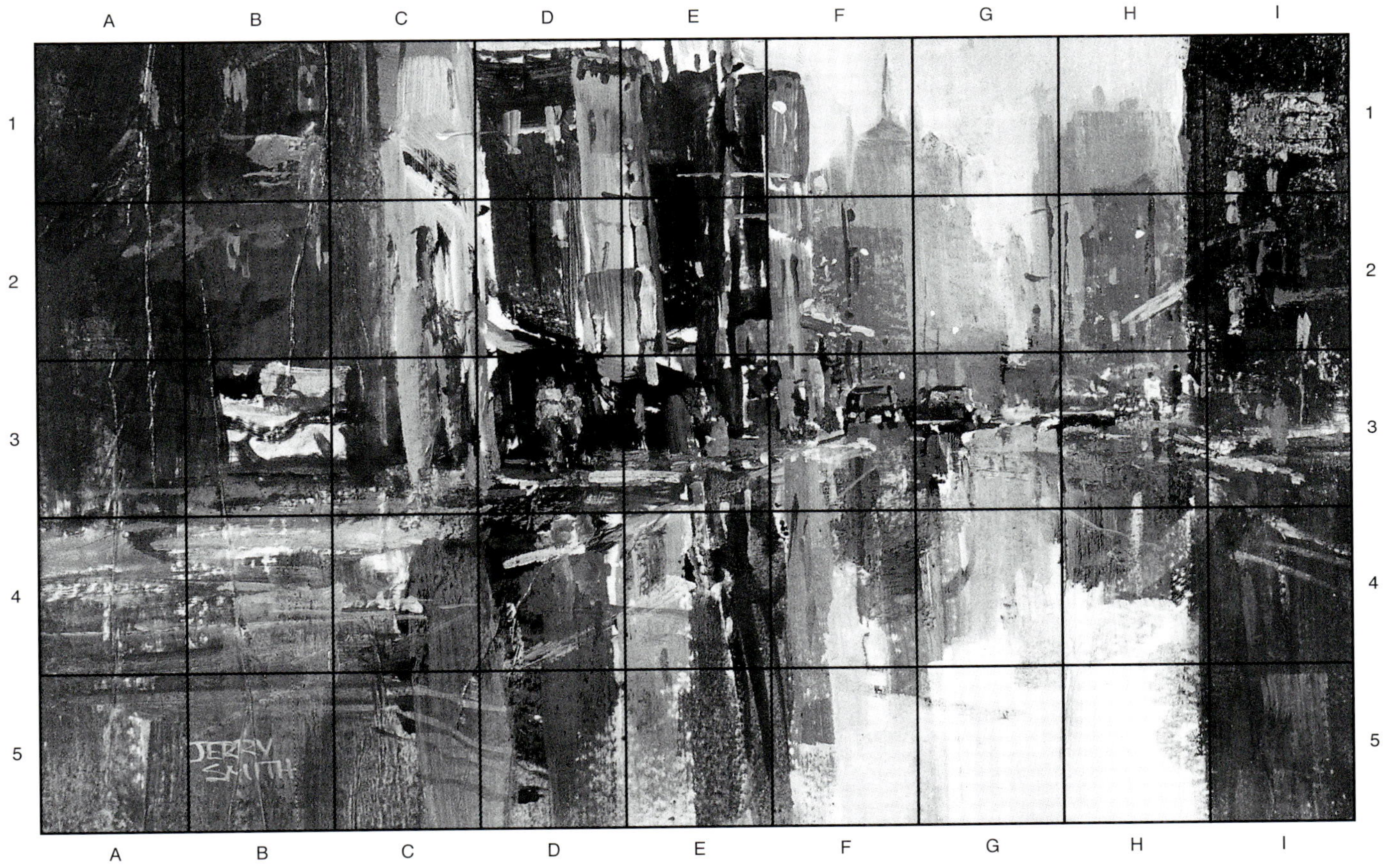

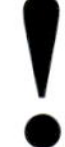

Bringing street scenes to life

Common elements such as figures, autos, signs, and so on, are essential in giving life and mood to street scenes. In loose, impressionistic painting it's best to render these items with a minimum of sketchy, direct brushstrokes to match the rest of the painting. These elements can be further simplified by grouping them together and combining them with other parts of the painting. The best way to become comfortable with this approach is to practice painting hundreds of the items on a separate scrap of paper until you gain confidence. Remember, you can quickly remove and repaint any brushstroke you don't like.

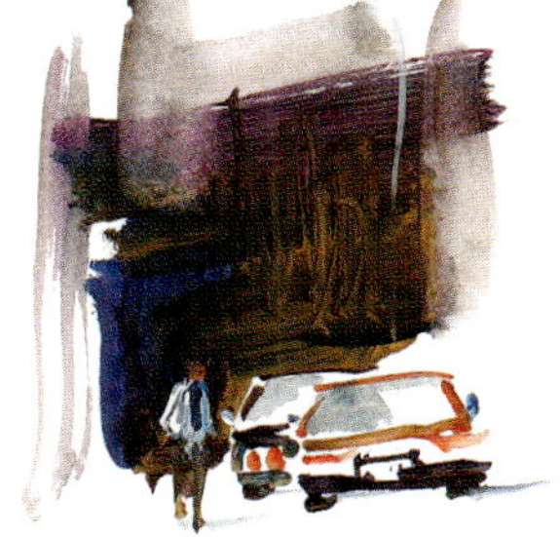

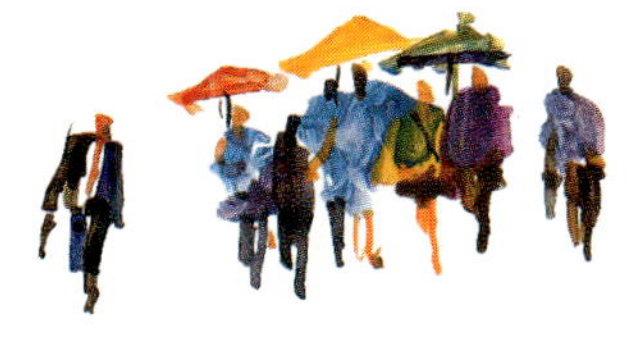

Put it all together

4. Start by blocking-in

Upon completion of the drawing, start with a block-in with darks and midtones, leaving as much of the underpainting and collage as possible.

5. Add details and highlights

Complete with the addition of details and lighter value highlights.

6. Expect surprises

Don't be surprised if your painting takes off in a slightly different direction than originally planned.

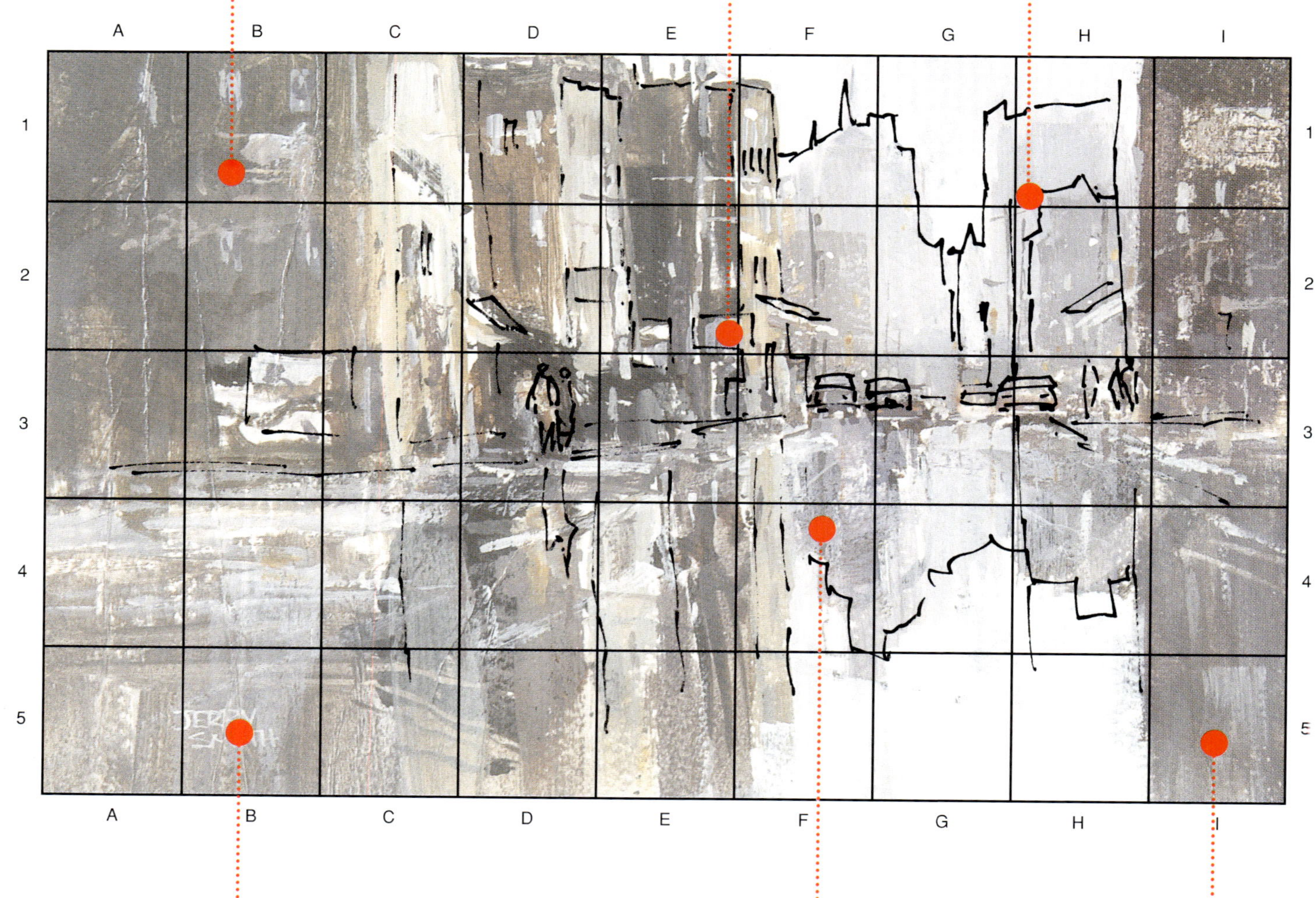

7. Welcome texture

Your drybrush texture will be evident throughout the entire foreground. You'll also notice some of the original, random underpainting showing through.

8. Add gray

Paint in the soft gray tones representing large distant buildings, keeping in mind that detail fades into the atmospheric shapes.

9. Coat with varnish

Finish the painting by brushing on satin polymer varnish.

Learning points

This project shows you how expressive painting can be jump started with underpainting and collage texture. It also shows you how discarded painting material can be recycled into finished paintings.

Detail

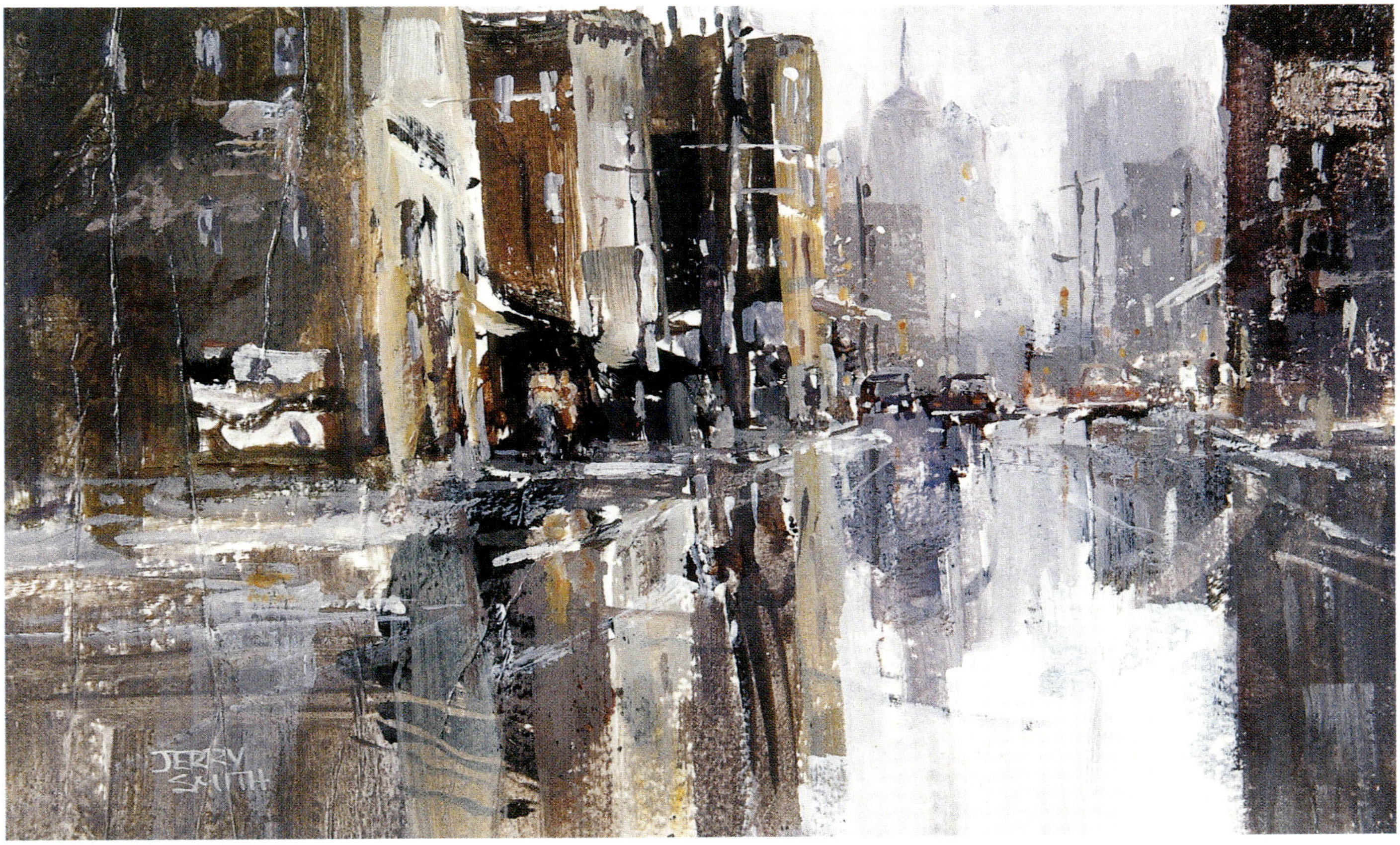

***Urban Reflections*, acrylic, 7 x 11" (18 x 28cm) by Jerry Smith ©**

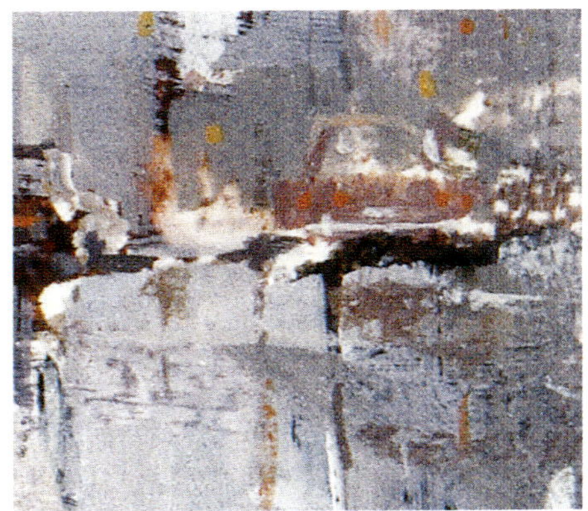

Detail

Detail

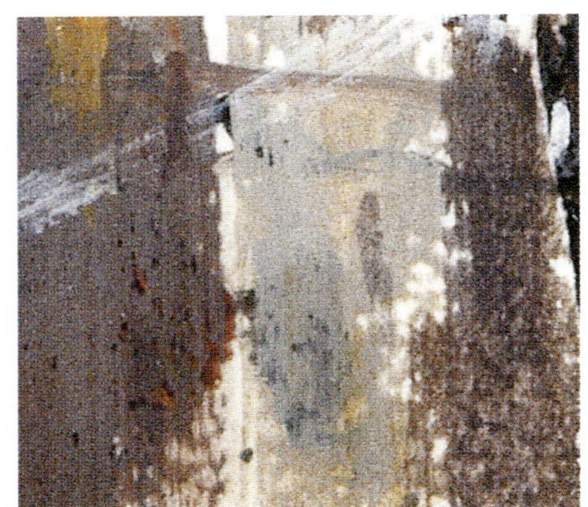

Detail

art map 13

Using perspective and negative shapes

Before you begin, read the entire project through so you know what's going to happen next.

You can see the positive shapes the buildings and trees form against the sky and foreground. Notice as well the role of the negative shapes of the sky and foreground snow in the overall design.

1. The image to be transferred using the art map.

Read the instructions to see how to map this image across to your painting surface.

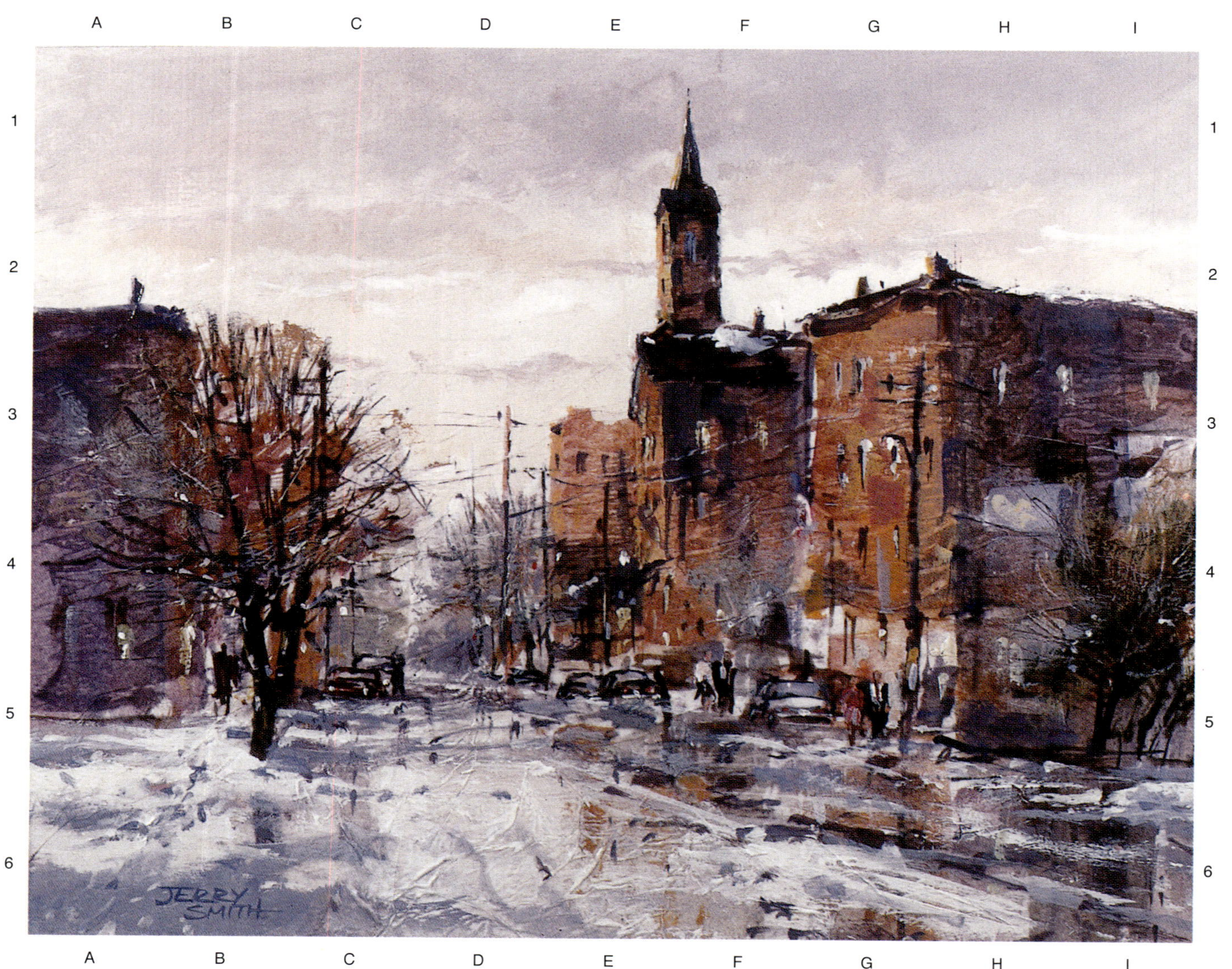

2. Map the image

With a 2B pencil, begin by LIGHTLY drawing a grid on your working surface that has the exact same number of squares as my grid. Your support can be the size of my original, or you can choose something proportionally larger or smaller. Your art map will be 6 squares down and 9 squares across. Put in the letters and numbers along the edges to make the next step easier.

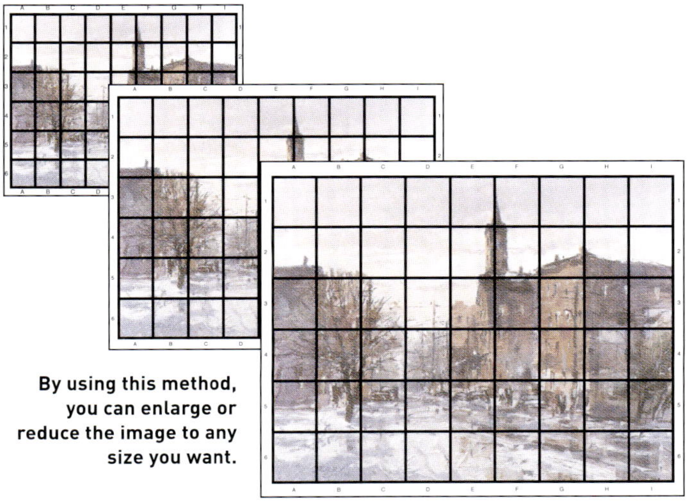

By using this method, you can enlarge or reduce the image to any size you want.

3. Use the art map to transfer the image

Now, still drawing very LIGHTLY with your pencil, copy the main contour lines of the object as shown in each square onto your working surface. It's not necessary to get every detail—just a simple line drawing will do. I recommend LIGHTLY and gently erasing the grid lines in the open, lighter areas before continuing.

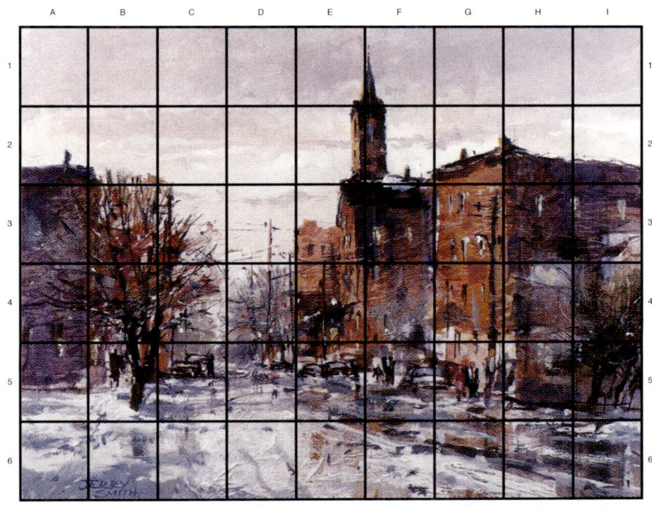

This is how your art map should look.

Here I've done the drawing in dark ink so you can see the idea, but you will do this lightly in pencil.

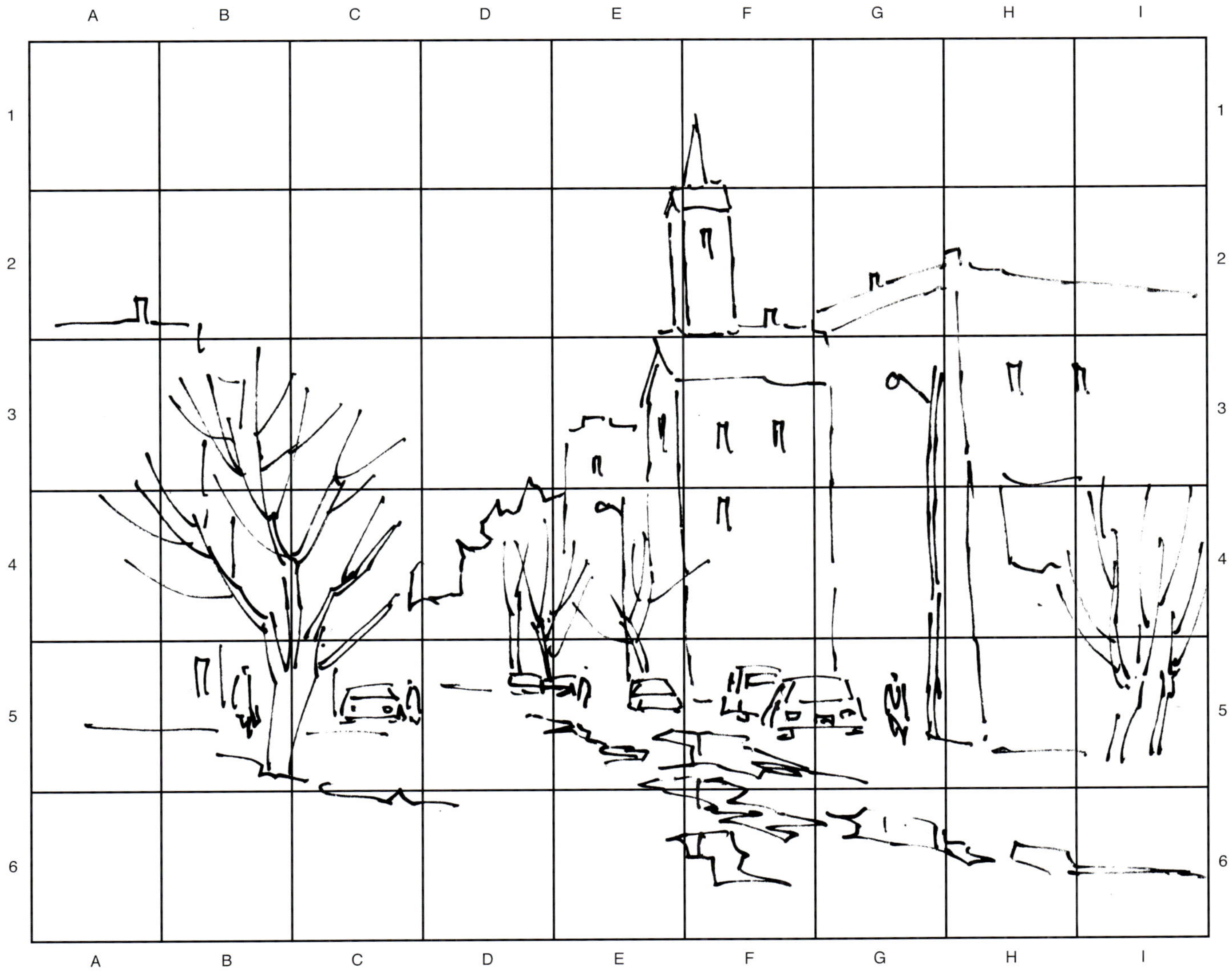

Study these pages before you start painting

4. A new approach

The approach to this project is slightly different.

Step 1.
Get a support board measuring 11 x 15" (27 x 38 cm) and cut a piece of tissue the exact same size.

Step 2.
With loose, wet washes, roughly paint the large positive shapes onto the support board with acrylic paint.

Step 3.
When the surface has thoroughly dried, crinkle the tissue paper and lay it on top of the board.

Step 4.
With very wet washes, then repeat the major shapes on the tissue, allowing random spots of color to soak through the tissue and onto the support board.

Step 5.
Remove the tissue and suspend it to dry. This provides two varied but related surfaces to combine through the collage technique.

Step 6.
From here on, the tearing and pasting process is left to your instincts. There is no right or wrong way to combine the shapes. I suggest you should not attempt to get the torn collage pieces back in the exact same position. The advantage of the technique is the interplay of shapes as they are repositioned.

Step 7.
Once the tissue pieces have been attached to your satisfaction, the entire "work-in-progress" should be allowed to dry before proceeding with the painting and refining process.

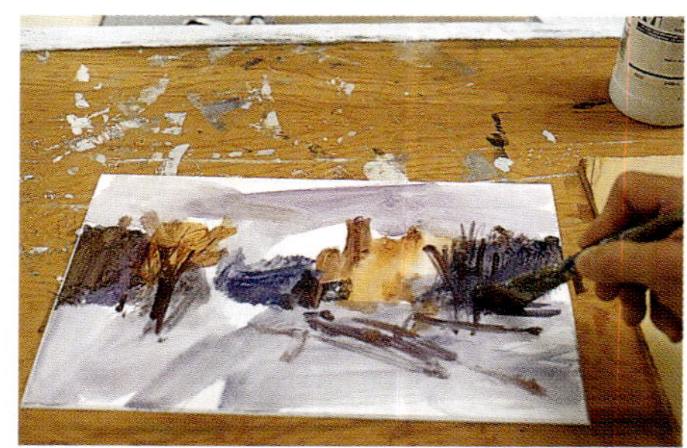

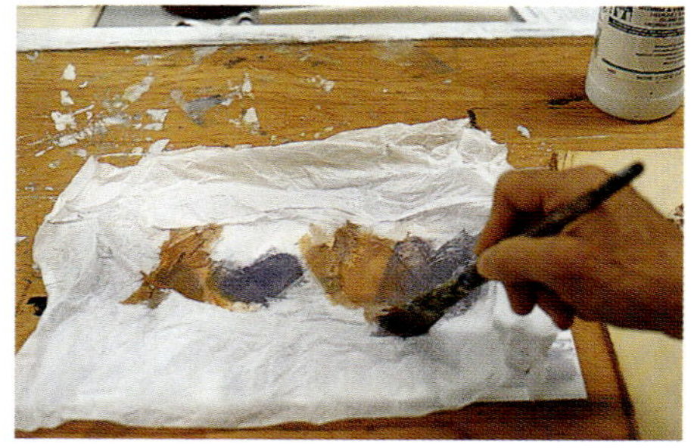

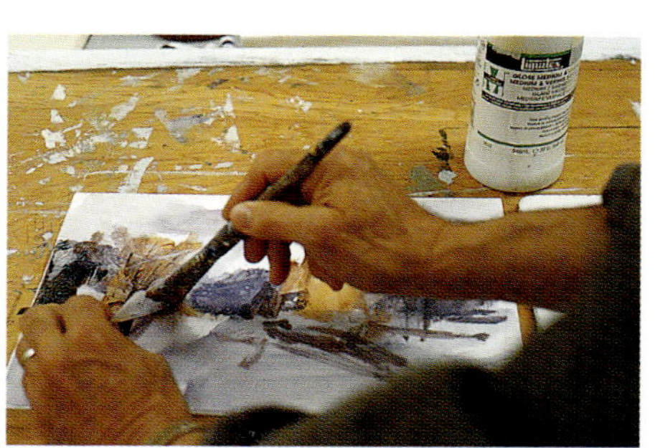

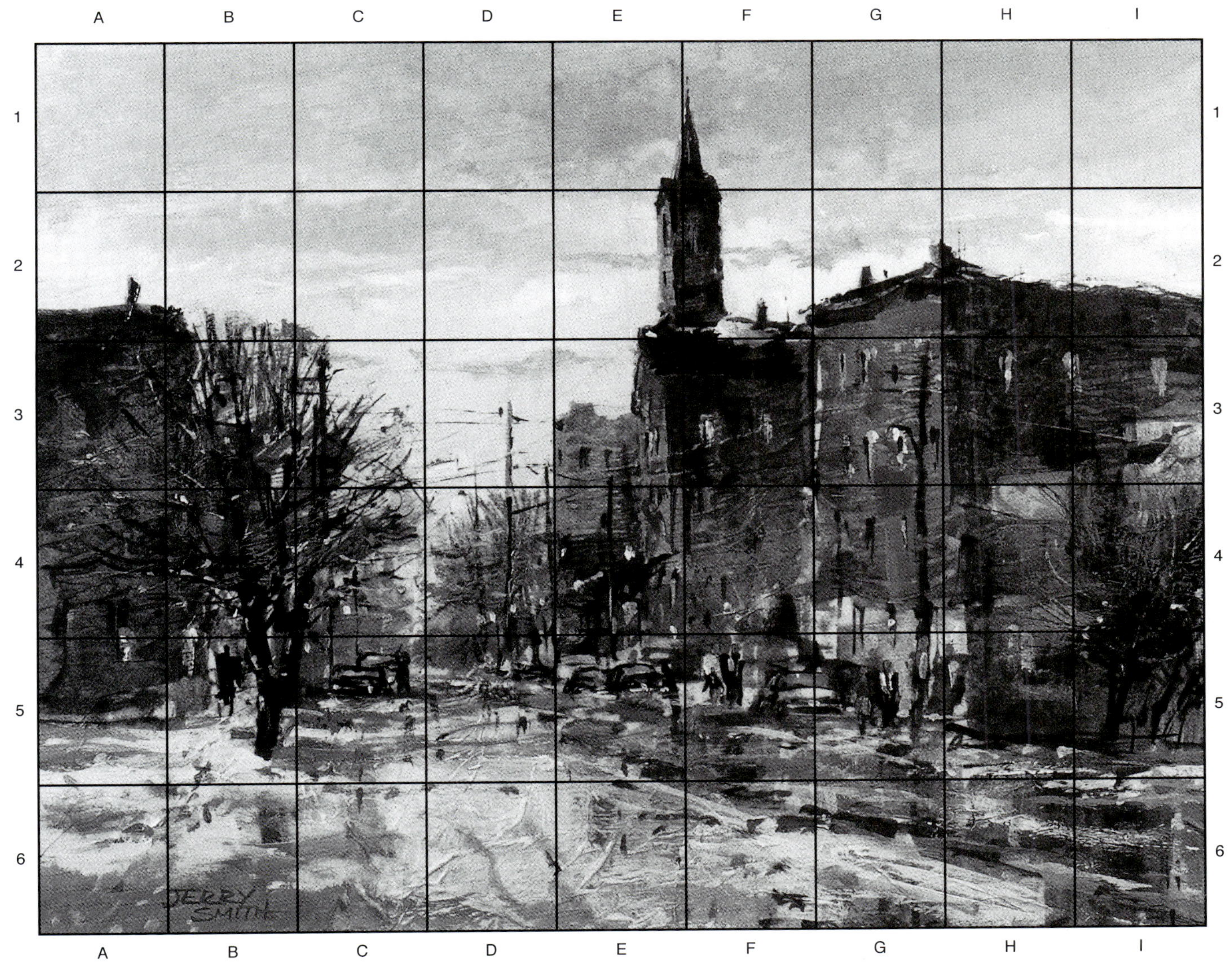

materials you'll need

painting surface
illustration board (an acid-free drawing paper mounted on a heavy paperboard) or museum board (an acid-free mount board)

brushes
1/4", 1/2" and 1" flats
nos. 4, 6 and 12 rounds
small rigger 1 or 2

other tools
2B pencil
ruler
palette
spray bottle to keep your palette moist
white tissue paper (the thinner the better)
acrylic gloss medium

your acrylic palette for this painting

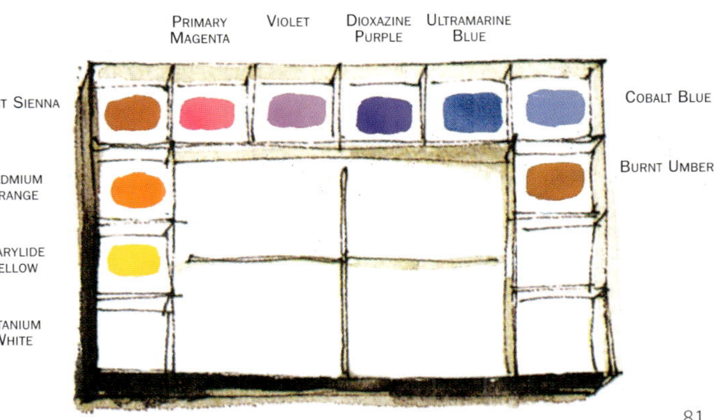

Put it all together

5. Collage and no collage

Note the influence of the collage technique throughout the painting. The sky is the only part of the painting that contains no collage treatment. It provides a large negative shape around the buildings.

6. Visual interplay

Note the interesting texture and colors created by the interplay of the underpainting, collage material, and the heavier overpainting.

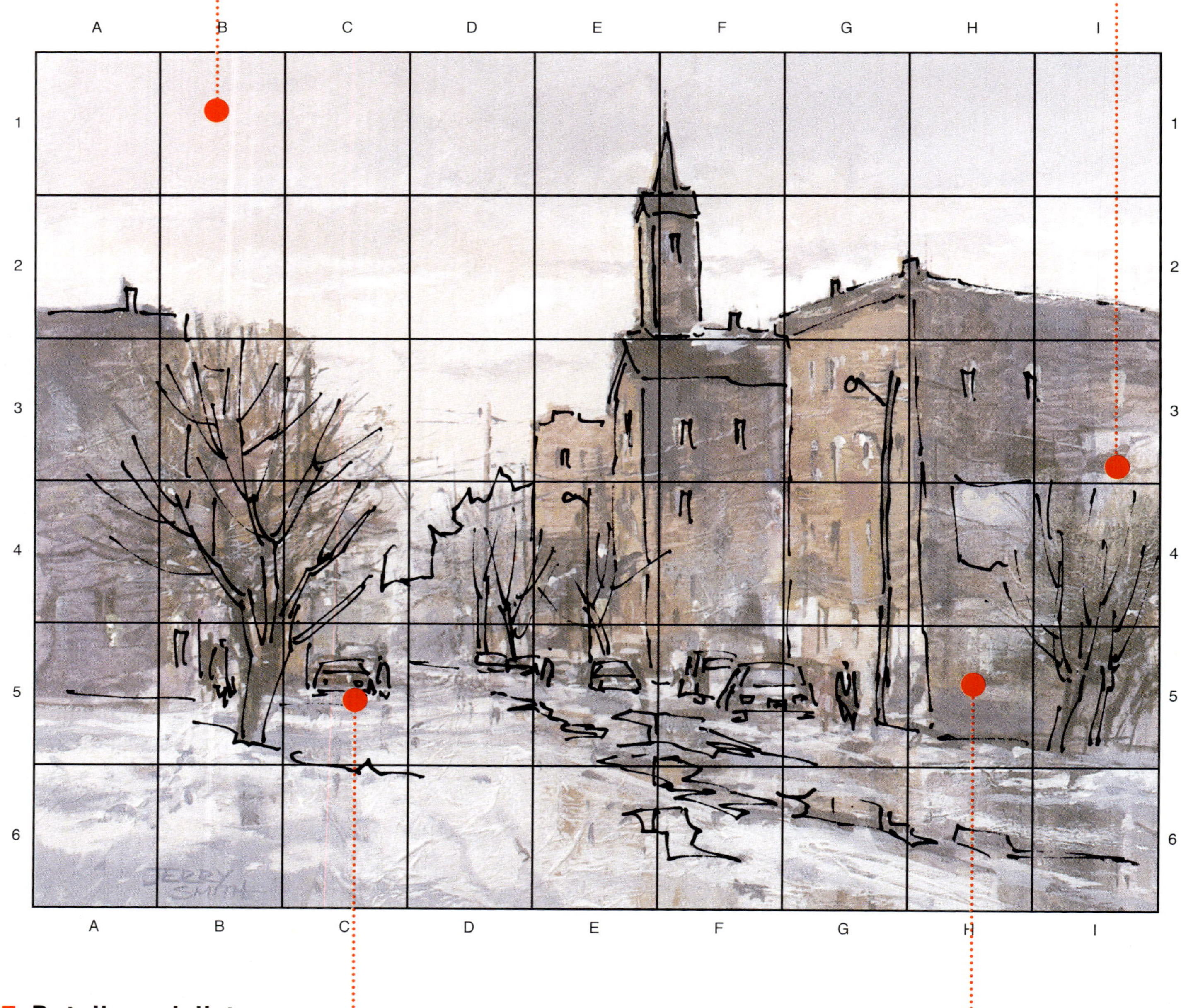

7. Details and distance

Most of the details are added with touches of acrylic paint on top of the collaged surface. Repeated elements such as trees and figures are progressively smaller as they recede into the distance. Puddle reflections are used to repeat building colors in foreground.

8. Balance

Large mass of buildings on right is balanced by the more intricate tree branches on the left side. The large white shape of the foreground snow is echoed and balanced by the smaller, but more prominent white shapes on the right.

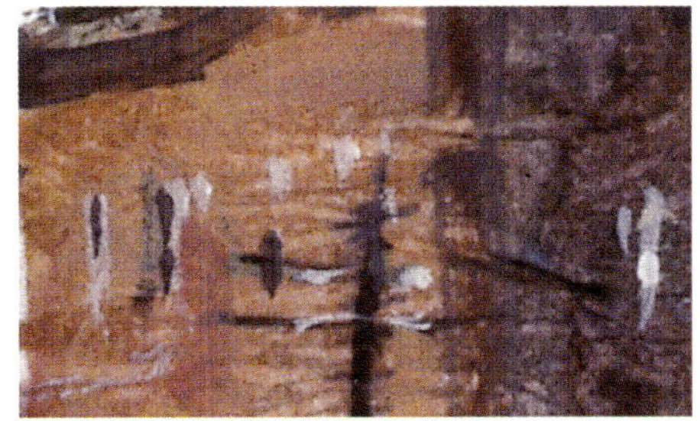

Detail

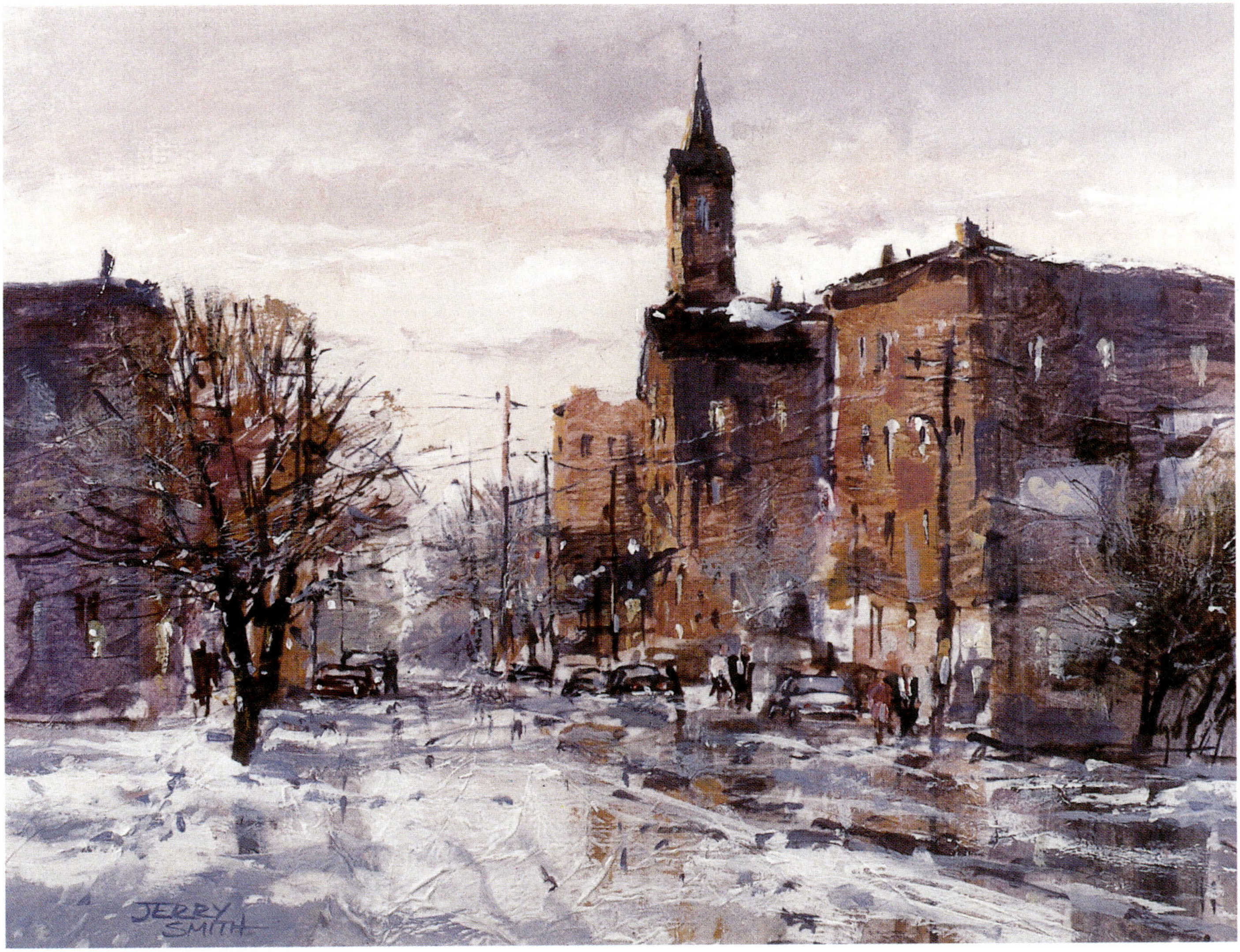

Meltdown, acrylic, 11 x 15" (28 x 38cm) by Jerry Smith ©

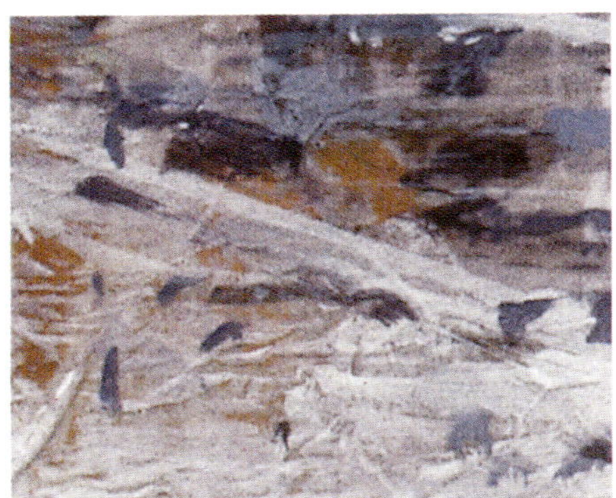

Detail

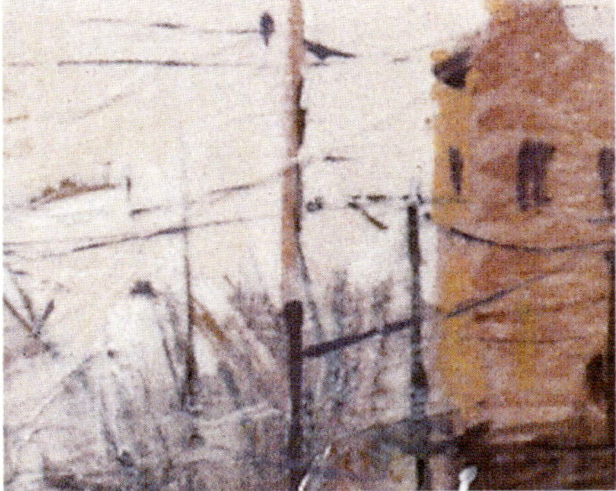

Detail

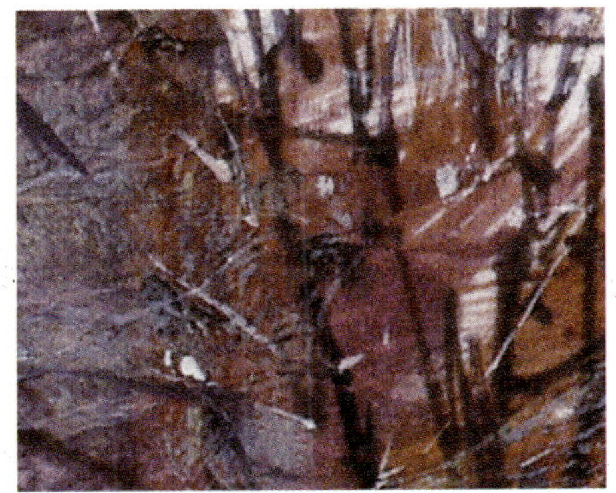

Detail

Before you begin, read the entire project through so you know what's going to happen next.

art map 14

Creating shape and texture with bold brushwork

We will now return to more traditional painting techniques for the final two exercises. Although the basic painting process in this project is essentially the same as in earlier ones, I recommend canvas for this one. Canvas texture is more uniform than that of gessoed board. Canvas has more "tooth," allowing thicker applications of paint, which means a little more time to manipulate the paint before it dries.

1. The image to be transferred using the art map.

Read the instructions to see how to map this image across to your canvas.

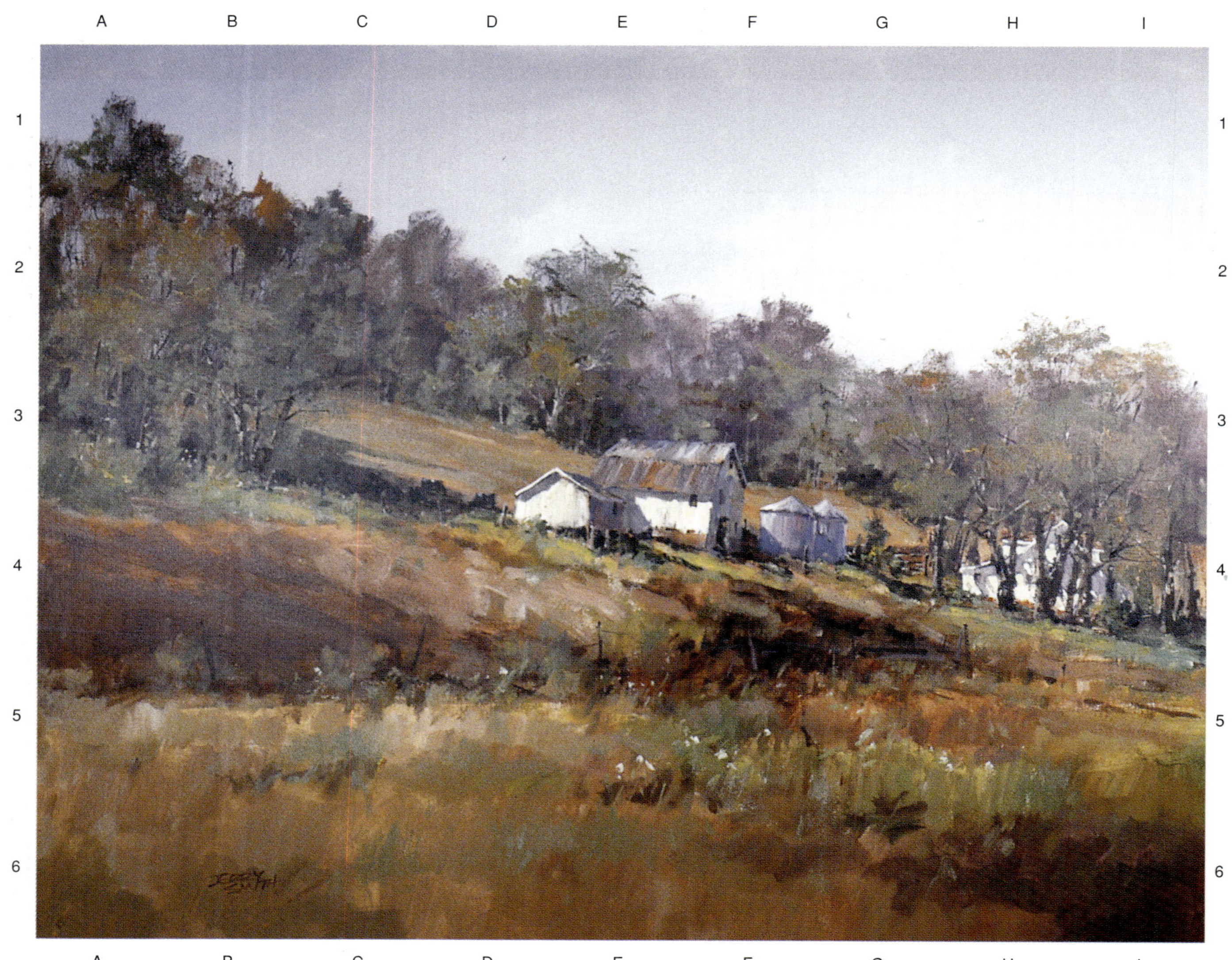

2. Map the image

With a 2B pencil, begin by LIGHTLY drawing a grid on your working surface that has the exact same number of squares as my grid. Your paper can be the size of my original, or you can choose something proportionally larger or smaller. Your art map will be 6 squares down and 9 squares across. Put in the letters and numbers along the edges to make the next step easier.

3. Use the art map to transfer the image

Now, still drawing very LIGHTLY with your pencil, copy the main contour lines of the object as shown in each square onto your working surface. It's not necessary to get every detail—just a simple line drawing will do. I recommend LIGHTLY and gently erasing the grid lines in the open, lighter areas before continuing.

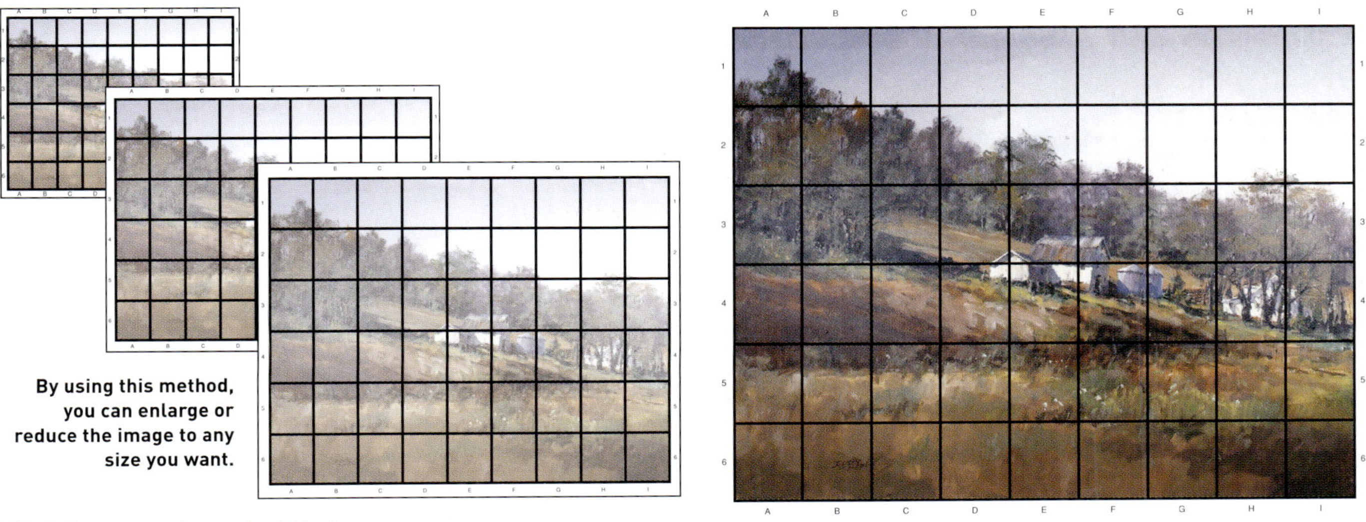

By using this method, you can enlarge or reduce the image to any size you want.

This is how your art map should look.
Here I've done the drawing in dark ink so you can see the idea, but you will do this lightly in pencil.

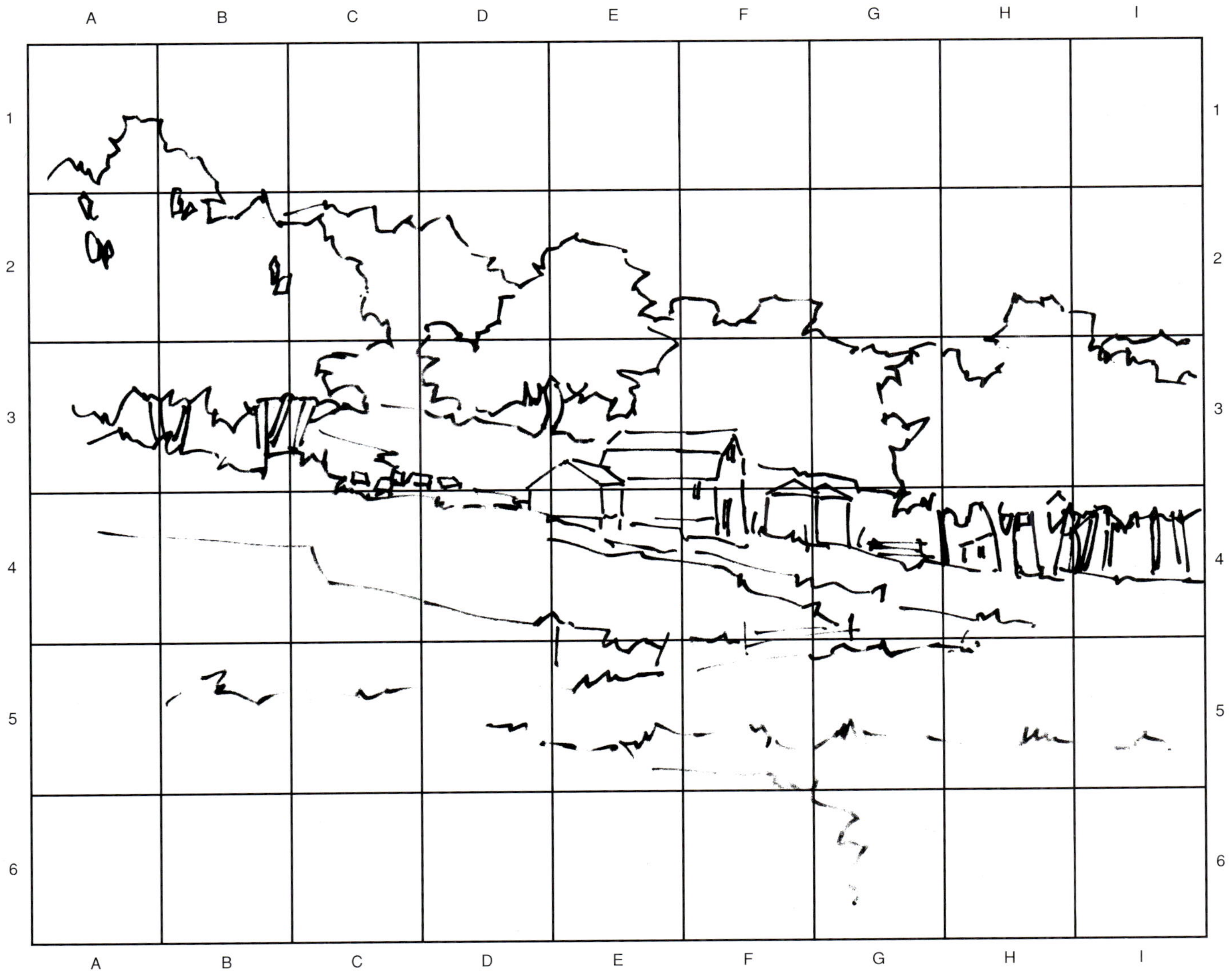

Study these pages before you start painting

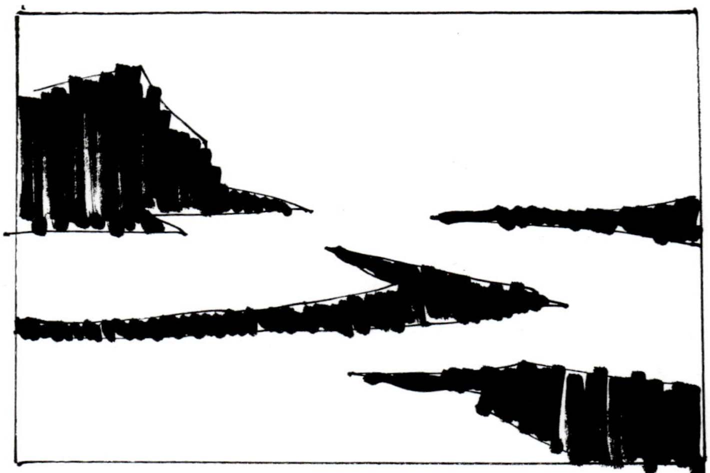

Design map
Relatively horizontal shapes provide a peaceful mood with some diagonals to create a little tension.

Shape map
Visual entry and movement through the painting is directed by the dark shapes.

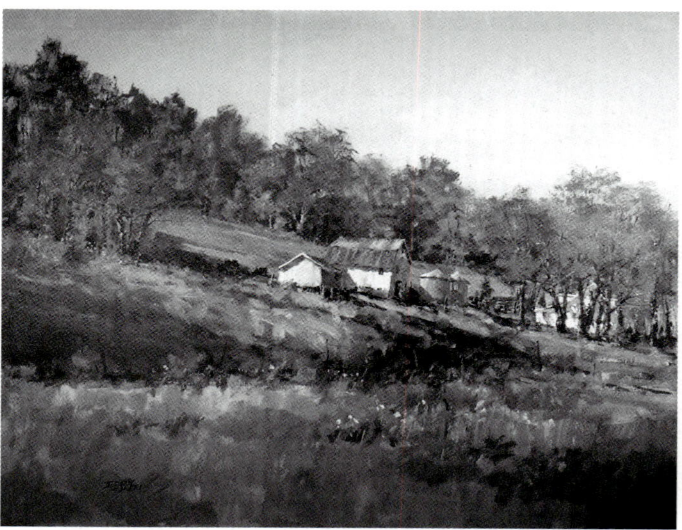

Tonal value map
A look at the tonal illustration of this painting reveals this as a color-dominated painting. Except for the sky and buildings, the tonal values are very close throughout.

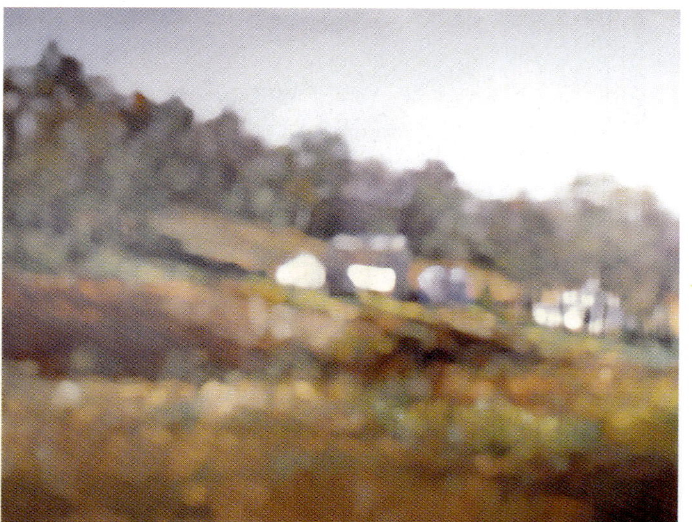

Color map (what you would see if you were to squint)

materials you'll need

painting surface
Gesso-primed canvas

brushes
¼", ½" and 1" flats
nos. 4, 6 and 12 rounds
rigger

other tools
2B pencil
ruler
palette
spray bottle to keep your palette moist

your acrylic palette for this painting

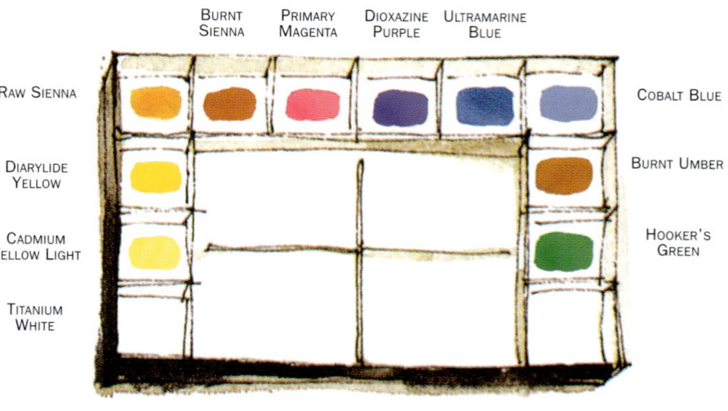

Consider the following elements

Light source

Strong light from left side creates prominent shadows that contribute to progression through the painting.

Brushwork

Let your brush describe the form. Variety adds interest.

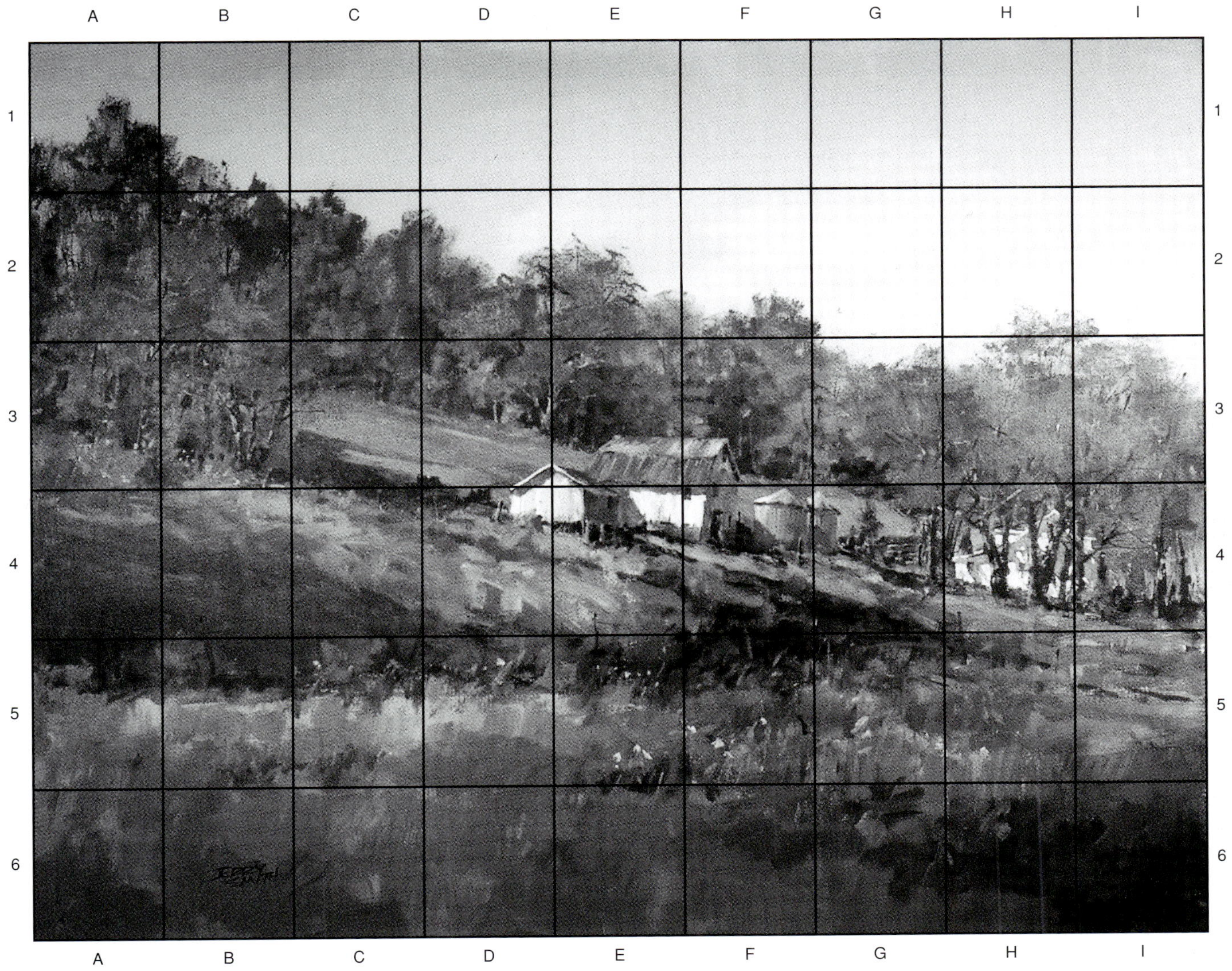

4. Highlight boldly

Execute the highlighted whites with bold, direct brush strokes. The trees on the far right frame the edge of the painting and hold the eye within.

Put it all together

5. Tone your canvas

Before transferring your drawing, you'll want to tone the canvas. To do this, first complete the sky down through the distant tree line. The remainder of the canvas, from the tree line down, should be a warm mixture of Raw Sienna and Burnt Sienna.

6. Begin in the distance

You'll begin your actual painting with the blue/gray layer of distant trees, then overlay with the brighter trees in front of them.

7. Block in the darks

Foreground darks and cast shadows are blocked in according to the design plan. Lighter values and brighter colors are introduced over the dark tones. The buildings are started with shadow colors and completed with highlights of Titanium White with a touch of Diarylide Yellow.

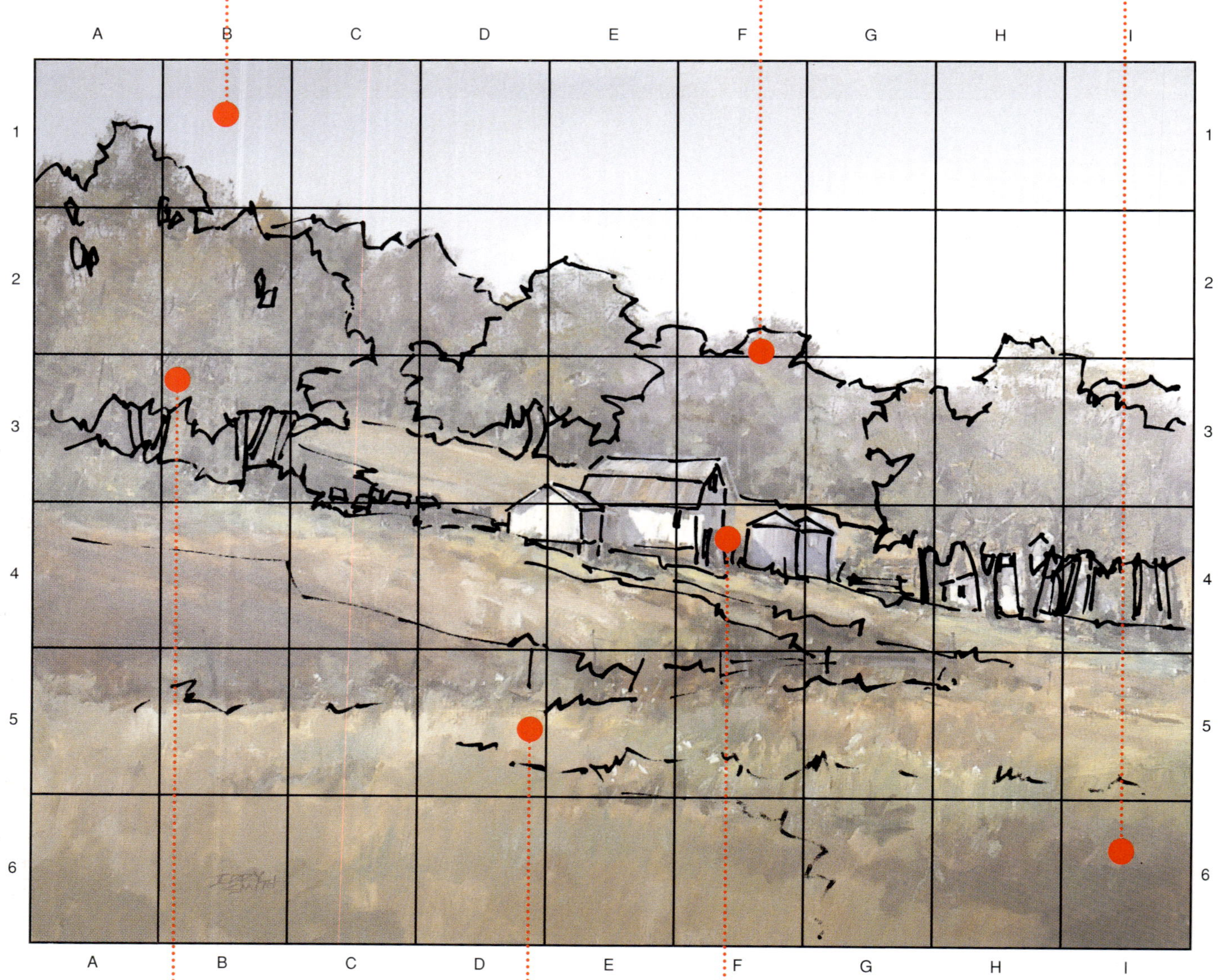

8. Mass the trees

Tree shapes are massed together. Atmospheric depth is illustrated by the contrast between the cool, distant trees and the warm greens in the trees closer to the viewer.

9. Break up the foreground

Bold brushwork and a hint of wildflowers break up the large foreground area. The subtle fence row is used to move the eye along without demanding too much attention.

10. Maintain focus

To maintain focus on the buildings, you'll put the cows in the middle distance and keep them in shadow, massing them together to merely suggest them.

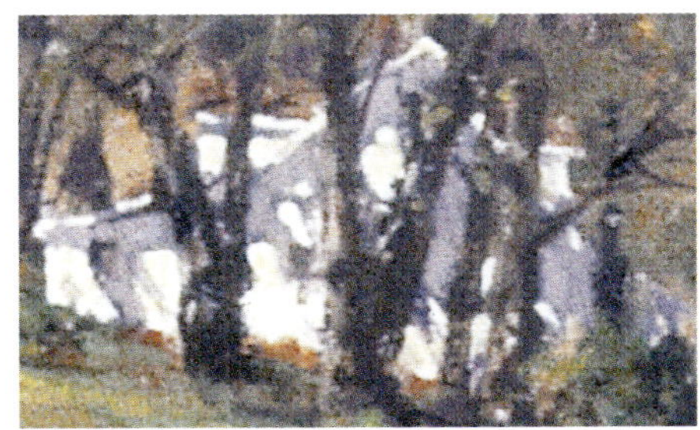

Detail

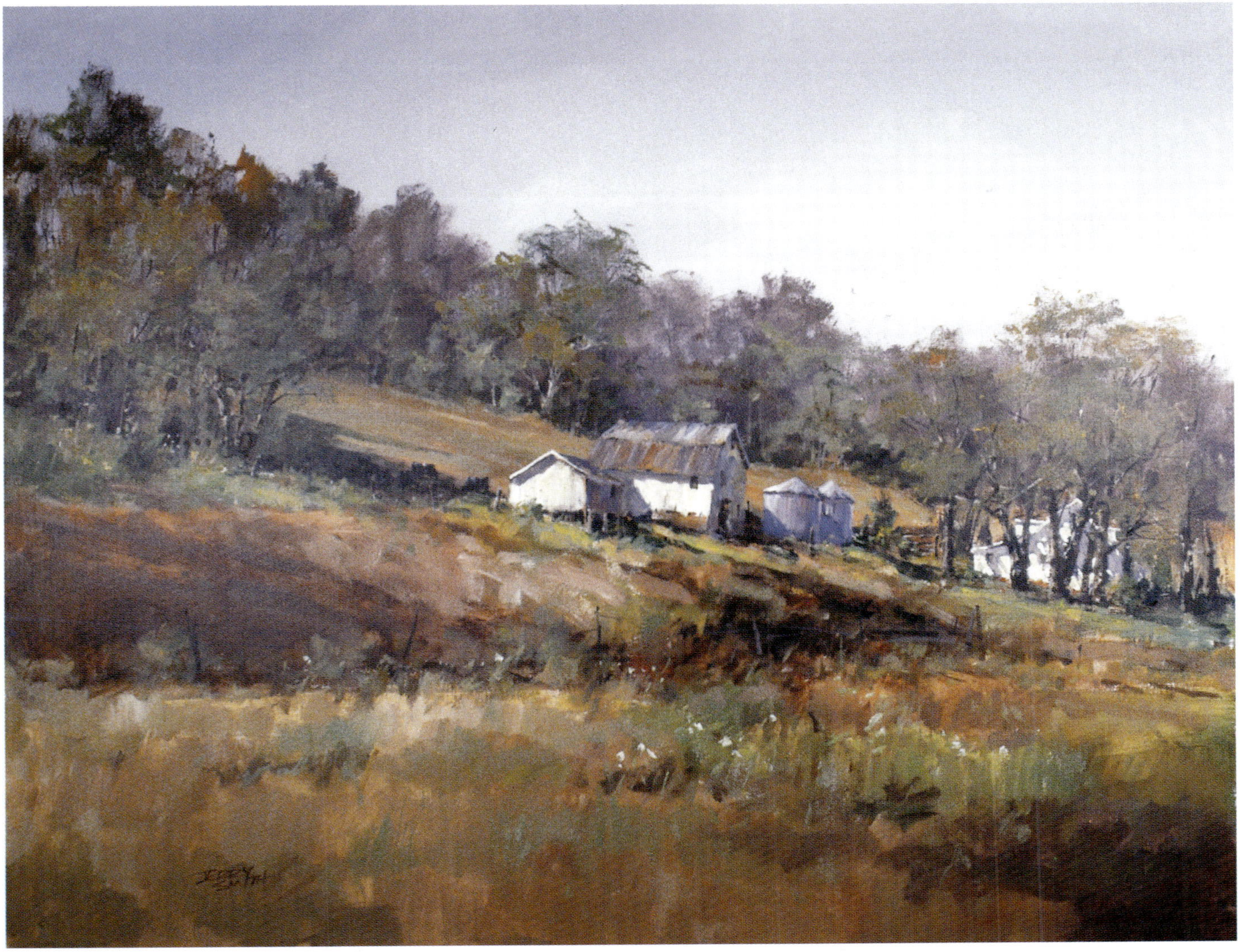

Hoosier Hillside, acrylic, 24 x 30" (61 x 76cm) by Jerry Smith ©

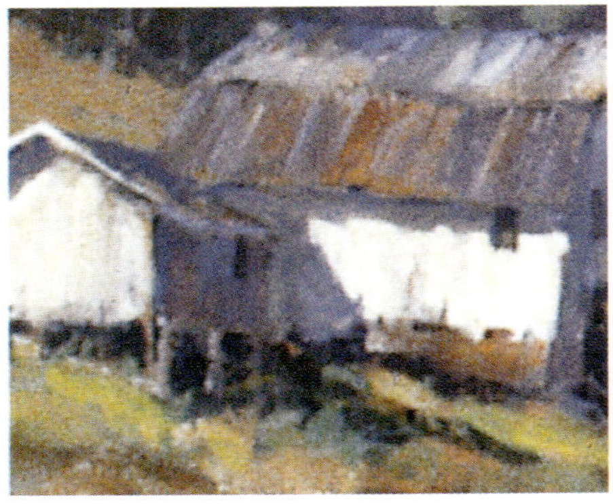

Detail

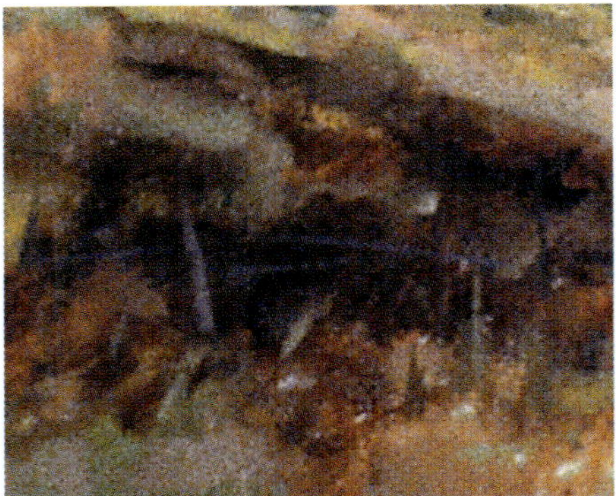

Detail

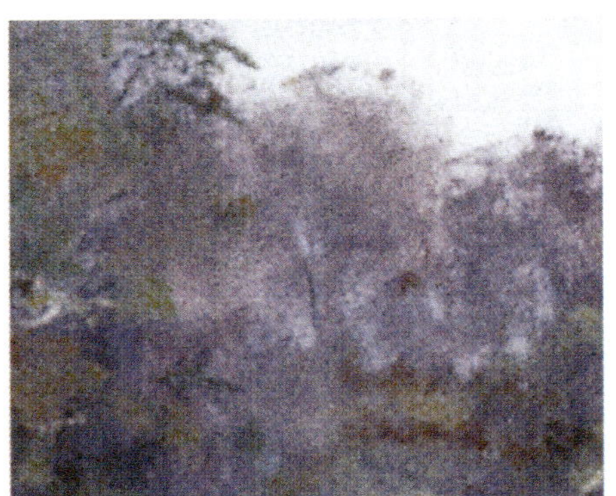

Detail

Before you begin, read the entire project through so you know what's going to happen next.

art map 15

Selecting and rearranging visual elements

This painting was done in my studio from a combination of sketches and photographs from the scene.

As you can see from the photos, this type of setting usually contains much more information than you need to make a concise statement. When tackling a subject like this, you'll need to be fairly selective in what elements you choose to include and how to they were arrange them.

1. The image to be transferred using the art map.

Read the instructions to see how to map this image across to your working surface.

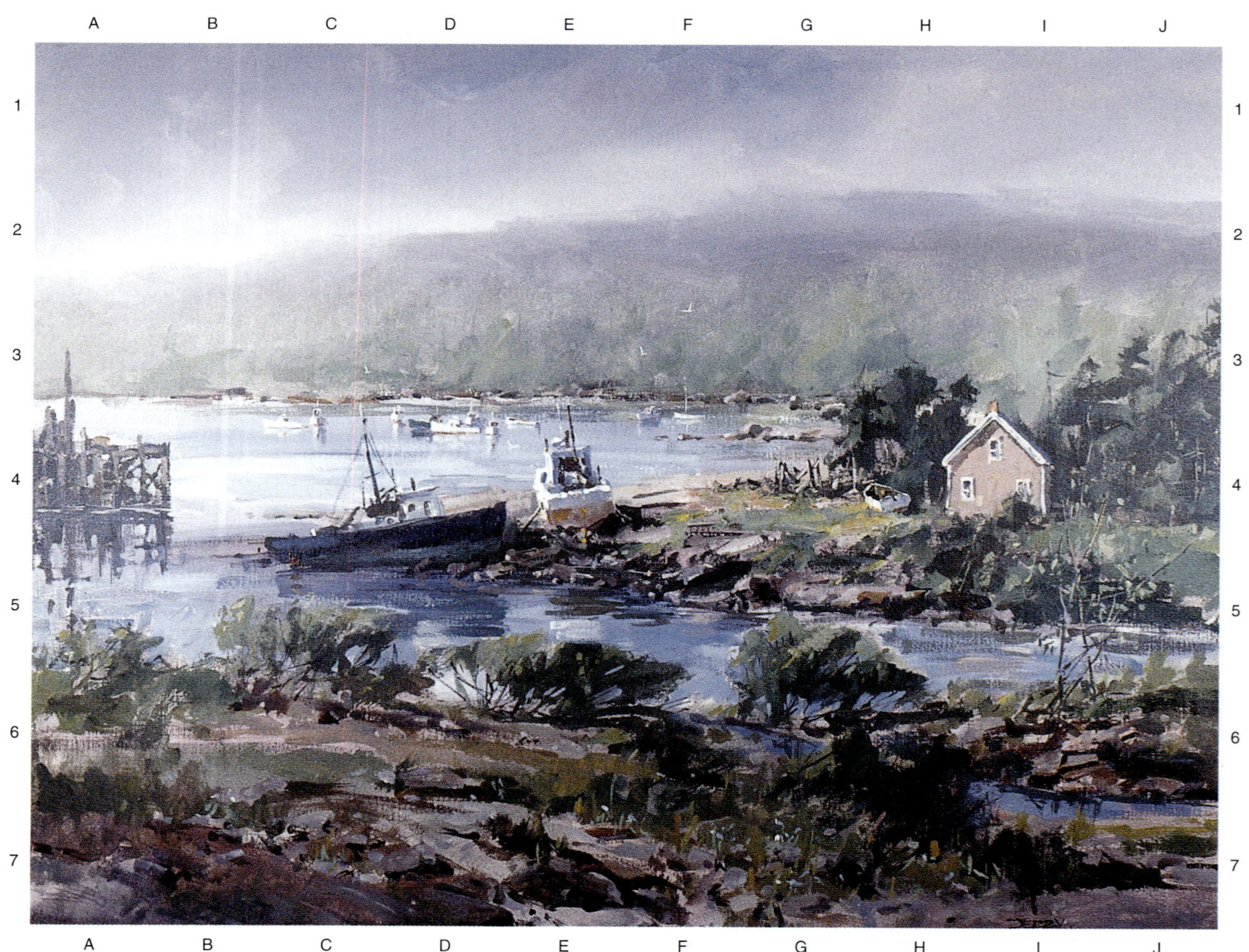

2. Map the image

With a 2B pencil, begin by LIGHTLY drawing a grid on your working surface that has the exact same number of squares as my grid. Your support can be the size of my original, or you can choose something proportionally larger or smaller. Your art map will be 7 squares down and 10 squares across. Put in the letters and numbers along the edges to make the next step easier.

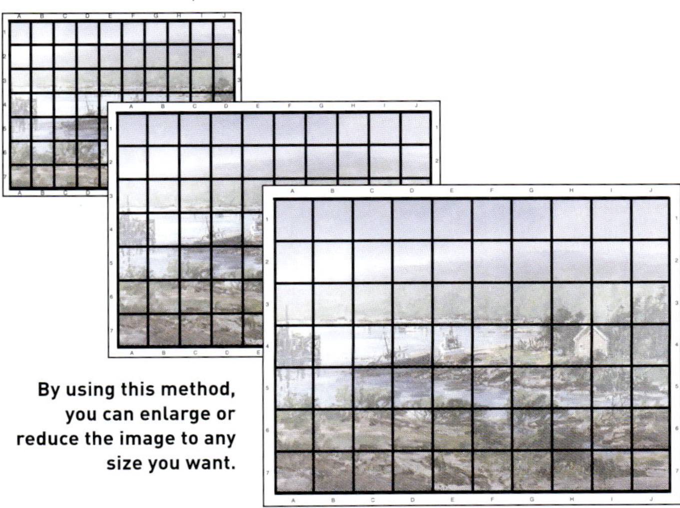

By using this method, you can enlarge or reduce the image to any size you want.

3. Use the art map to transfer the image

Now, still drawing very LIGHTLY with your pencil, copy the main contour lines of the object as shown in each square onto your working surface. It's not necessary to get every detail—just a simple line drawing will do. I recommend LIGHTLY and gently erasing the grid lines in the open, lighter areas before continuing.

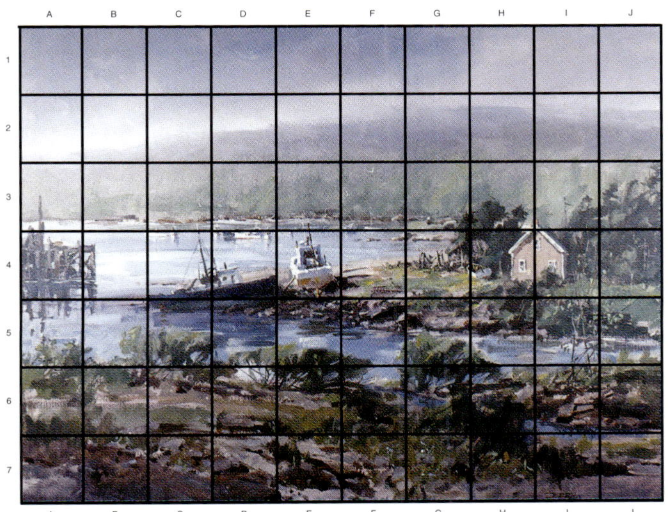

This is how your art map should look.

Here I've done the drawing in dark ink so you can see the idea, but you will do this lightly in pencil.

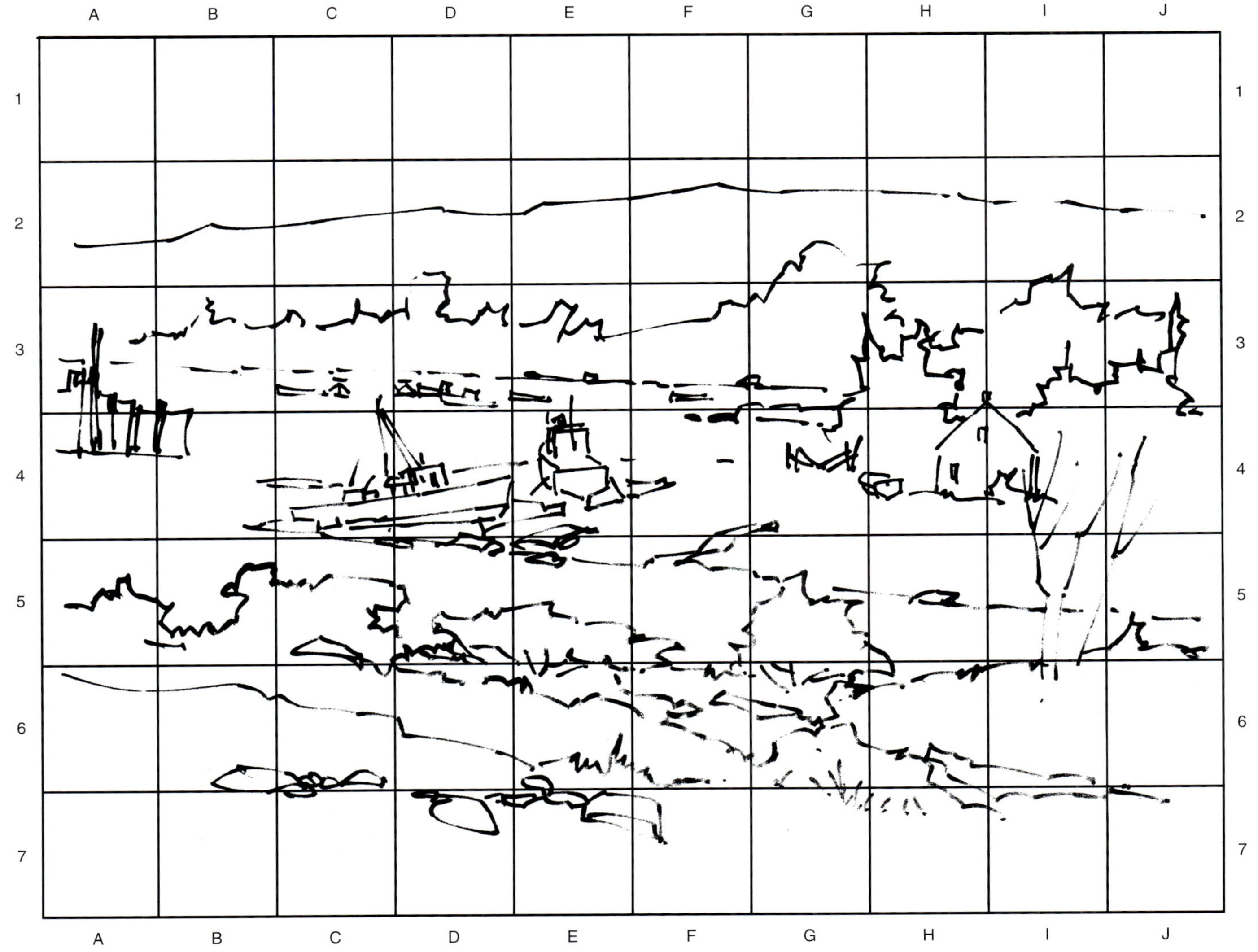

Study these pages before you start painting

Shape map

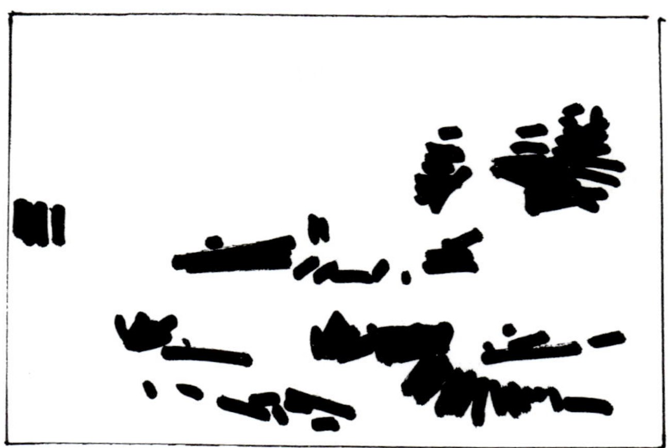

Design map

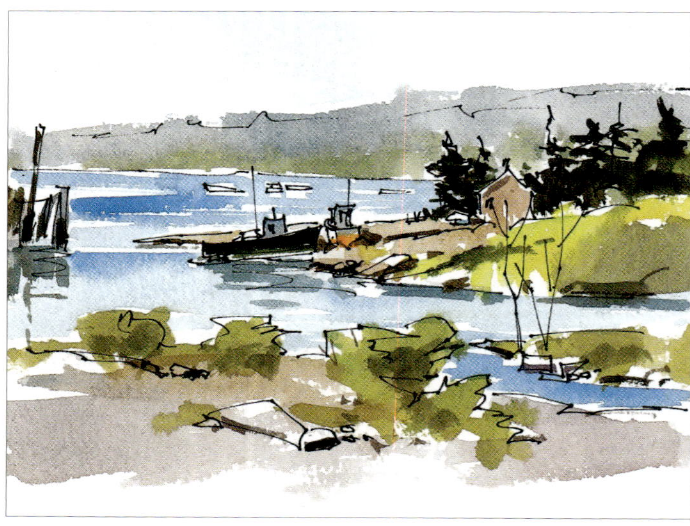

Thumbnail sketch

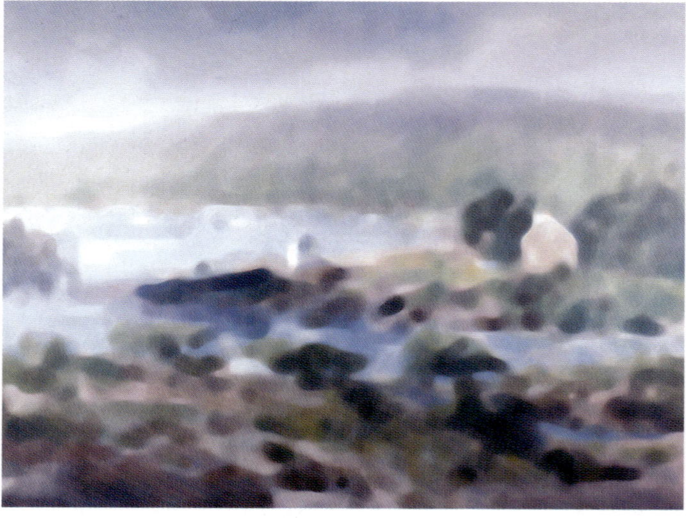

Color map (what you would see if you were to squint)
This painting has a red/green color plan with the greens dominating. Note the variety of greens used. Nothing will kill a "summer painting" more than using one constant green used throughout the painting.

materials you'll need

painting surface
canvas, board or paper

brushes
¼", ½" and 1" flats
nos. 4, 6 and 12 rounds
rigger

other tools
2B pencil
ruler
palette
spray bottle to keep your palette moist

your acrylic palette for this painting

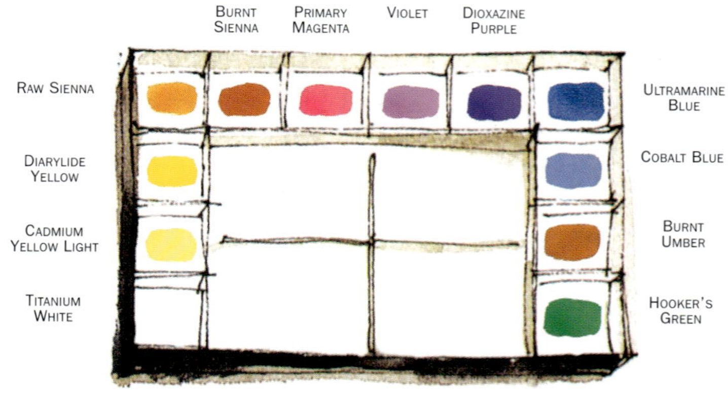

Consider the following elements

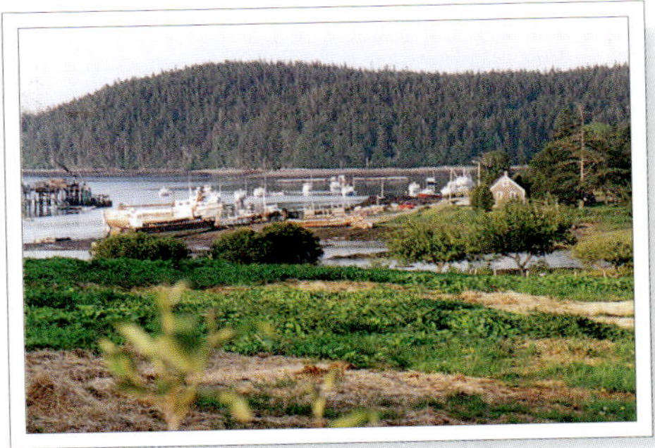

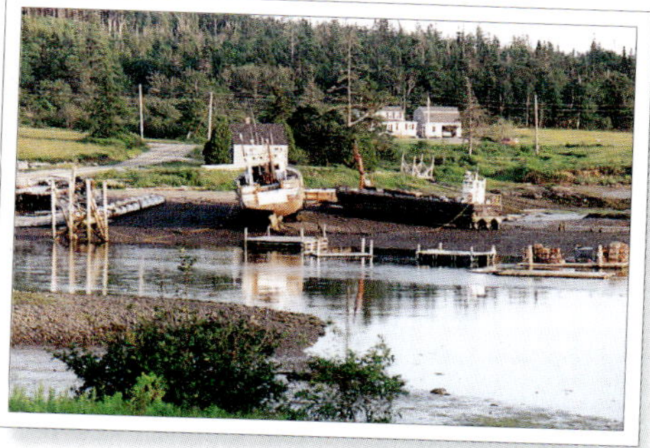

Compare these photos of the scene with my finished idea

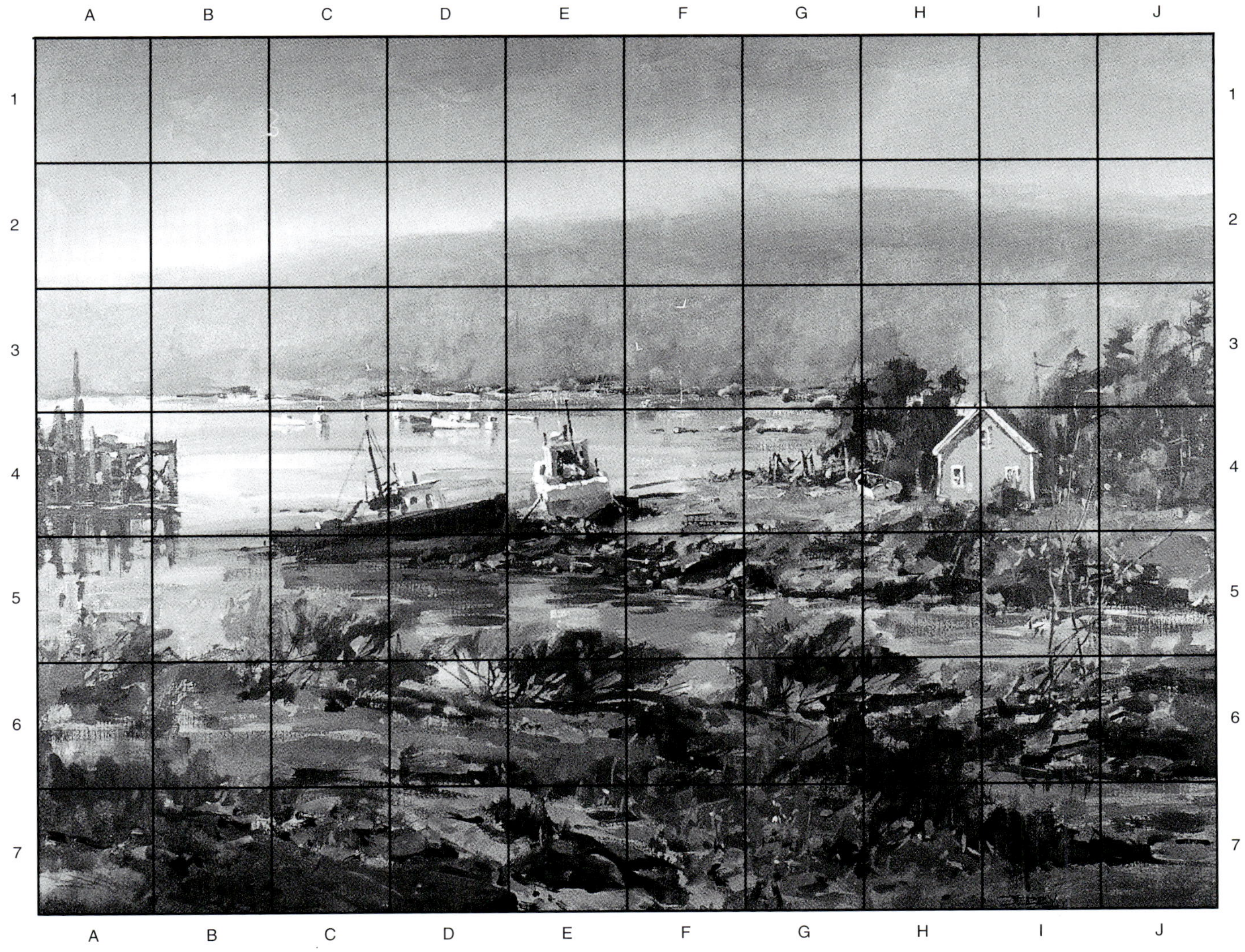

You'll notice several design variations from the scene photos in addition to the obvious elimination and simplification of details.

- The distant hills and trees were lightened in value and reduced in light to add atmosphere and depth.
- The large white boat was moved away from the darker boat and turned 90 degrees as pictured in the second photo.
- Values behind the dark boat were lightened for contrast.
- Dark trees were used to frame the small building and to tie middle distance and background together.
- The foreground bushes were placed to direct the viewer into the painting.

Put it all together

4. Block in the shapes

Block in the large shapes using blue/grays and Violet for the sky and background hills, and earthy tans for the foreground and middle distance. When I did this painting I had intended to repaint the sky at least one more time, but, as it turned out, I liked the color and the wispy brushstrokes in the initial block-in, so I left it alone.

5. Refine the background

Refine the muted background taking care to keep the top edge soft and varied.

6. Paint the water and reflections

The water can be painted in a couple of passes with long, horizontal strokes. Muted reflections are painted with grayed down versions of the colors being reflected.

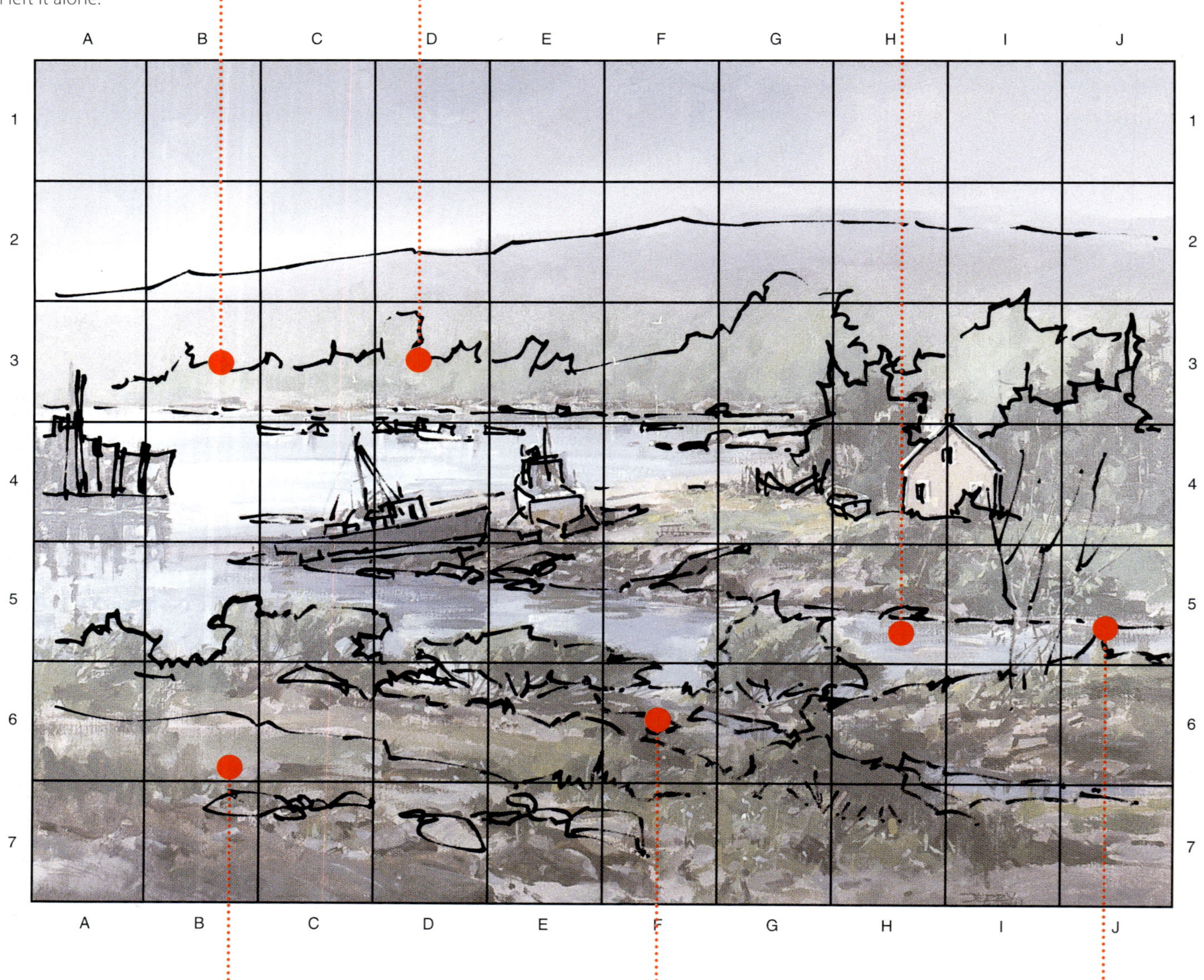

7. Keep the patterns in mind

See how the dark patterns are placed throughout the painting to carry the design. Simplified dock area directs the eye back into the painting and, along with its reflections, provides a bridge between the foreground and background. The boats are carefully positioned to move the eye through the painting. The more distant boats echo the shapes and provide scale.

8. Suggest detail and depth

Rigger strokes are selectively added throughout to suggest detail and to pull shapes together. "Lost and found" edges convey atmosphere and depth. Note how the edges are softer and how detail is limited in the corners.

9. Add highlights

Complete the painting with highlight touches on the beach, boats, trees, rocks, and building.

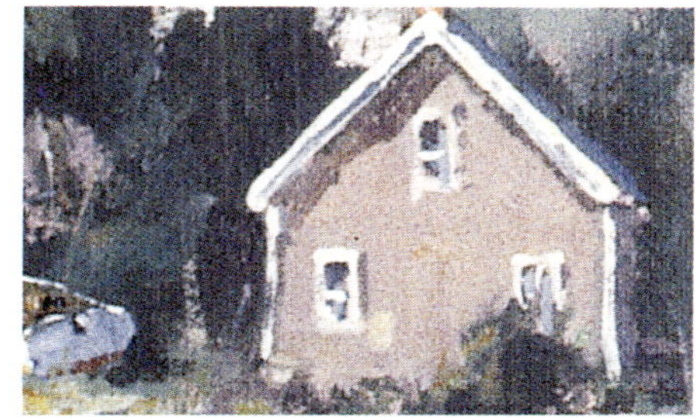

Detail

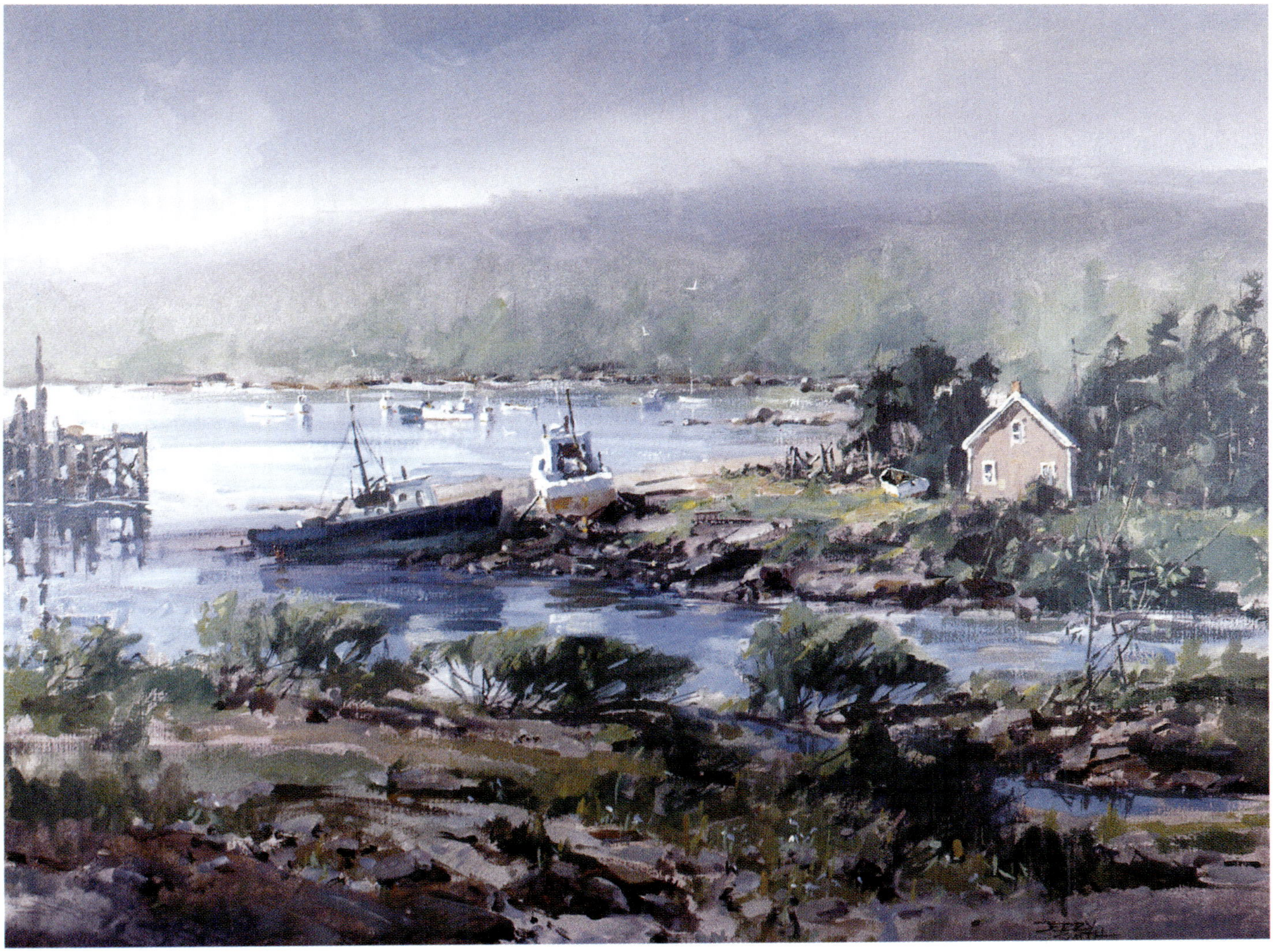

***Harbor Calm*, acrylic, 24 x 30" (61 x 76cm) by Jerry Smith ©**

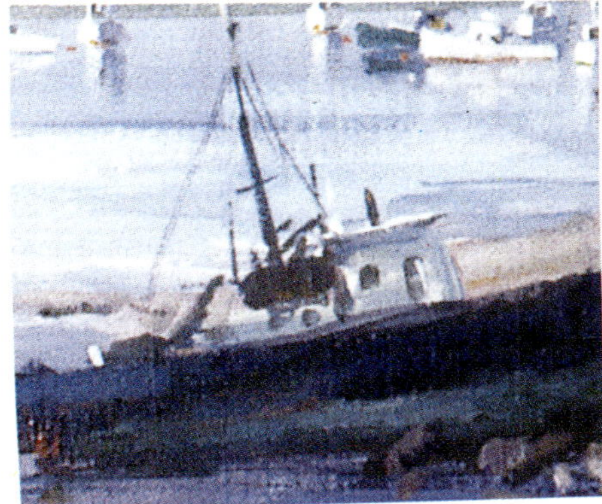

Detail

Detail

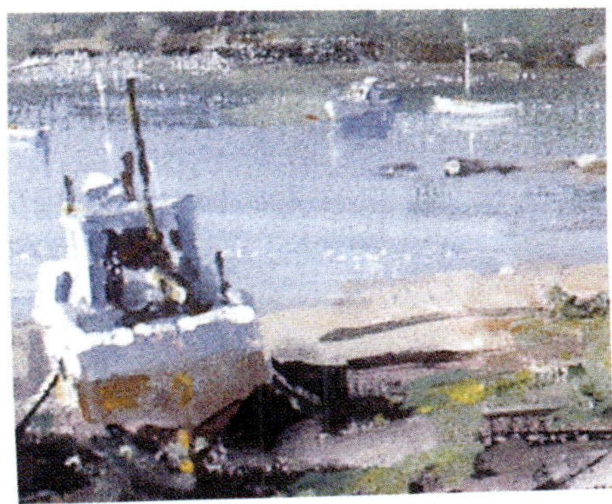

Detail